Library of Congress Cataloging-in-Publication Data

Peng, Mike W., 1968–
    Behind the success and failure of U.S. export intermediaries :
transactions, agents, and resources / Mike W. Peng.
      p. cm.
    Includes bibliographical references and index.
    ISBN 1–56720–152–0 (alk. paper)
    1. Export trading companies—United States. 2. Exports—United
States. I. Title.
HF1416.5.P46 1998
382′.6′0973—dc21   97–22747

British Library Cataloguing in Publication Data is available.

Library of Congress Catalog Card Number: 97–22747
ISBN: 1–56720–152–0

First published in 1998

Quorum Books, 88 Post Road West, Westport, CT 06881
An imprint of Greenwood Publishing Group, Inc.

Printed in the United States of America

The paper used in this book complies with the
Permanent Paper Standard issued by the National
Information Standards Organization (Z39.48–1984).

10 9 8 7 6 5 4 3 2 1

Copyright Acknowledgments

The author and publisher gratefully acknowledge permission for use of the following
material:

Excerpts from *Fortune,* August 5, 1996, pp. F1–F4. Reprinted with permission of *Fortune,* Global 500, © 1996 Time Inc. All rights reserved.

Excerpts from "Editorial: Nobody asked me, but . . . " by Leslie Stroh. *The Exporter
Magazine* May 16, 1996 (10): 2.

To Agnes,

Poet, Novelist, and Financial Analyst

Contents

Figures and Tables

Preface

The late twentieth century has witnessed greatly intensified international trade and competition. Of particular importance is the need to know why some firms are winning in this competition, while others are losing. This book is dedicated to such a task.

Most of the writings on international business focus on large corporations. As a result, we know more about the IBMs, GMs, and Toyotas of the world than we know about smaller firms. Moreover, much of our knowledge about large firms is based on manufacturing firms, despite significant contributions made by service firms. This large-firm bias is unfortunate, since many large corporations are now mostly in the business of "downsizing," "rightsizing," and "restructuring," and small businesses are increasingly being regarded as the primary engine for economic growth, employment generation, and export expansion. Our large-firm bias has resulted in limited knowledge about small firms in general, and small service firms in particular. The purpose of the book is to help correct the prevailing large-firm bias by investigating a particular type of small service firms, namely, export intermediary firms in the United States.

In 1982, with the passage of the Export Trading Company Act, Congress recognized that export intermediary firms may be the key to improving U.S. export competitiveness. Yet surprisingly, no previous study has sought to investigate what is behind the success and failure of these firms. The act has been widely viewed as ineffective in stimulating the development of these firms, and the country has been continuously plagued by persistent trade deficits. This book represents the first attempt to systematically provide a concrete answer to the question, What determines the success and failure of

U.S. export intermediaries? Such an answer is not only of significance for business practitioners and policy makers, but also fills an important gap in the scholarly literature.

This book is *not* about how to start or operate an export business; there are dozens of how-to books of this nature that interested readers can obtain. Rather, this book is about the fundamental determinants of export intermediary performance through rigorous application of strategic, economic, and organizational theories to this critical question. To the best of my knowledge, this is the one and only book that directly focuses on the performance determinants of U.S. export intermediaries, and no other book dealing with this topic can match it in analytical rigor and comprehensiveness.

The primary audience of this book is owners, principals, and managers of export intermediaries interested in improving their organizational performance; would-be entrepreneurs inclined toward the export business; manufacturing executives in search of export intermediary services; and government officials in charge of export promotion. The second audience is scholars and students in international business, strategic management, organizational economics, marketing channels, and entrepreneurship.

ACKNOWLEDGMENTS

I started writing this book when I was at the University of Washington in Seattle. Over the years, I have continued to work on it, first as a faculty member at the University of Hawaii and most recently as a visiting professor at the Chinese University of Hong Kong. At Washington, I thank Professors Charles Hill and Richard Moxon, who patiently read each of the following chapters as they were completed and offered wise counsel. Charles was instrumental in the theoretical development stage of the study. Dick was supportive at various stages of the study, from funding arrangements to final copyediting.

I also thank Professor Anne Ilinitch of the University of North Carolina, since this book grew out of a joint project on export performance that I undertook with her. In our attempt to uncover what was behind the "quantum leap" in export involvement among some small manufacturers with no previous overseas experience, we came to realize the importance of export intermediaries in facilitating more exports among these companies. As a result, my attention gradually shifted to export intermediaries, which eventually led to this book. Therefore, Anne deserves my special thanks for pointing out the directions of this study.

Many other colleagues also contributed to the book by challenging my ideas and critiquing earlier drafts. Among them were Professors Howard Becker, Fahad Khalil, Dorothy Paun, and Hirokuni Tamura of the University of Washington, Yadong Luo, Laurence Jacobs, James Richardson, and Nancy Wong of the University of Hawaii, Masaaki Kotabe of the University of Texas, Ken Smith of the University of Maryland, Ed Coyne of Nova Southeastern University, Paul Godfrey of Brigham Young University, Philip Phan of York University, Peter Walters of the Hong Kong Polytechnic University, David Tse of the City University of Hong Kong, and H. F. Lau of the Chinese University of Hong Kong. Portions of this work were presented at the Academy of International Business conferences in Boston, Massachusetts, and Seoul, Korea (Peng, 1994b; Peng and Ilinitch, 1995), and the Academy of Management conference in Vancouver, Canada (Peng, 1995b). In addition, five universities invited me to present seminars based on this study (Universities of Hawaii, Kentucky, Maryland, and San Francisco, and California State University at Hayward). The quality of the work has certainly benefited from such interaction with a wide range of colleagues. Nevertheless, I was still surprised—and thrilled—to find out that my work on which this book is based (Peng, 1996) was voted as one of the top-four best dissertations at the Barry Richman Competition at the Academy of Management conference in Cincinnati, August 1996.

I would also like to express my appreciation to the Center for International Business Education and Research (CIBER) at the University of Washington, which generously supported this study from the very beginning through a grant from the U.S. Department of Education. Specifically, I want to thank the dedicated CIBER staff, Elizabeth O'Shea, Kathryn Shields, and Claire Lu, for their great help in the logistics of the study. In addition, I thank Dean William Bradford and his assistant Georgia Mosher for assistance in preparing the cover letters for the mail survey, which I am sure helped increase the survey response rate. I also thank Professor Peter Frost and his assistant Jamie Banaag in the Doctoral Program Office for their support. In addition, fellowships from the Edna Benson Foundation in Seattle and President Chiang Ching-kuo Education Foundation in San Francisco supported preliminary investigation which eventually led to this book.

Most data analysis of the study was completed at the University of Hawaii. I thank Dean David Bess and Department Chairman Hugh Folk, as well as my colleagues, most notably Oded Shenkar, Yadong Luo, David Yang, Richard Brislin, Lane Kelley, Bob Doktor, D. Bhawuk, Elaine Bailey, Jim Richardson, Glen Taylor, David Bangert, David McClain, Jack Suyderhoud, Nicholas Ordway, Laurence

Jacobs, Dana Alden, Nancy Wong, Shirley Daniel, Eric Harwit, and Alvin So, for their interest in having me. I also acknowledge the funding support from the UH CIBER and CBA Research and Faculty Development Committee. I am especially grateful to the Office of Research Administration, which offered a course release during the spring 1997 semester which enabled me to finish the manuscript.

More recently, I have had an opportunity to spend a year in Hong Kong, the dynamic center of Asia business and destination of a lot of American exports. At the Chinese University of Hong Kong, I thank Department Chairman H. F. Lau and my new colleagues, Kevin Au, John Fukuda, Thamis Lo, K. C. Mun, Kent Neupert, Gongming Qian, Raymond So, Denis Wang, Kitty Young, Julia Yu, and Lu Yuan, for their interest in my work. I also appreciate the Seed Money Grant provided by Dean K. H. Lee. Forrest Chan, an MPhil student, provided excellent research assistance during the "home run" stretch to finish the final product.

In addition, I would like to thank Professors Mary Rieder and Mary Gander of Minnesota State University in Winona for helping me start my academic career. I also acknowledge the support from Professors Carlis Anderson, Roger Carlson, and Joseph Foegen during my studies there.

Outside the academic community, I want to thank all the government officials and export intermediary owners and managers whom I interviewed in six cities (Boston, Dallas, Honolulu, Portland [Oregon], Seattle, and Santa Fe [New Mexico]), the twelve case study participants, and the 195 respondents of the mail survey for sharing their insights and experience with me. Among these people who are too numerous to list here individually, I would like to thank Kenneth Pai of the Port of Seattle, Roman Tkachenko of Asia-Pacific Trading, and Akio Sano of Mitsui & Co. (USA) for their help. The assistance from Don Stow of the Export Trading Company Office, U.S. Department of Commerce, Washington, DC, is also acknowledged. Furthermore, my thanks go to Patrece Banks of Pacific Tide International, who, in addition to being my informant and interviewee, became a good friend of mine during the course of the study. I also appreciate the support from Donna and Rim Miksys for sharing the joy and excitement with me. In addition, I thank Leslie Stroh, publisher of *The Exporter Magazine*, for his interest in my work and for his kindness in publicizing this study in his editorial pages (Stroh, 1996, 1997).

At Quorum, I thank my publisher, Eric Valentine, not only for his interest in this work, but also for his speedy responses to my inquiries. Deborah Whitford, my production editor, and Suzanne Solensky, my copy editor, also deserve a great deal of thanks for their indispensable help in turning my manuscript into a book.

I reserve the last, but certainly not the least, acknowledgment for my family. To my wife, Agnes, who has exercised a degree of forbearance far beyond what I have any right to expect, I owe the greatest debt. The demands of working on this book have often pushed family responsibilities into secondary place and thrown my life into a state of what I call "highest-level military alert." Agnes has not only endured the hardship of working on this seemingly never-ending project, but has also made direct contributions to its quality as evidenced in the graphs and interviews for case studies. Her unfailing love, passion, and support have made me feel less guilty than I should have. A great deal of thanks also goes to my parents. They have always believed in my ability and encouraged me to set ambitious goals. This book represents an answer to their call for excellence. I also thank Aunt Zhikang, whose support and encouragement have greatly influenced who I am now. Finally, I thank my late grandfather, who passed away before I was born, but whose early studies in the 1920s–1930s have provided much needed guiding light for my own journey. To all of you, my thanks and my love.

CHAPTER 1

Introduction

This is a book about export intermediary firms in the United States. Specifically, it is about the fundamental determinants of their performance. Usually dubbed "traders" or "middlemen," export intermediaries are a group of specialized service firms connecting domestic manufaturers and foreign buyers. Trading across borders, some of them thrive, while others struggle. This book investigates what is behind the success and failure of these entrepreneurial firms.

THE IMPORTANCE OF EXPORTS

Exports are crucial to the economy of the United States and export intermediaries can play an important role in facilitating exports, especially among small and midsize manufacturers. Since the colonial era, the United States has been able to generate a large number of exports that are sold in different parts of the world. Many politicians, academics, and business practitioners have stressed the importance of exports to a healthy U.S. economy (Porter, 1990; Reich, 1991; Thurow, 1993; Tyson, Dickens and Zysman, 1988). Such concern takes on added importance in light of increasing trade deficits and the perceived decline of U.S. industrial competitiveness in the late twentieth century (President's Commission on Industrial Competitiveness, 1985; *Wall Street Journal*, 1997). Compared with protectionist policies such as curtailing imports, erecting trade barriers, or manipulating exchange rates, export expansion has been identified by many experts as an effective solution for reducing the nation's trade deficit problem and stimulating the economy (Cohen,

Paul and Blecker, 1996; Feldstein, 1987; Lenway, 1985; Richardson and Rindal, 1995).

Currently, most U.S. exports have been concentrated in large multinational enterprises which have extensive foreign direct investment and in-house export capabilities (Dunning, 1993). Most small and midsize firms in the United States, on the other hand, shy away from exporting, due to perceived risks, limited resources and lack of knowledge regarding foreign markets (Ilinitch and Peng, 1993, 1994; Root, 1994). At the outset of the 1990s, small and midsize firms employed more than 50 percent of the total work force and produced almost half of the gross national product. However, they were vastly underrepresented in the export sector, contributing only 10 percent of total U.S. exports in 1990 (Small Business Administration, 1991). Given the significant role that small businesses play in the domestic economy, it has become increasingly clear that they must participate more fully in the export sector if the U.S. economy is to function more efficiently.[1] As a result, increasing small business involvement in exporting has become one of the main goals for improving U.S. competitiveness in the global economy (Small Business Administration, 1989, 1991; U.S. Senate, 1982).

THE IMPORTANCE OF EXPORT INTERMEDIARY FIRMS

When exporting, large firms tend to develop their export capabilities in-house, through an export department, an international division, a foreign-based sales and distribution subsidiary, or a production facility abroad (Buckley and Pearce, 1984). Small exporters, on the other hand, may have to rely more on export intermediaries to help them overcome barriers to exporting (Becker and Porter, 1983; Mattson, 1990; Peng and Ilinitch, 1997). At the outset of the 1990s, export intermediaries collectively handled approximately 5 to 10 percent of U.S. manufactured exports (Perry, 1990: 148; Root, 1994: 102). In comparison, well-developed trade intermediaries handled over 40 percent of total Japanese exports (*The Economist*, 1995: 57). Given the persistent reluctance to export among small firms in the United States (Delacroix, 1984; O'Rourke, 1985; Small Business Administration, 1989, 1991), American export intermediaries clearly need to play an active role in stimulating more export involvement among small firms. As such, the effectiveness of export intermediaries will directly affect the export performance of small firms, which in turn will affect the overall competitiveness of U.S. exports in the global economy.

Against this background this book sets out to investigate what is behind the success and failure of export intermediary firms in the

United States, which are commonly called "export management companies" (EMCs) and "export trading companies" (ETCs). These firms leverage on intangible resources such as their knowledge about foreign markets and their efficiency in marketing products abroad. They help their manufacturing clients, which are mostly small and midsize firms, enter foreign markets in a way that their clients are unable to do on their own.

Historically, much of the early international trade was conducted by such forerunners of modern trade intermediary organizations as the East India Company (Cho, 1987). In the United States, "Yankee traders" spearheaded much of the early development of the economy (Galenson, 1986; Rosenberg, 1982; Wilkins, 1970). However, a substantial volume of today's world trade is handled by subsidiaries of multinational enterprises with presence spanning the globe (Dunning, 1993; Ohmae, 1985, 1989). This pattern of using in-house export channels and production abroad to boost foreign sales is especially profound for large U.S. firms, thus suppressing the demand for export intermediary services. As a result, the export intermediary sector is less developed in the United States than it is in other countries such as Japan (Cho, 1987; Kotabe, 1984; Sarathy, 1985). Since the early 1980s, when the Export Trading Company Act of 1982 was passed by Congress, export intermediaries have gained renewed attention in the United States in an effort to tap residual export potential in small firms in order to boost exports and combat trade deficits.

In summary, export intermediary firms represent a potentially important link in improving the competitiveness of U.S. exports. Specifically, they can tap into the export potential of small and midsize manufacturers, which may have difficulties in exporting on their own.

THE CENTRAL QUESTION

The central question that this book attempts to answer is "What determines the success and failure of U.S. export intermediaries?" Despite the apparent importance of increasing exports to the U.S. economy and the renewed interest in export intermediary firms, surprisingly, no previous study has directly and rigorously addressed this important question. Instead, most of the existing work has focused on how manufacturers can enter overseas markets directly by themselves (Anderson and Gatignon, 1986; Hill, Hwang and Kim, 1990; Leonidou and Katsikeas, 1996). However, such research is simply irrelevant for many small manufacturers that are unable to export by themselves due to their limited resources (Root, 1994).

Although some of these firms may be anxious to enter overseas markets, initially they have to rely on export intermediaries to help them venture abroad. For managers at these smaller firms, this question is very practical. They will not be concerned with public policy issues such as using export intermediaries to help the nation decrease its trade deficits. Rather, they will be interested in knowing more about what determines export intermediary performance, in order to select the winning intermediaries instead of placing their export business in the hands of losing ones.

Unfortunately, existing research in the scholarly, trade, and professional literature has not provided a satisfactory answer to this question. Compared with the large body of research on export manufacturers, the scholarly literature on export intermediaries is sparse (Peng and Ilinitch, 1997). In Leonidou and Katsikeas's (1996: 538) encyclopedic review of the research literature on export development, only one *paragraph* was devoted to the role of export intermediaries, which were mentioned in passing as an indirect export method. In earlier reviews of the literature in international marketing (Aaby and Slater, 1989; Aulakh and Kotabe, 1993) and international management (Ricks, Toyne and Martinez, 1990), export intermediaries were not even mentioned. Since there was hardly any underlying research to draw upon, standard university textbooks in international business (Czinkota, Ronkainen and Moffett, 1996; Daniels and Radebaugh, 1998; Hill, 1997) and international marketing (Albaum, et al., 1994; Douglas and Craig, 1995; Terpstra and Sarathy, 1994; Young, et al., 1989) provided only sketchy coverage on export intermediaries. For instance, in Albaum and colleagues' (1994: 177–87) 480-page textbook, only ten pages were used to describe indirect export, which involves the use of export intermediaries.

Within the limited literature on export intermediaries, most studies were descriptive, only documenting the demographic profiles of U.S. export intermediaries and providing little information about their performance (Batra, 1991; Bello and Williamson, 1985a, 1985b; Brasch, 1978; Coopers and Lybrand, 1984; Hay Associates, 1977; Howard and Maskulka, 1988; U.S. Department of Commerce, 1990). While more analytical, the work of Amine (1987), Cho (1987), and Perry (1990, 1992) focused on the evolution, instead of the performance, of these firms. These authors remained silent on what determines the success and failure of export intermediaries. As a result, there is a paucity of knowledge about export intermediary performance. Denis (1990: 104), for example, commented that "perhaps the most serious lack of knowledge . . . [regarding the export process] lies in the area of the services provided by intermediaries."

In the only published study that addressed the performance question of export intermediaries, Haigh (1994: 66) found that the performance of these firms is below the expectations of manufacturers more than half the time. However, since Haigh chose to survey manufacturers instead of intermediaries, no conclusion can be drawn from his study about the determinants of export intermediary performance. In other words, it is not certain whether such lackluster performance is due to manufacturers' expectations which may be too high, or due to intermediaries' capabilities which may be too low. Thus, no research-based guidelines can be formulated to help manufacturers select appropriate export intermediaries.

In addition to its academic significance, the answer to the export intermediary performance question is obviously important to owners, managers, and employees who currently operate these firms, as well as to would-be entrepreneurs interested in entering the export business. Currently, there are a large number of how-to books that try to help these people. Recent titles in this category include *Exporting: From Start to Finance* (Wells and Dulat, 1996), *Export Import: Everything You and Your Company Need to Know* (Zodl, 1995), *How to Make Your Small Company an Export Tiger* (Ake, 1995), *Keys to Starting an Import-Export Business* (Jonnard, 1996), *Start Your Own Import-Export Business* (Staff, 1994), and *The Entrepreneur Guide to Starting an Import-Export Business* (*Entrepreneur Magazine*, 1995). These books generally had two major shortcomings. First, many of them, such as Ake (1995), Wells and Dulat, (1996), and Zodl (1995), were written for managers at manufacturing firms interested in exporting, and did not focus on export intermediaries. For example, the voluminous, 613-page book by Wells and Dulat (1996: 103–7) had only four pages on "exporting through an EMC/ETC." The shorter, 151-page book by Zodl (1995: 5–6) had only two *paragraphs* on EMCs and ETCs. Not surprisingly, they had no coverage on what determines export intermediary performance. Second, even for books that were intended for readers interested in setting up their own export business, they were usually unable to pinpoint proven key success factors, since there is hardly any research evidence. Instead, they provided largely experience-based anecdotes and suggestions, some of which are dubious. In short, while the scholarly literature has not provided an answer to the export intermediary performance question, the how-to trade and professional books do not help either.

Finally, from a public policy perspective, the answer to the export intermediary performance question has profound implications. Many federal agencies, such as the Department of Commerce, the Small Business Administration, and the Export-Import Bank, as well as numerous state and local government agencies are mandated to promote U.S. exports. However, they have generally focused their efforts on manufacturers and paid less attention to the needs of service firms such as export intermediaries. A case in point is the Export Trading Company Act of 1982. Despite congressional support, the business community showed a distinct lack of interest (Czinkota, 1984; Howard and Maskulka, 1988; Kryzanowski and Ursel, 1993). After fifteen years the act has been widely viewed as ineffective both in promoting more U.S. exports in general and in stimulating the development of export intermediaries in particular (Christensen, 1989; Perry, 1992). While there are many factors that led to the failure of this act, retarded understanding of the key question— namely, What determines export intermediary performance?—is certainly a part of the legacy of the failed act. Improved under- standing of this critical question, on the other hand, will help formulate better policies that address the needs of export inter- mediaries, which in turn will contribute toward improved export competitiveness of the nation.

In summary, the export intermediary performance question is extremely important for managers at small and midsize manufac- turers interested in using export intermediaries to enter overseas markets, for current and would-be entrepreneurs in the export business aiming at improved organizational performance, and for public policy makers concerned with U.S. export competitiveness. The current scholarly, trade, and professional literature, however, has failed to provide an answer to this question. It is believed that improved knowledge in this area of inquiry will not only increase the effectiveness of export intermediary firms, but also enrich the scho- larly literature. Therefore, this book intends to fill the gap in our current knowledge by attempting to answer this critical question.

ANALYTICAL APPROACH:
TRANSACTIONS, AGENTS, AND RESOURCES

This book employs a rigorous analytical approach drawing on strategic, economic, and organizational theories to tackle the pre- viously unexplored question about export intermediary perfor- mance. Specifically, an integrative approach based on three major theoretical perspectives will be adopted to shed new light on this question. To readers interested only in the practical aspects of the study, these theories are by no means abstract or inaccessible. Instead, they can be summarized in three simple yet powerful words: transactions, agents, and resources.

Transactions grow out of transaction cost theory in organizational economics. This theory focuses on the particular attributes of economic transactions and the strategies employed by buyers and sellers to minimize costs associated with these transactions—hence the term "transaction cost" (Coase, 1937; Williamson, 1975, 1985). This theory is particularly relevant to this study, because the nature of export transactions entails very high costs due to the "liability of foreignness" that exporters have to overcome (Hymer, 1976; Zaheer, 1995). The role of export intermediaries is to help lower the export-related transaction costs for their manufacturing clients, and the performance of export intermediaries depends on how successful they are in lowering these costs. As a result, transaction cost theory helps define the problem and provides insights to the answer.

Agents refer to agency theory, another major branch of organizational economics. Agency theory is concerned with the inherent conflict of interest between principals and agents in economic relationships, such as the relationship between manufacturers and export intermediaries. Specifically, since agents may not share the principals' goals and because agents have better information about the details of the task, agents may have both the motivation and the opportunity to behave in a way that is at odds with the principals' interests (Alchian and Demsetz, 1972; Jensen and Meckling, 1976). To principals, the costs of dealing with agents are called "agency costs," and principals are naturally interested in minimizing these costs. However, principals face a dilemma: They often have to rely on agents to perform certain tasks. This dilemma is evident in the manufacturer-intermediary relationship. Many principals, such as small and midsize manufacturers, have to rely on intermediaries as agents to enter foreign markets. As a result, agency theory is able to provide insights on the dynamic and complex relationship between manufacturers and intermediaries, whose outcome determines export intermediary performance.

Finally, *resources* represent resource-based theory in the strategic management literature, which focuses on firm resources and capabilities as fundamental determinants of performance (Barney, 1991, 1997; Conner, 1991; Wernerfelt, 1984). This theory suggests that only by possessing valuable, unique, and hard-to-imitate resources and capabilities can firms build up their competitive advantage, which may lead to entrepreneurial success in the marketplace (Schumpeter, 1942). Given that U.S. export intermediaries are usually of small size, this book is also about small businesses and entrepreneurs that operate them. Despite their size, small businesses may present "the simplest, cleanest, and easiest environment in which to see the basic strategic management tasks" and "the place where pure entrepreneurial character may be seen best" (Schendel and Hofer, 1979: 6).

In the case of export intermediaries, their knowledge and expertise in foreign markets and export processes represent their principal resources and capabilities, which give rise to their competitive advantage. And it is the value, uniqueness, and hard-to-imitate nature of these resources and capabilities that provide a rationale for the existence of export intermediaries. Otherwise, if these abilities can be easily acquired and imitated, then manufacturers will attempt to develop export capabilities in-house, thus diminishing the chances for export intermediaries to exist and succeed. Indeed, many large manufacturers have developed such capabilities, and forced export intermediaries to concentrate on small and midsize firms that are unable to acquire export capabilities. In short, with its focus on firm resources and capabilities as drivers of firm performance, resource-based theory is also highly relevant to the export intermediary performance question.

Each of these three theories partially solves the puzzle of export intermediary performance. Collectively, they will be used to derive an integrated model that provides a concrete answer to explain what is behind the success and failure of export intermediaries. Conceptually, the model is complete with its definition, assumptions, propositions, and hypotheses. Methodologically, a combination of qualitative and quantitative studies will be employed, involving six case studies and a nationwide mail survey drawing on a 1,000-firm sample. The findings of these studies provide strong evidence to support the integrated model, thus answering the question about export intermediary performance with strong confidence and generalizability.

In summary, a distinctive analytical approach will be employed drawing upon three theoretical perspectives. Focusing on transactions, agents, and resources, these theories lead to an integrated model that provides an answer to the previously unexplored question. As a result, this book, to the best of my knowledge, represents the one and only book that directly focuses on the performance determinants of U.S. export intermediaries.

ORGANIZATION OF THE BOOK

There are eight chapters in the book. After this introductory chapter, Chapter 2 starts with definitions. Next, Chapter 3 provides a global perspective on the worldwide development of export intermediary firms as a basis for comparing their evolution in the United States. Chapter 4 then describes the state of the art of U.S. export intermediaries as reported by previous studies. The integrated model drawing on three major theoretical perspectives is then articulated in Chapter 5. Chapters 6 and 7 report the findings from six case studies and a large-sample, nationwide mail survey of these firms, respectively. Finally, discussions, implications, and conclusions are drawn in Chapter 8. For readers interested in the research process, the detailed appendix on research methodology and background data provides a more technical description of the methodology and also presents some of the more quantitative data analysis that supports the main findings reported in the book.

NOTE

1. Consistent with the Small Business Administration definition, "small businesses" are defined in this book as those small and midsize enterprises with fewer than 500 employees. This is also consistent with standard business size classes established by the Office of Management and Budget on May 18, 1982, to be used by all federal agencies when publishing statistical data (Small Business Administration, 1989: 18). The categories noted are the following: (a) Very small: < 20 employees; (b) Small: 20–99 employees; (c) Medium: 100–499 employees; and (d) Large: > 500 employees.

CHAPTER 2

Export Intermediaries: Definitions

As Adam Smith insightfully pointed out over two hundred years ago in *The Wealth of Nations*, trading is perhaps one of the most extensively conducted economic activities around the world since the beginning of human history. Whenever there is a need for trading, trade intermediaries (or middlemen) will emerge to connect producers and buyers. When such transactions take place across international borders, these intermediaries become international traders bringing goods and services to other lands. This book focuses on traders who market American goods and services abroad—in other words, export intermediaries. This chapter first provides a general definition of export intermediaries, then reviews the use of terminologies such as "export management company" and "export trading company" in the literature, and ends with an operational definition of U.S. export intermediary to be used throughout this book.

WHAT THEY ARE AND WHY THEY EXIST

Intermediaries perform an important economic function by acting as a link between individuals and organizations that otherwise would not have been connected (Cosimano, 1996). Such a function is especially critical in export transactions characterized by the geographical and cultural separation between sellers and buyers. Export intermediaries are specialized service organizations that play an important part in the distribution channel of the manufacturer that sells abroad. In a marketing classic, Kotler (1983: 354) defined *distribution channel* as "the set of firms and individuals that take title, or assist in transferring title, to the particular good or service as it moves from the producer to the consumer." With little difficulty, this definition can be extended to suggest that *export intermediaries* are "the set of firms and individuals that take title, or assist in transferring title, to the particular good or service as it moves from the producer in one country to the consumer in another country."[1]

The existence of export intermediary firms relies on the producer's willingness to outsource some of the export marketing job to them (Bello, Urban and Verhage, 1991). For the producer, the choice of distribution channel is a strategic decision (Rosenbloom, 1987; Stern and El-Ansary, 1992; Stern and Reve, 1980). Indeed, "a company's channels of distribution represent a foundation for its other marketing policies" (Lilien, Kotler and Moorthy, 1992: 452). As Figure 2.1 shows, when marketing abroad, the producer basically has three strategic choices as follows:

1. Foreign direct investment: Set up foreign production and/or sales facilities through foreign direct investment where products can be marketed abroad.[2]

2. Direct export: Directly export to foreign customers from the home country through in-house export channels.

3. Indirect export: Rely on export intermediaries, which either take title or work on commission, to market products abroad.

Figure 2.1
Strategic Choices in Export Channel Selection

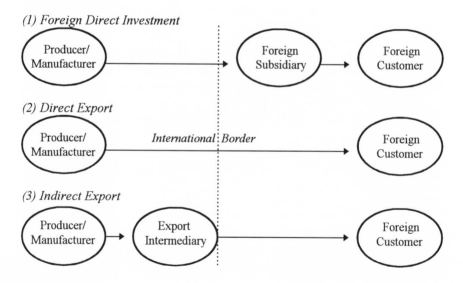

(1) Foreign Direct Investment

(2) Direct Export

(3) Indirect Export

The first two choices rely on the producer's in-house channels, which are direct, while the last one uses an external agent, which lengthens the distribution channel. As such, from the producer's point of view, the optimal strategy of channel choice is determined by the relative costs and benefits of each alternative. In-house channels can ensure coordination of the production and marketing functions, and control over distribution channels, as well as avoid the need to share profits with an outside intermediary. However, in-house channels would also require substantial investment on the producer's part. Setting up subsidiaries abroad through foreign direct investment (choice 1) is an enormous, complex, and costly undertaking, which many firms, especially small and midsize ones, have neither the capital nor the expertise to handle (Root, 1994). Most of the firms active in such activities are large multinational enterprises (MNEs) which have built up their financial and organizational resources over a long period of time (Bartlett and Ghoshal, 1989; Dunning, 1993; Vernon, 1971, 1977; Wilkins, 1970, 1974).

Direct exporting (choice 2), while less demanding, also requires substantial commitment from the producer's resources: progressing from having dedicated salespeople handling export orders, to setting up an export department, to establishing an export/international division (Cavusgil, 1984a, 1984b; Reid, 1981; Stopford and Wells, 1972). In dealing directly with foreign customers, the manufacturer would incur various expenditures due to the need to overcome the "liability of foreignness" (Hymer, 1976; Zaheer, 1995). These include the costs of searching foreign markets and potential customers, negotiating deals, and fulfilling the contractual obligations. Taken together, these expenditures can be viewed as *export-related transaction costs* (Peng, 1996; Williamson, 1975, 1985). Unable to absorb these costs, most small firms have neither the expertise nor the resources to handle direct exports (Axinn, 1988; Bonaccorsi, 1993; da Rocha, Christensen and da Cunha, 1990; O'Rourke, 1985).[3]

Like the other two choices, the use of export intermediaries (choice 3) also entails costs and benefits for the producer. By using intermediaries as agents, producers have to incur *agency costs* when dealing with them in this principal-agent (manufacturer-intermediary) relationship (Bergen, Dutta and Walker, 1992; Eisenhardt, 1989a; Jensen and Meckling, 1976). The longer the channel length, the greater are the aggregate markup and the profits that must be shared with intermediaries, and, consequently, the higher the prices that foreign customers are charged for the final product. The primary benefit of using export intermediaries is their superior efficiency in marketing products abroad. Through their contacts, experience, specialization, and scale of operation, they economize on exporting costs more so than the producer can achieve on its own. In other words, the benefits of using export intermediary firms are the transaction cost savings that they may provide to manufacturers, compared with what manufacturers would incur if they handle the exports by themselves. At the same time, as agents, export inter-mediaries also introduce agency costs to manufacturers in this relationship.

The literature on the internationalization process of the firm suggests that most firms progress through several stages: from a purely domestic producer to an occasional exporter, then to a committed exporter, and later to a foreign investor through the establishment of subsidiaries abroad (O. Anderson, 1993; Beamish, 1990; Bilkey, 1978; Bonaccorsi, 1993; Johanson and Vahlne, 1977; Kamath et al., 1987; Melin, 1992; Reid, 1981). During initial stages, the typical, internationally inexperienced firm not only lacks finan-cial resources to establish in-house channels, but also lacks commit-ment from top management to seriously engage in export sales (Axinn, 1988; Cavusgil, 1984a, 1984b; Cavusgil and Kirpalani, 1993; Dichtl, Koeglmayr and Mueller, 1990; Gomez-Mejia, 1988). It is at this point that export intermediaries can provide value-added to the inexperienced exporter (Becker and Porter, 1983; Mattson, 1990). Prior research has shown that intermediaries can significantly speed up the learning process of inexperienced exporters, thus allowing for "quantum leaps" in their export commitment (Ilinitch and Peng, 1993, 1994).

For export intermediaries, there is a constant dilemma. A very profitable relationship with the producer, based on successful pro-motion of the producer's products abroad, can also be an unstable one since the producer that has reached a large export volume and has developed exporting skills may find it more economical to switch to in-house channels. In other words, there is a "built-in mortality" of client firms for export intermediaries, which face manufacturers' constant threat to establish in-house export channels and phase out the need for export intermediary services. Therefore, as agents, export intermediaries have the potential incentive not to exert the maximum effort (Jensen and Meckling, 1976). However, performing at a level that is totally unsatisfactory to manufacturers will result in the danger of being replaced, by another export intermediary, by manufacturers' own in-house export channels, or by a foreign-based, import intermediary (Bello and Lohtia, 1995; Rosson and Ford, 1982). Therefore, the success of export intermediaries will depend on how they can increase the odds of being selected and retained by manufacturers. Specifically, they need to assure their manufacturing clients that the transaction cost savings of using intermediaries outweigh the agency costs of using intermediaries. Otherwise, if the agency costs are too high, intermediaries will be replaced, thus losing any chance to be involved in the export process.

Since larger, more experienced manufacturers tend to develop in-house export capabilities, export intermediaries generally serve producers that tend to be internationally inexperienced and less committed to an export strategy. Typically, such firms are small and midsize manufacturers that take a "sales" approach to exports without much export commitment or planning (Cooper and Klein-schmidt, 1985; Liang, 1995; Peng and Heath, 1993; Walters, 1993; Walters and Samiee, 1990). Many of them are not committed to exporting, and some of them are only interested in exports when domestic markets enter a recession (Rao, Erramilli and Ganesh, 1990). However, when these manufacturers grow larger and become more sophisticated in their international operations, they tend to adopt a more systematic approach in foreign sales and the needs for export intermediary services decline.

In summary, export intermediaries are specialized service firms that connect domestic producers and foreign customers by providing value-added to the export process. As an important part of the indirect export mode, they help their client firms realize lower export-related transaction costs when dealing with foreign custo-mers. However, they also introduce agency costs to the manufac-turer-intermediary relationship. Their clients tend to be small and midsize manufacturers that are internationally inexperienced and less committed to exporting. Next, we move on to introduce the terminologies that have been used to describe these firms.

EXPORT MANAGEMENT COMPANIES

Different authors have employed an impressive array of terms to describe export intermediary firms, ranging from a broad term such as "international trade intermediary" (Perry, 1990, 1992) to a very restrictive one such as "export-only, merchant export management company" (Batra, 1991). The following contains a partial list of the labels, in alphabetical order, that have been applied to describe U.S. export intermediaries in the literature:

1. Export management company: Batra (1991); Brasch (1978); *Directory* (1987); High (1994); Howard and Maskulka (1988); Root (1994); U.S. Department of Commerce (1985)

2. Export middleman: Bello, et al. (1991)

3. Export service provider: Czinkota (1984)

4. Export specialist: Brasch (1981)

5. Export trade intermediary: U.S. Department of Commerce (1990)

6. Export trading company: Amine (1987); Bello and Williamson (1985a); Kaikati (1984); U.S. Sente (1982, 1986)

7. International trade intermediary: Perry (1990, 1992)

8. Trading house: Suzuki (1989)

9. Yankee trader: Wilkins (1970)

Since the colonial era, export intermediaries have existed in the United States (Galenson, 1986; Wilkins, 1970). While they have been described using various labels, the generic term "export management company" (EMC) is perhaps the most commonly used in the contemporary literature. An *export management company* has been defined by Root (1994: 102) in an authoritative text as "an international marketing specialist that functions as the export department of several manufacturers in noncompetitive lines."

In other words, an EMC, as an outside export department, is expected to do the same in terms of formulating and implementing an export strategy for its clients (usually manufacturers) that their in-house export channel would do. It selects international target markets, formulates an international marketing strategy, and executes and modifies the strategy according to the performance requirements set by its clients (Brasch, 1978, 1981; Haigh, 1994). Traditionally, the term EMC stands for an export intermediary which works as reps on commission and does *not* take title to the goods sold (Perry, 1992). However, more and more EMCs have begun to take title. Surveys by Batra (1991), Brasch (1978), Hay Associates (1977), and the U.S. Department of Commerce (1990) all suggested that close to half of them *always* take title, and only 8 to 22 percent of them never take title. As such, the distinction between the merchant-EMC which takes title and the agent-EMC which does not take title has become blurred (Barovick and Anderson, 1992).

Since setting up an EMC in the United States requires no incorporation, an official record with a complete list of EMCs does not exist, and "no one knows the exact size of that population" (Root, 1994: 102).[4] Various authors have given different estimates. For example, Root (1994: 102) estimated that there may be 1,200 such firms. Kaikati (1984: 60) believed that there are some 3,700 to 3,800 of them. Batra (1991: 60–61), relying on a directory published by the

CHAPTER 3

Global Evolution and U.S. Development: A Historical Excursion

While this book focuses on the success and failure of U.S. export intermediaries, I believe that without a proper understanding of the evolution of such an organizational form within a global context, any isolated analysis confined to the United States would result in a parochial exercise (Boyacigiller and Adler, 1991; Peng and Peterson, 1994). A historical overview of the worldwide evolution of such unique, specialized service organizations may present useful "base line" models against which one can compare variations in the United States.[1] Indeed, the diffusion of such an organizational form from Europe to North America and Japan in the 1800s, and more recently to a wide variety of countries in the late twentieth century, has become one of the most noticeable examples of global organizational learning and diffusion (Cho, 1987).

The worldwide evolution of export intermediaries can be conceptualized into three distinct stages: (a) early, (b) late modern, and (c) global diffusion (Peng, 1994b, 1995b). In this chapter I first examine these three periods of evolution on a worldwide basis, and then review the development of this type of organization in the United States during each of these three periods. Finally, contemporary implications of such a historical excursion are discussed.

GLOBAL EVOLUTION OF EXPORT INTERMEDIARIES

In early human history, since borders were not well defined, trading across "borders" with nearby tribes or "countries" was common. From the period of the earliest known civilization in 2500 B.C., Sumerian merchants found in their foreign commerce that they needed specialized personnel to receive, store, and sell their goods (Wilkins, 1970). Later, Roman traders exchanged goods with foreign merchants at more distant points, advancing as far east as central Asia to meet silk caravans from China through the famous Silk Road (Fairbank, Reischauer and Craig, 1989). During the Middle Ages, numerous Italian trading companies, most notably the Commenda, dominated caravan and maritime trade in medieval Europe (North, 1985).

While the importance of traders had long been recognized, experts on export intermediary firms generally agree that the year 1600 represented a major demarcation separating the "old" trading activities, which were mostly confined within the continent, from the "new" activities, which largely involved transoceanic movement of goods facilitated by a different breed of export intermediaries (Amine, 1987; Cho, 1987). Moreover, the historical evidence from 1600 onward is more available and accurate due to better documentation by these firms. Therefore, our historical excursion starts from that period, and an overview of the principal events can be seen in Table 3.1.

Stage I: Early Trading (1600–1876)

In 1600, the East India Company received royal charter in London from the Crown to monopolize the India trade (Cho, 1987). Several decades later (in 1670 and 1672), the Hudson's Bay Company and the Royal African Company were granted monopoly for fur trading within the drainage basin of Hudson Bay and for the British slave trade along the coast of West Africa, respectively (Carlos, 1992; Carlos and Nichols, 1990; Davies, 1957). Similar trading houses were established in the Netherlands (e.g., Oost-Indische Compagnie) and France (e.g., Société Commerciale de l'Ouest African and Compagnie Française de l'Afrique Occidentale) during the era of colonialism (Amine, 1987; Prakash, 1985).

Unlike their medieval predecessors, most of these companies were directly set up or supported by the state and enjoyed its patronage as long as they advanced the state's economic and political objectives (Dunning, 1993: 98). Specifically, each of these early trading companies was furnished with royal charters by its home country, which gave it not only the right to engage in trade, but also a blanket endorsement for making war, concluding treaties, and acquiring territories (Davies, 1957; Mill, 1958). The distinguishing feature of these organizations was their possession of monopoly control over the region where they conducted trading activities, such as the British in India, the Dutch in the East Indies (the present-day

Table 3.1
The Worldwide Evolution of Export Intermediary Firms
(1600–Present)

Stage	1. Early (1600–1876)	2. Late Modern (1876–1972)	3. Global Diffusion (1972–present)
Principal Events of Demarcation	1600: East India Company chartered in London 1670: Hudson's Bay Company chartered 1672: Royal African Company chartered	1876: Mitsui established in Japan 1889: Mitsubishi established 1892: Nichimen established	The year of passing legislation or issuing government decrees to promote export intermediaries 1972: Brazil 1975: South Korea 1977: Taiwan 1978: Thailand 1980: China 1980: Turkey 1982: USA
Representative Countries and Export Intermediaries	Great Britain: East India Company, Hudson's Bay Company, Royal African Company France: Compagnie Française de l'Afrique Occidentale, Société Commerciale de l'Ouest African The Netherlands: Oost-Indische Compagnie	Japan: Nine *sogo shosha*, i.e., Mitsui, Mitsubishi, Nichimen, Itochu, Sumitomo, Marubeni, Nisso Iwai, Tomen, Kanematsu	Japan: Same *sogo shosha* as in Stage II Brazil: Interbras, Maxitrade, Cobec South Korea: Samsung, Ssangyong, Daewoo Taiwan: E-Hsin, Pan Overseas, Nanlien Thailand: Saha Union, Siam Cement China: CITIC, Shanghai Foreign Trade Corporation Turkey: Enka, Anadolu USA: Sears World Trade, Commerce International, U.S. Surimi Commission

Source: M. W. Peng (1995b), *Tracking the Global Diffusion and U.S. Development of Export Intermediary Organizations: Evolution, Rationale, and Implications*, paper presented at the Academy of Management annual meeting, Vancouver, Canada, August.

Indonesia), the Spaniards in the Philippines, and the French in Indochina. As a result, within each of the given colonies, the competition between these organizations was minimal, and they were able to promote exports from their mercantilist motherlands to remote outposts around the globe (Prakash, 1985). This stage of relatively low-intensity competition went on for almost three centuries after the establishment of the East India Company.

While the activities of these intermediary firms certainly had a "dark" side ranging from colonialism to slave trading, they did perform one important function, namely, expanding the total scale and scope of global trade at a time when international trade was extremely limited, primitive, and hazardous.[2] Specifically, they facilitated a large number of exports among domestic manufacturers which faced tremendous barriers in entering foreign markets by themselves.

Stage II: Late Modern (1876–1972)

The worldwide evolution of export intermediary firms entered a second stage in 1876, when Mitsui was established in Japan. During the next 100 years or so, European trading companies met with increasingly vigorous challenges from Japan.

In the mid-nineteenth century, European trading houses such as the East India Company and Oost-Indische Compagnie expanded their business territories first from India to Indochina and then from China to Japan. Within years after Japan's Meiji Restoration in 1868, which opened the country for international trade, European traders quickly penetrated the Japanese market and commanded 95 percent of Japan's foreign trade volume by 1876 (Reischauer, 1974). Alarmed by such economic dependency on European trading houses, the progressive Meiji government established indigenous export intermediary firms as the trading arm of respective industrial groups (the *zaibatsu*), such as Mitsui (1876), Mitsubishi (1889), and Nichimen (1892). Competing with the Europeans for Japan's growing trade volume, these companies captured 12.5 percent of the total volume by 1887, 39.3 percent by 1900, and over 80 percent by 1918 (Cho, 1987). In other words, a great deal of organizational learning occurred to transplant the organizing principles of a Western concept, namely, the export intermediary firm as an organizational form, into the Japanese context (Westney, 1987).

During this second stage, despite the devastating defeat in World War II, the Japanese preserved and strengthened the trading company form. During the postwar decades, the prewar *zaibatsu* were first dissolved and later transformed to *keiretsu* groups (Johnson, 1982). The trading companies survived such economy-wide restructuring, and continued to serve as agents for Japan's manufacturing firms, especially for members of their respective *keiretsu* groups

(Gerlach, 1992; Kotabe, 1984). Since the late 1950s, a dozen or so gigantic trading companies associated with the *keiretsu* have been referred to by the Japanese press as the *sogo shosha*, loosely translated as "general trading companies" (Kojima and Ozawa, 1984; Yoshihara, 1982). This top group aside, the remaining Japanese trading companies consist of some 8,000 to 9,000 small and midsize trading companies, called the *senmon shosha*, each specializing in a few products and limited services (Amine, 1987; Sarathy, 1985).

During this stage, especially during the postwar period, trading companies, most notably the *sogo shosha*, greatly spearheaded the expansion of Japanese exports (Cho, 1987; Kotabe, 1984; Young, 1978). Describing their role as the "vanguard" of the Japanese economy (Yoshihara, 1982), Bello and Williamson (1985a: 60) wrote:

As marketing intermediaries, Japanese general trading companies have been extraordinarily successful in developing world markets for Japan's domestic industries. Japanese [general] trading companies are enormous global marketing firms with extensive investments in foreign offices, communication centers, and logistic facilities. With those resources, Japanese [general] trading companies achieve significant economies of scale in international trade and provide a full range of low cost export services to Japanese producers.

In no small part, trading companies, especially the *sogo shosha*, contributed toward Japan's export-led economic success during the first few decades after World War II. While this organizational innovation did not originate in Japan, the Japanese improved upon the form and perfected its use (Cho, 1987; Westney, 1987). The level of competition during this period might be considered as moderate, since the initial exports which Japanese trading companies brought to world markets concentrated on the low end and were often neglected by the then dominant American and European firms, which tended to cover high-end markets. Toward the end of this period, American firms increasingly engaged in foreign direct investment and transformed themselves into multinationals (Vernon, 1971; Wilkins, 1970, 1974). European trading companies, with a few exceptions such as the Hong Kong-based Jardine Matheson, gradually withdrew from their former colonies.

In summary, export intermediaries, such as the *sogo shosha*, lowered the export-related costs for a large number of Japanese manufacturers during this period. Spearheading Japan's spectacular export expansion during the postwar decades, these firms have become a strong force in the global economic landscape.

Stage III: Global Diffusion (1972–Present)

In the 1970s, despite the two Oil Shocks which devastated much of the world economy, Japan was found to be able to absorb such shocks and continue to expand its exports while vigorously upgrading its economy. Such "Japanese miracle" received worldwide attention (Johnson, 1982). As the world economy has become more turbulent and competitive since the 1970s, industrialized countries are not the only ones interested in expanding their exports to counter balance domestic fluctuation; many developing countries, led by export-oriented newly industrialized countries (NICs) from East Asia, also want to join the export competition (So and Chiu, 1995; Rubner, 1987; Wortzel and Vernon-Wortzel, 1983). In this process, export intermediary firms, especially the large *sogo shosha*, have been identified as a major source of Japan's competitive advantage and have attracted a great deal of imitation—almost to the extent of a *"sogo shosha* mania" in the 1970s and 1980s (Amine, 1987; Cho, 1987; Dziubla, 1982). As such, the development of export inter- mediaries has entered a global diffusion stage, as more and more nations strive to carve out a larger niche in the world marketplace through the use of sophisticated intermediary organizations (Kim, 1986).

The recent global diffusion stage started about twenty-five years ago. In November 1972, Brazil passed the Presidential Decree Law No. 1298 to create *sogo shosha*-type export intermediaries in order to boost exports. This legislation represented the first in any nation directly aiming at imitating the Japanese trading companies (Amine, 1987). As listed in Table 3.2, a number of countries followed suit in the 1970s and early 1980s, including South Korea (1975), Taiwan (1977), Thailand (1978), Turkey (1980), China (1980), as well as the United States (1982), all using legislation or government decrees to spur the development of *sogo shosha*-type export intermediaries intended to improve export performance (Cho, 1987; Czinkota, 1984; Lardy, 1992; MacBean, 1996; Wortzel and Vernon-Wortzel, 1983). While the specific U.S. efforts during this stage of global diffusion will be addressed in a later section, it is worth noting here that the passage of the Export Trading Company Act (ETC Act) in 1982 was not an isolated incident. Rather, it was against this institutional background of global diffusion of export intermediaries that Congress passed the act (Rubner, 1987).

The total volume of global trade expanded enormously during the postwar period. From 1950 to the mid-1980s, world merchandise ex- ports increased about nine times in volume (Grimwade, 1989: 51–53).

Table 3.2
The Global Diffusion of Export Intermediaries

Export Intermediaries	Country (Year)	Legislation/Government Regulations Issued
General trading company (*sogo shosha*)	Japan (1876)	Meiji government mandate
Export trading company	Brazil (1972)	Presidential Decree Law No. 1298
General trading company	South Korea (1975)	Ministry of Commerce and Industry ordinance
Large trading company	Taiwan (1977)	Ministry of Economy ordinance
International trading company	Thailand (1978)	Board of Investment ordinance
Foreign trade corporate company	Turkey (1980)	State Planning Organization decree
Foreign trade corporation	China (1980)	Ministry of Foreign Economic Relations and Trade decree
Export trading company	United States (1982)	Export Trading Company Act passed by Congress

Sources: Brazil: L. S. Amine (1987), Toward a conceptualization of export trading companies in world markets, *Advances in International Marketing*, 2: 216–220; Japan, South Korea, Taiwan, Thailand, and Turkey: D.-S. Cho (1987), *The General Trading Company: Concept and Strategy* (Lexington, MA: Lexington Books), 43–84; China: N. R. Lardy (1992), *Foreign Trade and Economic Reform in China, 1978–1990* (Cambridge and New York: Cambridge University Press), 39–40; United States: U.S. Department of Commerce (1985), *A Competitive Edge for U.S. Exports: The Export Trade Certificate of Review Program* (Washington, DC: Department of Commerce, International Trade Administration), 2.

During this period, as more and more countries launched export intermediary firms, often subsidized by their governments, the Japanese could no longer rely on selling low-end products and had to upgrade product offerings and expand their range of services (Mitsui, 1991a, 1991b; Yoshihara, 1982). As a result, they have substantially moved beyond the traditional export/import role, and have been extensively involved in foreign direct investment, turn-key "mega" projects, and third-country trade (Amine, 1987; Kotabe, 1984; Young, 1978). In doing so, they have achieved superb diversification in terms of products, areas, and functions, selling virtually everything "from noodles to missiles" (Cho, 1987). Moreover, they have grown enorously in size. Recent statistics show that seven of the nine *sogo shosha* were among the top twnety-five largest firms in the world, as measured by sales volume, including all the top three positions in 1995 (*Fortune*, 1996). The other two *sogo shosha* were also among the top 100 group. As Table 3.3 indicates, their sheer size makes them formidable competitors in the international marketplace.

Given the global scope of export intermediary development and persistent country-specific differences (Porter, 1990), it seems clear that the organizational capability to develop export intermediaries would be different for firms from different countries. Kogut (1991) suggested that the diffusion of organizing principles such as the export intermediary organization is slower than the diffusion of tangible technologies across national borders. In this regard, the Japanese have proven their remarkable ability in internalizing an externally developed organizational concept, namely, the export intermediary form (Mansfield, 1988; Westney, 1987). The results of other countries' efforts to emulate the *sogo shosha* vary. According to Cho (1987: 80–81), by the early 1980s, more successful *sogo shosha* emulators in Korea and Turkey commanded 51 percent and 38 percent of their countries' exports, respectively. In comparison, less successful emulators in Taiwan and Thailand only contributed 1 percent and 5 percent of their total exports, respectively. U.S. efforts in this regard, detailed in the next section, have been largely ineffective.

Summary

In this section, the 400-year history of worldwide evolution of export intermediary firms has been reviewed. There is a clear pattern of gradual diffusion over the world of this unique yet powerful organizational form specializing in export trade. With such worldwide evolution as a backdrop, next I turn to the historical development of export intermediaries in the United States.

DEVELOPMENT OF EXPORT INTERMEDIARIES IN THE UNITED STATES

Following the pattern of global evolution, one can divide the development of U.S. export intermediary firms into three stages (see

Figure 3.1), which approximately correspond to the three stages of global evolution discussed in the previous section, the major difference being the divergence during the second stage (Peng, 1994b, 1995b, 1996).

Table 3.3
Top Twenty-five of the World's Largest Corporations in 1995 (Measured by Revenue)

Worldwide Ranking		Primary Industry	Home Country	Revenue (US$ millions)
1.	**Mitsubishi**[*]	trading	Japan	184,365.2
2.	**Mitsui**	trading	Japan	181,518.7
3.	**Itochu**	trading	Japan	169,164.6
4.	General Motors	automotive	USA	168,828.6
5.	**Sumitomo**	trading	Japan	167,530.7
6.	**Marubeni**	trading	Japan	161,057.4
7.	Ford Motor	automotive	USA	137,137.0
8.	Toyota Motor	automotive	Japan	111,052.0
9.	Exxon	petroleum	USA	110,009.0
10.	Royal Dutch/Shell	petroleum	UK / Netherlands	109,833.7
11.	**Nissho Iwai**	trading	Japan	97,886.4
12.	Wal-Mart	retailing	USA	93,627.0
13.	Hitachi	electronics	Japan	84,167.1
14.	Nippon Life	insurance	Japan	83,206.7
15.	NTT	telecommunications	Japan	81,937.2
16.	AT&T	telecommunications	USA	79,609.0
17.	Daimler-Benz	automotive	Germany	72,256.1
18.	IBM	computer	USA	71,940.0
19.	Matsushita	electronics	Japan	70,398.4
20.	General Electric	electronics	USA	70,028.0
21.	**Tomen**	trading	Japan	67,755.8
22.	Mobil	petroleum	USA	66,724.0
23.	Nissan Motor	automotive	Japan	62,568.5
24.	Volkswagen	automotive	Germany	61,489.1
25.	Siemens	electronics	Germany	60,673.6

[*] Highlighted are Japan's general trading companies (*sogo shosha*). Other *sogo shosha* in the *Fortune* global 100 group include: Nichimen (#35, $50,842 million in 1995 sales) and Kanematsu (#37, $49,838 million in 1995 sales).

Source: *Fortune* (1996), The global 500 list, August 5: F1-F4. Reprinted with permission of *Fortune*, Global 500, © 1996 Time, Inc. All rights reserved.

Figure 3.1
Export Intermediaries: Global Development
versus U.S. Variations

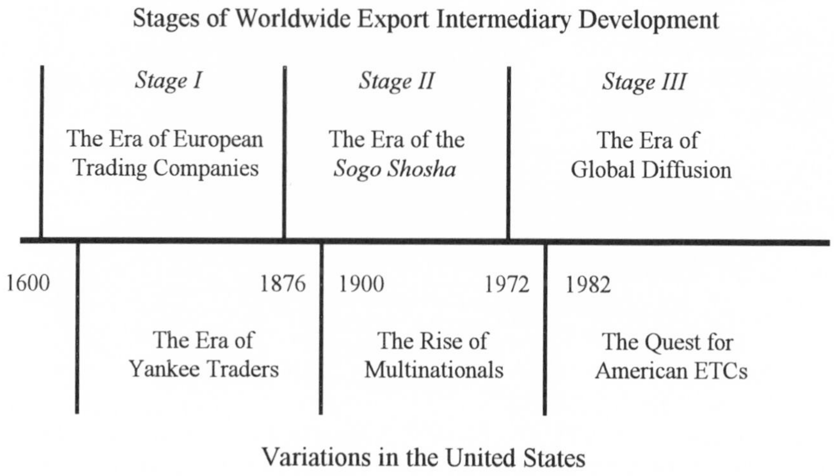

Stages of Worldwide Export Intermediary Development

Stage I	*Stage II*	*Stage III*
The Era of European Trading Companies	The Era of the *Sogo Shosha*	The Era of Global Diffusion

1600	1876	1900	1972	1982
	The Era of Yankee Traders	The Rise of Multinationals		The Quest for American ETCs

Variations in the United States

Source: M. W. Peng (1996), *Behind the Success and Failure of U.S. Export Intermediaries*, doctoral dissertation (Seattle: University of Washington), 64.

Stage I: Early Trading (Up to 1900)—The Era of Yankee Traders

This was a period when Yankee traders, intermediaries modeled after European trading houses, first dominated America's export trade and then spearheaded the development of many overseas markets. But later on, intermediaries were increasingly eclipsed by U.S. manufacturers' foreign investment and in-house export efforts.

Colonial America depended on foreign trade. Since essential manufactured products had to be imported from Great Britain, locally produced goods had to be exported to pay for the imports (North, 1961). "In a land with a small population, poor internal communication, and therefore a limited domestic market, foreign trade offered to colonial businessmen the best prospects for wealth" (Wilkins, 1970: 4). During this era, while European traders dominated much of the New World's trade, there rose a new class of American intermediary firms, dubbed Yankee traders, whose presence and influence became increasingly known (Galenson, 1986).

After the Revolution, American businesses had to adjust to new political as well as economic realities; no longer were Yankee traders given Empire preference by the British. To compensate for the reduction in dealings with the British right after the Revolution, Americans sought two solutions. One was to develop local industry and expand internal trade. The other was to seek new and distant foreign markets and U.S. export intermediaries spearheaded these endeavors (North, 1961; Rosenberg, 1982; Wilkins, 1970). However, since many of the existing trading areas such as India were dominated, and to a large extent monopolized, by Europeans, Yankee traders had to seek new markets where the Europeans had not established their dominance yet, such as the Pacific Northwest, the Far East, and Latin America.

In the early years of the American republic, trade with the Pacific Northwest was "foreign" business. For instance, in 1808, the American Fur Company was incorporated as an intermediary that traded with the Indians, exchanging American and European manufactured goods for fur. By 1812, in search of fur trading opportunities, this company penetrated the northwest coast of the present-day Washington state (Wilkins, 1970: 7).

In the Pacific basin, Yankee traders established themselves as the predominant trading force, creating trading outposts and settlements in Fiji and Hawaii by the early 1800s. Across the Pacific, they actively participated in the Canton (the present-day Guangzhou) trade with China, representing nine out of fifty-five foreign firms there by 1836. By that time, American traders had also firmly established themselves in Manila (Wilkins, 1970: 9).[3]

In the Western Hemisphere, American export intermediaries were extensively found in places such as Mexico, Cuba, Chile, Peru, and Argentina by the 1830s. Across the Atlantic, Yankee traders became an increasingly viable force competing with the European trading houses. By the 1830s, a large number of Yankee traders resided in Europe, bringing an increasing quantity of American goods to the Old World. At that time, however, American traders were still under the shadow of the gigantic European trading houses in terms of scale, scope, and sophistication (Wilkins, 1970: 10).

During the latter half of the nineteenth century, along with the closure of the western frontier, Americans' nation-building efforts culminated in a sizable domestic economy with an enormous market (North, 1961; Pusteri, 1988). Its strengths included an efficient internal transportation system, a high degree of specialization and mechanization, rapid scientific and technological advance, as well as the foundations of ground-breaking organizational innovations such as Taylorism and Fordism, which blossomed in the early twentieth century. All these strengths translated into globally competitive positions in a great number of industries, ranging from agriculture to textiles, from steel to transportation (Chandler, 1990). The result of such competitiveness in the global marketplace was a drastic increase in U.S. exports worldwide at the turn of the century, which was called the "American export invasion" by some Europeans (Rosenberg, 1982).

The value of American exports surged from $800 million in 1895 to $2.3 billion in 1914, an increase of almost 240 percent. Until 1914, nearly half of U.S. exports were generated by the agricultural sector, which exported nearly 20 percent of its total output. In 1914, agricultural exports were eclipsed by the volume of manufactured products. The growth of manufactured goods alone during the 1895–1914 period was nearly 500 percent (Rosenberg, 1982: 16–18).

The growth of American exports at the turn of the century, however, did not spur the development of large, diversified trade intermediary organizations in the United States. Rather, an increasing number of these exports were handled by manufacturers themselves through in-house export channels as well as foreign production. During the twentieth century, there rose a great number of U.S.-based multinational enterprises whose integrated foreign production and sales capabilities rendered the need for intermediary services minimal. As a result, despite their earlier contributions, Yankee traders gradually became eclipsed by the multinationals.

Stage II: Late Modern (1900–1982)—The Rise of Multinationals

The rise of U.S. multinational enterprises (MNEs) during much of the twentieth century has been documented by a large body of literature, including major contributions by Aharoni (1966), Bartlett and Ghoshal (1989), Stopford and Wells (1972), Vernon (1971, 1977), and Wilkins (1970, 1974), among others. Theoretical analysis of the rationale for MNEs, as opposed to smaller firms trading with each other across national borders, can be found in the works of Buckley and Casson (1976), Caves (1995), Dunning (1980, 1988, 1993), Hennart (1982), Hymer (1976), Penrose (1959), and Rugman (1981). A detailed review of this literature is beyond the scope of this historical excursion. What is most interesting here is the propensity of U.S. manufacturers to handle the exports by themselves through foreign direct investment (FDI) rather than through export intermediary firms.

Wilkins (1970: Chap. 1) suggested that Americans' first FDI was made by traders well before the Civil War. Until the turn of the century, most of these investments were made by Yankee traders for the purpose of controlling foreign supplies and agents. For example, in Hawaii, Ladd & Co. transformed itself from a trader to a sugar plantation developer in 1835 (Wilkins, 1970: 12). Similarly, in Peru, W. R. Grace & Co., which was an important trading and shipping company, acquired sugar estates as payment for a debt and eventually became Cartavio Sugar Co. in 1891 (Rosenberg, 1982: 24).

However, beginning in the latter half of the nineteenth century, significant FDI was initiated by U.S. manufacturers, thus eclipsing the role of export intermediaries. The acceleration of American manufacturing FDI since the 1890s formed the basis of many of today's huge MNEs. The Singer Sewing Machine Company, established in 1851, was a pioneer in this process (Rosenberg, 1982: 20–22; Wilkins, 1970: 37–47). Within 17 years since the company's inception, Singer had achieved rapid progress in international business involvement. It first exported through indirect channels by selling to European trading houses and later relied on direct export channels by establishing sales subsidiaries abroad. In 1868, it set up an assembly plant in Glasgow, Scotland, to serve major European markets, thus becoming the first U.S. manufacturer to have foreign production facilities through FDI.

While remarkable, Singer's experience was by no means unique. Reflecting their growing confidence in their ability to compete abroad, large American manufacturers increasingly adopted entry modes that were in favor of more control through the use of equity investment abroad (Dunning, 1993: Chap. 5). Numerous factors contributed to such FDI-based multinational expansion, including

- Circumventing foreign tariff walls (Wilkins, 1970, 1974)

- Moving closer to raw materials or markets (Rosenberg, 1982)

- Extending product life cycles (Vernon, 1966, 1971)

- Hedging foreign exchange risks (Aliber, 1983)

- Utilizing offshore cheap labor (Moxon, 1975)

- Taking advantage of integrated production (Kogut, 1989)

- Protecting technological knowhow (Hennart, 1982)

- Maintaining options abroad (Peng, 1995a)

The scale and scope of such multinational expansion by American MNEs were especially profound after the end of World War II. Immediately following World War II, as the only major developed nation with its economy unscathed, the United States accounted for 75 percent of the world's total output, and its MNEs dominated much of the world trade (Vernon, 1971). Such FDI-based multinational expansion was so widespread that, to some observers, it represented another "American challenge" (Servan-Schreiber, 1968), similar to the earlier "American export invasion" at the turn of the century.

One of the results of such multinational expansion through FDI was that the importance of export intermediary firms declined vis-à-vis that of manufacturers' in-house export capabilities and foreign production and sales subsidiaries. While available statistics do not indicate exactly when the sales of U.S. business abroad surpassed U.S. exports, maybe as early as 1914, according to Wilkins (1974: 374), U.S. exports were already being eclipsed by the sales of American MNEs' foreign branches, affiliates, and subsidiaries. After World War II, sales of U.S. subsidiaries abroad routinely outperformed U.S. exports (Wilkins, 1974: 375). Moreover, the bulk of U.S. exports were concentrated in a small number of very large MNEs through in-house export channels. In comparison, the volume of exports handled by U.S. export intermediaries was small, estimated at 5 to 10 percent of total manufactured exports (Perry, 1992: 148; Root, 1994: 102).

In summary, after the turn of the century, especially during the postwar decades, American companies experienced unprecedented growth in international business. However, it was manufacturing MNEs, not export intermediaries as was the case in Europe or Japan, that spearheaded such expansion. As a result, export intermediary firms in the United States experienced a decline in size, function, and importance, and there were no large *sogo shosha*-type general trading companies that evolved from the early trading days. Long gone was the heyday of the Yankee traders.

Stage III: Since 1982—The Search for American ETCs

After almost seven decades of multinational expansion after the turn of the century, the U.S. performance in the global economy began to weaken since the 1970s and into the 1980s (Carvounis, 1987; Krugman, 1990). For the first time since 1914, the United States turned from a net contributor of FDI to a net recipient of FDI and became a debtor nation (Destler, 1986; Lodge and Crum, 1985). The same period also witnessed record high levels of inflation and unemployment, with rising trade deficits and fluctuations in interest rates and in the value of the dollar (Krugman, 1990). Overall, the competitiveness of U.S. industry was seriously questioned by a large number of experts (President's Commission on Industrial Competitiveness, 1985; Scott and Lodge, 1985; Teece, 1987).

While the American share in the global economy has declined (from contributing an all-time high of 75 percent of the world's total output immediately after World War II to less than one-quarter [approximately 22 percent] today), MNEs from other parts of the world have risen to challenge the U.S. dominance (Ohmae, 1985, 1989; Thurow, 1993). In contrast to the earlier "American export invasion" found in Europe, there was an "import invasion" in the United States: By 1984 Americans were spending 20 cents of each dollar on imports, ranging from automobiles to toys, from electronics to shoes (*Business Week*, 1984). At the same time, 70 percent of the goods produced in the United States competed with merchandise from abroad (President's Commission on Industrial Competitiveness, 1985). With the U.S. trade deficit constantly on the rise, such a situation in turn sparked pressure on Congress to protect American industry (Cohen, et al., 1996). Compared with protectionist policies such as curtailing imports, erecting trade barriers, and manipulating exchange rates, export expansion has been identified as an effective solution for reducing the trade deficit and stimulating the economy (Johns, 1985; McFadden, 1987; Richardson and Rindal, 1995).

Since the 1980s, exports from the United States have grown rapidly. Specifically, between 1986 and 1994, exports more than doubled, to $696 billion, or more than 10 percent of total gross domestic product (GDP). At a rate of 9 percent adjusted for inflation, exports grew four times faster than GDP during that period (*Fortune*, 1995: S1). Despite significant improvement, U.S. export performance still pales when compared with that of its major trading partners, such as Canada, France, Germany, Great Britain, Japan, and the Netherlands (see Table 3.4). During the same period, the amount of imports also increased significantly. As a result, the export boom was unable to compensate for import increases, and the U.S. trade deficit remained at a high level. In 1987, it rose to a record $171 billion (Czinkota, et al., 1996: 17). The deficit went down somewhat afterward due to the recent export boom. However, in 1996, it again hit an eight-year high for the period 1988–96, at $114 billion (*Wall Street Journal*, 1997: A2). Annual trade deficits in this range are insupportable in the long run, since they add to the U.S. international debt which must be serviced and eventually repaid (Cohen, et al., 1996). In short, while export growth since the 1980s is evident, it is not enough given the strong demand for imports and the high level of trade deficits. Further increases in exports, therefore, continue to be a major public policy concern, particularly since one billion dollars' worth of exports creates, on average, 2,000 jobs (Czinkota, et al., 1996: 17).

Then how can the United States significantly increase exports? It was found that large firms in the United States, most notably the MNEs, have already been extensively involved in exporting and FDI. While they still have huge potential, they will not become new sources of significant export growth. In contrast, the export potential for small and midsize firms remains largely untapped and it is these firms that represent the country's best hope to combat trade deficits. The Department of Commerce estimated that in the mid-1980s, among 250,000 U.S. manufacturing firms, only 10 percent exported; and of that 10 percent, less than one percent accounted for more than 80 percent of the total export volume (Kaikati, 1984: 59). On the other hand, some 20,000 small firms manufactured internationally competitive products but did not attempt to market them abroad. Recently, exports among small and midsize firms have increased noticeably, thus contributing toward the export boom since the late 1980s. For example, 49 percent of companies with annual revenues of less than $100 million exported products in 1993, up from 36 percent of such companies in 1990 (*Wall Street Journal*, 1994: B2). However, the United States is still behind its major trading partners

Table 3.4

International Trade Performance: The United States and Its Major Trading Partners (1992–1994)

	Merchandise Exports as % of GDP (1992)	Exports Per Capita in 1994 (US$)	Imports Per Capita in 1994 (US$)
Canada	24%	5,898	5,258
France	20	4,037	3,953
Germany	25	5,204	4,630
Great Britain	17	3,596	3,989
Japan	10	3,162	2,193
Netherlands	44	8,765	7,938
United States	9	1,965	2,546

Source: M. R. Czinkota, I. A. Ronkainen and M. H. Moffett (1996), *International Business*, 4th ed. (Ft. Worth, TX: Dryden), 16–17.

in this regard. In Germany, for example, companies with fewer than 500 employees—equivalent to the small and midsize businesses defined by the U.S. Small Business Administration—account for approximately 30 percent of that nation's exports. The comparable figure for this country is about 10 percent (*Business Week*, 1991: 64–65).

Given the persistent reluctance among small firms to export, the key to further increasing U.S. exports by tapping into the export potential of small and midsize manufacturers seemed to lie in the development of export intermediaries. This was the view embraced by Congress, whose members believed that only through rigorous development of export intermediary firms, modeled after Japan's *sogo shosha*, could the export potential of small firms be fully tapped (U.S. Senate, 1982). However, the country lacked large-scale, *sogo shosha*-type intermediaries that would greatly facilitate export trade (Christensen, 1989; Kaikati, 1984). Existing export intermediaries, mostly export management companies (EMCs) and export trading companies (ETCs), generally were small and undercapitalized, and found it difficult to obtain export financing. Moreover, U.S. antitrust laws were perceived by many manufacturers as a barrier to creating export alliances (Dziubla, 1982). As a result, U.S. export intermediaries could not match the strength and sophistication of integrated, well-financed trading companies from abroad, especially the *sogo shosha*.

It was against this background that the Export Trading Company Act (ETC Act) was passed and signed into law by President Ronald Reagan on October 8, 1982, aiming at strengthening the U.S. export intermediary sector.[4] For the first time since the early days of the Yankee traders, the importance of export intermediaries has again been recognized in this country, thus echoing the efforts to emulate the *sogo shosha* concept in countries such as Brazil, China, South Korea, Taiwan, Thailand, and Turkey since 1972. Under the heading of the Export Trading Company Act of 1982, there are four subtitles:

1. The Export Trading Company Act

2. The Bank Export Services Act

3. The Export Trade Certificates of Review Act

4. The Foreign Trade Antitrust Improvements Act

In its entirety, the ETC Act has two major provisions: (a) allowing banks to participate indirectly in exporting and (b) easing antitrust constraints for registered export trading companies. A major weakness of U.S. export intermediaries until then was their lack of close ties to financial institutions, which resulted in their being small and thinly capitalized (U.S. Senate, 1982). Part of the reason for that situation was that U.S. banks were not allowed to invest in trading companies, reflecting the post-New Deal tradition of keeping commerce and banking separate. However, such restrictions made it extremely difficult for export intermediaries to obtain trade-related financing, which would be necessary to take title to goods (Willsher, 1995). As the first exception to the long-standing U.S. banking tradition, the ETC Act allows bank holding companies and certain other banking organizations to invest up to 10 percent of their capital and surplus in export trading companies. "This is landmark legislation in that it allows a banking organization to have an equity interest, including complete ownership, in a commercial business venture" (U.S. Department of Commerce, 1990: 2). Supporters of the act argued that because of banks' financial expertise and international knowledge as well as their capital, they stand in a unique position to help facilitate the export trade (Howard and Maskulka, 1988). Some even suggested that banks themselves may spin off "one stop" export trading subsidiaries to serve the needs of potential exporters (Christensen, 1989; Kaikati, 1984).

The second major provision of the ETC Act is to grant antitrust immunity, with concurrence from the Justice Department, to those "export trading companies" certified by the Commerce Department. As noted earlier in Chapter 2, an ETC is defined as any individual or organization that specializes in export trade. Congress believed that such a provision would allow U.S. firms to join forces through the use of an ETC to compete abroad, even though antitrust laws bar them from cooperating within the United States (U.S. Senate, 1982).

While the ETC Act's encouragement of banks' involvement in export trade is new, the idea of granting antitrust immunity to ETCs as a means of promoting exports is not new. Back in 1918, Congress passed the Export Trade Act of 1918 (commonly known as the Webb-Pomerene Act) for many of the same reasons that it passed the ETC Act of 1982. The 1918 act waived certain antitrust law coverage for companies to form export-oriented associations. However, the hope that the act would result in the formation of hundreds of associations serving as joint selling agencies for small firms had not materialized (Federal Trade Commission, 1967). At their peak, Webb-Pomerene associations numbered 57 and accounted for 19 percent of total U.S. exports in the 1930s. By 1979, the number dropped to 33 associations, responsible for less than 2 percent of total exports (Kaikati, 1984).

Part of the reason that the 1918 act failed was the ambiguity surrounding the antitrust immunity (Kaikati, 1984). Congress hoped that by clearly specifying the antitrust coverage, as well as allowing bank participation in export trade, the ETC Act of 1982 would create a new generation of export intermediaries that can significantly boost U.S. exports and compete successfully in the global market-place. Specifically, the Department of Commerce predicted that there would be an increase of 5 to 20 percent in U.S. exports over the first five-year period after the passage of the ETC Act, with a minimum gain of $11 billion in exports and 350,000 jobs (Baldridge, 1982; U.S. Senate, 1982).

Despite such high-profile, large-scale efforts to promote the deve-lopment of export intermediary firms in the United States, the actual results have been largely disappointing (Christensen, 1989; Egan, 1987; Howard and Maskulka, 1988; Kryzanowski and Ursel, 1993; Perry, 1992). In 1986, the Department of Commerce reported to Congress that despite efforts to publicize the ETC Act, the business community showed a distinct lack of interest or enthusiasm (U.S. Senate, 1986). Similar lack of interest was also reported by Czinkota (1984) and Howard and Maskulka (1988). Lacy (1987: 191) estimated that the ETC Act accounted for over $1 billion in exports, which was only about 1.3 percent of the increase in U.S. exports of $76 billion in constant dollars, from 1983 to 1987. This was far short of the gains predicted by the Department of Commerce (Baldridge, 1982).

In the fifteen years since the passage of the ETC Act, certified ETCs have remained as a minority among thousands of U.S. export intermediaries. Christensen (1989: 266–67) surveyed forty-five banks which had to some extent participated in ETCs and found that twnety-seven of them were totally inactive by 1989. Of the eighteen banks still active in ETC operations, only four would meet the operational definition of export intermediaries used for this book (i.e., located within the United States, independent, and engaging in export sales), and the rest were offering either some financing or consulting. Banks' involvement with ETCs was not very successful, to say the least (DeNoble and Belch, 1986). Financial markets even reacted negatively to banks' announcement that they would engage in export trade due to banks' perceived lack of expertise in that area, despite the contrary expec-tations held by advocates of the ETC Act (Kryzanowski and Ursel, 1993).

For nonbank ETCs, during the period of 1983 to 1992, the first decade since the passage of the ETC Act, there were only 148 organizations that applied for an ETC certificate from the Depart-ment of Commerce for antitrust immunity, among which only 104 remained active in 1992 (Peng, 1996: 266). Few of these certified

ETCs are of any size, and most of them are similar in nature to existing export management companies.[5] Their share of total U.S. exports, according to an official at the Export Trading Company Affairs Office at the Commerce Department, which is mandated by Congress to monitor the implementation of the ETC Act, would be "minimal" by 1994.[6]

Given such lackluster performance, several researchers have concluded that despite strong hopes, the ETC Act of 1982 has failed to successfully spur the development of large-scale, *sogo shosha*-type export intermediary organizations in the United States (Christensen, 1989; Egan, 1987; Howard and Maskulka, 1988; Perry, 1992). While ETCs certified by the Commerce Department may not have made much impact, in the 1980s the ETC Act did stimulate the establishment of several large uncertified ETCs by well-known U.S. corporations, such as Sears, General Electric, and Control Data. Among them, Sears World Trade, established in 1981 before the passage of the ETC Act, was considered to be on the order of a Mitsui or Mitsubishi and to represent the best model for an American *sogo shosha*. With a $100 million investment from the parent company, Sears World Trade intended to be a "one stop" trading shop which could trade anything, anywhere. However, in 1987, after losing $59 million in about four years, Sears World Trade closed up. Similarly, Commerce International, the high-tech trading subsidiary of Control Data, ceased operations in 1986. General Electric's trading unit is now an in-house trader again (Amine, 1987; Christensen, 1989).

In short, "the dust raised by the ETC Act has settled" (Perry, 1992: 29). Despite the renewed interest in developing the export intermediary sector, large-scale trade intermediary firms that might have been able to facilitate exports for small firms, as the supporters of the act hoped, simply have not survived the times. Overall, the act has been widely viewed as ineffective and thus ignored. In a new, 311-page text entitled *Fundamentals of U.S. Foreign Trade Policy* (Cohen, et al., 1996: 153), only one paragraph was devoted to describe the ETC Act of 1982. In a random survey of 1,046 export intermediary owners, principals, and managers I conducted in 1995, a striking 29 percent of the respondents had not even heard of the act, and only 3.5 percent of the respondent firms were registered with the Department of Commerce as an ETC (Peng, 1996).

Fifteen years after the passage of the ETC Act, the United States is left with what it had in the beginning—the thousands of small, undercapitalized EMCs, ETCs, and other intermediary firms, plus offices of the large Japanese *sogo shosha* that are among the largest U.S. exporters. While some of them have been remarkably successful, most of them have not made much impact. It is surprising to learn that before, during, and after the policy debate surrounding the passage of the ETC Act of 1982, no one has seriously studied what determines the performance of export intermediaries. Although no one knows the actual mechanisms of how these firms can add value to the export process and what makes them perform better, the act was passed as a part of the global wave of "*sogo shosha* mania" (Kim, 1986). Once it became clear that it did not work, old sayings such as "Trading companies only work in Japan" and "The individualistic U.S. business culture does not appreciate the role of intermediaries" resurfaced to explain this phenomenon. At the same time, many small and midsize manufacturers continue to be frustrated by the lack of guidance on how to find the best-performing intermediaries that will help them enter foreign markets, and the nation's trade deficit remains at a high level.

Summary

This section has reviewed the development of export intermediary firms in the United States since the colonial era. Such an evolution demonstrates the close linkage between the demand for export intermediary services and the exporters' primary mode of foreign entry. Manufacturers during the early period relied on indirect exports, thus creating strong demand for intermediary services. However, the enormous development of American MNEs after the turn of the twentieth century lowered the demand for such services. More recently, as the nation attempts to tap the residual export potential mostly resident in small firms in order to combat the growing trade deficit, there seems to be some renewed interest in the development of this sector, especially since the passage of the ETC Act of 1982. The results, however, have been largely unsatisfactory.

CONCLUSIONS

Although export intermediary firms have existed for a long time, the widespread adoption of this organizational form has been a more recent phenomenon. Over time, such an organizational form has experienced a process of global diffusion, first from Europe to North America and Japan in the 1800s, and later on to a wide variety of countries in this century. Moreover, as more and more nations have recognized the role of export intermediaries in facilitating their exports, the diffusion of such an organizational concept has accelerated during the late twentieth century, a period which is characterized by heightened global integration and intensified competition. As the world economy becomes more competitive and interdependent (D'Aveni, 1994; Levitt, 1983; Ohmae, 1985, 1989; Thurow, 1993), exporters from various countries compete not only on *product competitiveness*, but also on *process competitiveness*, namely, the efficiency of the export process. It is this competition on export process efficiency that has stimulated the global diffusion of export intermediaries in recent decades (Peng, 1994b, 1995b). As exporters attempt to find ways to become more efficient when entering foreign markets, they have found that increased "outsourcing" of the export sales function to knowledgeable export intermediaries makes sense.

This trend of manufacturers' increased realization of the benefits of using export intermediaries is also consistent with the general trend of service outsourcing. During this "postindustrial" era (Piore and Sable, 1984), services and service technologies are revolutionizing global competition (Quinn, 1992).[7] In this process, increasing the outsourcing of many service functions which the traditional manufacturing firm performs in-house becomes a necessity in order to cut costs and boost efficiency. At the same time, such growing needs for outsourcing service functions allow for the increasing specialization of service firms, thus enabling them to achieve new heights of competitive advantage. As such, the role of export intermediaries as specialized service firms in the improvement of export efficiency has been increasingly recognized around the world lately.

While there are many reasons behind the failure of the ETC Act of 1982, statements such as "The trading company is a Japanese tradition that will not work well here" and "The U.S. business culture does not appreciate the role of intermediaries" reflect historical ignorance (Peng, 1996). Our historical excursion of the evolution of American export intermediaries suggests otherwise. There was an important period in U.S. history when export intermediaries played a significant role. In other words, export intermediaries did work in the United States, and there is no cultural reason that they should be unable to play an important role in expanding this country's exports in the contemporary era. Despite the relative decline of this sector during much of the twentieth century, the strong demand to tap the nation's residual export potential in small firms has created an urgency to improve the effectiveness of these firms.

In conclusion, specialized export intermediary firms may be regarded as an organizational innovation with accelerated diffusion throughout the world during the past few centuries. "The diffusion of organizational innovations within industries, across industries, and across cultures—both in terms of the mechanics of the diffusion process and the economic consequences—warrants more investigation" (Williamson, 1975: 262). It is with this motivation that I set out in this book to investigate what is behind the success and failure of U.S. export intermediaries.

NOTES

1. Weber (1947) first pioneered the idea of constructing base line models based on "ideal types" against which we can examine variations and changes.

2. Some of them were also instrumental in shaping some of the present-day nation states, such as the East India and Hudson's Bay Companies, whose early activities later led to the nation-building efforts of India and Canada, respectively (James, 1994).

3. The Japan trade was a different story. Instead of having the private sector, namely, individual trading companies, penetrate the market first, as Americans did in Hawaii, China, and the Philippines, the U.S. government took the lead to open the Japan market. In 1853, Commander Matthew Perry of the U.S. Navy and his four ships forced the Japanese rulers to abandon their complete isolationist policy. However, the principal beneficiaries of such American efforts were not American trading companies, but Europeans. Moreover, it was the European dominance over Japan's foreign trade that aroused the nationalistic movement in Japan, which culminated in the Meiji Restoration in 1868 (Reischauer, 1974: 93–95). As discussed earlier, one of the principal achievements of the new Meiji government was to spur the development of indigenous trading companies, thus starting a new era of global development of export intermediary firms.

4. Public Law 97–290, 96 Stat. 1233 (1982), codified at 12 U.S.C. 372, 635a–4, 1843 (c) (14), 15 U.S.C. 6a, 45 (a), 4001–4003, 4011–4021 (1982).

5. A small number of ETCs certified by the Commerce Department have been set up by quasi-public agencies such as port authorities. For example, shortly after the ETC Act was passed, the Port Authorities of New York and New Jersey created XPORT in order to aid the region's small exporters. Similarly, the Virginia Port Authority and the Port of Montana (Butte) had their ETCs certified. Although these public-sector ETCs are believed to be ideally situated to provide trading services to small exporters, there has been little sustained interest on the part of quasi-public agencies in forming ETCs. Since the emphasis of this book is on private-sector export intermediaries, I leave this issue unexplored. It may be interesting to pursue the issue of public-sector ETCs in future research.

6. Telephone interview with an official in the Export Trading Company Affairs Office, U.S. Department of Commerce, Washington, DC, May 1994.

7. Quinn's (1992) influential "knowledge- and service-based paradigm for intelligent enterprise" rests on two statistical facts of the competitive dynamics of the "postindustrial" era: (a) During this era in every advanced economy, the service sector employs the majority of the work force (e.g., 70 percent of U.S. workers and 59 percent of Japanese workers in 1988); and (b) Even within "manufacturing" firms, 75–95 percent of their employees engage in nonmanufacturing activities and 60–75 percent of nonmaterial costs typically lie in internal services, such as design, engineering, accounting, information systems, sales, and distribution.

CHAPTER 4

The State of the Art

Now that we have undertaken the historical excursion covering the global evolution and U.S. development of export intermediary firms, it is time to investigate what is currently known about the state of the art of these firms in this country. This chapter first reviews the survey literature on these firms and then summarizes the trade and professional literature. Finally, the scholarly literature is discussed.

THE SURVEY LITERATURE

Since the 1970s, at least five studies, summarized in Table 4.1, have attempted to survey export intermediaries in the United States: Hay Associates (1977), Brasch (1978), Coopers and Lybrand (1984), U.S. Department of Commerce (1990), and Batra (1991). These surveys confirmed what many familiar with the industry have long thought to be true: U.S. export intermediaries are generally small (60–70 percent of them have fewer than 10 employees), with small sales revenues (around 70 percent of them have gross revenues of less than $5 million) and thin capital bases (over 80 percent of them have less than $1 million in equity capital). Notwithstanding their relatively small size, more than half of them have been in business for more than 10 years and their principals have substantial experience in exporting (averaged 26.5 years in exporting, as reported by Howard and Maskulka [1988]). As might be expected, a vast majority of them are located within proximity of a coastal city and they export to a wide variety of world markets. What is noteworthy is that approximately half of them always take title to the goods they sell, and only 8 to 22 percent of them never do so.

Table 4.1
Demographic Profiles of U.S. Export Intermediaries
since the 1970s

Studies*	(1)	(2)	(3)	(4)	(5)
Size (U.S. employees)					
1–4			37%	60%	44%
5–9			29	14	27
10–24			22	10	17
25–49			6	15**	6
50 and over			6		6
Gross Revenues					
Under $5 million	74%		69%	68%	68%
$5–9.99 million	12		14	9	13
$10–49.99 million	14		15	11	13
$50 million and over	0		2	5**	6
Equity Capital					
Under $100,000	28%				37%
$100,000–999,000	72%				46
$1 million and over					17
Age					
0–5 years		19	18%	15%	10%
6–10 years		32	20	25	18
11–20 years		49	26	24	38
21 and over			36	34**	34
Taking Title to Goods					
Always	46%			59%	50%
Sometimes	46			19	38
Never	8			22	12
Major Export Markets					
Canada			19%	28%	
West Europe			25	61	
Pacific Rim			38**	68	
Latin America				72	
Middle East				54	
East Europe				13**	

* These five studies are listed on the next page.
** The percentages do not add to 100.

Sources: (1) Hay Associates (1977), *A Study to Determine the Feasibility of the ETC Concept as a Viable Vehicle for Expansion of U.S. Products* (Philadelphia: Hay Associates); (2) J. J. Brasch (1978), Export management companies, *Journal of International Business Studies*, 9 (1): 59–70; (3) Coopers and Lybrand (1984), *Export Management Companies* (Washington, DC: Coopers and Lybrand); (4) U.S. Department of Commerce (1990), *Report to Congress on Export Trade Intermediaries* (Washington, DC: Department of Commerce, International Trade Administration); (5) M. M. Batra (1991), *An Exploratory Analysis of Organizational Characteristics and Business Strategies of U.S. Export Management Companies*, doctoral dissertation (Madison: University of Wisconsin).

In addition to demographic profiles, Bello and Williamson (1985a, 1985b) focused on the particular type of services and contract structures used by export intermediaries to deal with their clients. They (1985b) identified three contract structures that are used when dealing with manufacturers: (a) formal contract; (b) informal agreement; and (c) no agreement, which is subject to negotiations on a case-by-case basis. In another study using the same data set, they (1985a) suggested three key service areas that export intermediaries must be able to perform: (a) promotion (i.e., participating in trade shows, preparing advertising and sales literature); (b) contact (i.e., personal contacts abroad, visiting foreign buyers); and (c) consolidation (i.e., ability to provide one-stop service). Their findings suggested the "ideal" level of services, in terms of these three key service areas, that intermediaries must provide to match manufacturers' specific needs as determined by their export volume (low or high) and the type of products exported (differentiated or undifferentiated). However, the performance issue—namely, how EMCs can actually meet manufacturers' needs—is left largely unanswered.

Moving beyond the services provided and contract types, Howard and Maskulka (1988) argued that in order to be successful, the American "export trading company," as envisioned by advocates of the ETC Act of 1982, must have three components: (a) bank participation; (b) manufacturers' collective effort; and (c) international marketing expertise, which existing export intermediaries such as EMCs can provide. However, their survey results indicated that EMCs are afraid of bank domination and manufacturers' bypassing their service once such an all-encompassing, conglomerate-type ETC is established. Therefore, only 29 percent of EMCs had contacted someone, most frequently a bank, concerning the possibility of forming an ETC to be certified by the Department of Commerce. More than three-fourths (78 percent) of them were only interested in leasing their services to a Commerce Department-certified ETC, thus maintaining their own autonomy.

These studies have been noticeably silent on the issue of export intermediary performance. Haigh's (1994) study represented the only effort in the literature attempting to provide information on the performance of these firms. He surveyed 2,000 manufacturers which have used export intermediary services. From 423 responses, he reported that the performance of EMCs is below the expectations of manufacturers more than half the time. Nevertheless, he concluded that using intermediaries "can be a very effective strategy for entering foreign markets if care is taken to select an appropriate [export intermediary] company" (Haigh, 1994: 66). The finding that export intermediaries' performance is below their clients' expectations more than half the time is striking. Yet Haigh did not provide an answer as to why this is the case. Since he only surveyed manufacturers as opposed to intermediaries, we have to speculate whether such a lackluster performance is due to manufacturers' expectations which may be too high, or due to intermediaries' capabilities which may be too low.

Overall, the existing surveys of export intermediaries have painted a picture of an industry that is populated by a large number of small firms. They vary in the services they offer and contract structures they use. Moreover, they do not seem to be very interested in moving toward the direction that advocates of the ETC Act of 1982 would like to see. In terms of performance, according to the only such study by Haigh (1994), these firms seem unable to meet the expectations of manufacturers most of the time. While useful in terms of presenting basic demographic profiles of the export intermediary population in the United States, this literature has very little information on what determines the performance of these firms.

THE TRADE AND PROFESSIONAL LITERATURE

This literature has primarily been written by practitioners to share their industry experience and by government officials to promote the use of export intermediaries. Based largely on the authors' personal experience, this literature appears to follow two major thrusts. The first one focuses on how to locate and select proper export intermediaries, represented by Barovick and Anderson (1992), Brasch (1981), Miller (1981a, 1981b, 1981c), and Zodl (1995). These writings introduced the range of services export intermediaries provide and the criteria for the manufacturer to evaluate their capabilities. For example, Brasch (1981) suggested that an ideal intermediary for a small manufacturer is one that (a) specializes in the manufacturer's product type; (b) has a well-organized foreign distribution system in place; (c) is well financed and managed; and

and capabilities that enable them to deter environmental turbulence and "thrive on chaos" (Peters, 1987). If we extend this line of thinking to export intermediaries, we can suggest that the reasons why certain export intermediaries are successful and others fail must lie in the differential among their internal resources and capabilities.

In summary, Perry's model (1990, 1992), calling for withdrawals from unattractive markets, is in the spirit of traditional strategic analyses which emphasize environmental determinism. A better model should be able to explain what is behind the success and failure of these firms, *independent* of environmental conditions (Rumelt, 1991). In addition, qualitative findings based on a small sample of firms reported by Perry (1992) may be difficult to generalize to the population of export intermediaries in the United States.

CONCLUSIONS

Overall, there is clearly a paucity of research that can help answer the important question of export intermediary performance. There are three primary barriers that have prevented research on export intermediaries from making significant progress in recent years (Peng and Ilinitch, 1997). The first barrier seems to be cultural, since research outcome is inherently influenced by researchers' own culture and by the broader environment in which research questions are selected (Hofstede, 1994: 10). Despite their significant role in earlier periods, American export intermediaries have not played a major role in the economy since the turn of the century. As a result, the majority of American writers may have overlooked the potential role that export intermediaries may play.

The second barrier is the methodological difficulty of investigating the performance of export intermediaries. Unlike their manufacturing clients, export intermediaries do not produce tangible products, their "output" is difficult to measure, and very little published archival data are available on these firms (Root, 1994). Currently, with the exception of the Japanese *sogo shosha* and a few remaining European trading houses, most export intermediaries are small. As a result, their behavior is hard to capture, and their performance is difficult to assess.

Finally, at a conceptual level, research on export intermediaries has grossly lagged behind the work on manufacturing exporters both in terms of volume and sophistication. According to Leonidou and Katsikeas (1996), a number of conceptual models, such as innovation adoption, organizational learning, and relationship marketing, have been adopted to study the strategy and performance of manufacturing exporters. In contrast, scholarly efforts in the research on export intermediaries have been very limited (Denis, 1990). No previous study in the survey, trade and professional, or scholarly literature has attempted to rigorously investigate what is behind the success and failure of export intermediaries in the United States.

Given the gap in our knowledge about export intermediary performance, there will be significant benefits to advancing research in this area. The challenge for undertaking such research, however, remains considerable. Specifically, since the most rigorously derived conceptual model to date (Perry, 1990, 1992) has failed to generate testable hypotheses, new research needs to develop hypotheses that can rigorously test the performance determinants of export intermediaries. The next chapter will take on such a challenge by focusing on transactions, agents, and resources as three fundamental building blocks of export intermediary performance.

CHAPTER 5

An Integrated Model of Export Intermediary Performance

While research directly focusing on the success and failure of export intermediary firms in the United States is scant, there is a large body of related interdisciplinary literature that one can draw upon to investigate the determinants of export intermediary performance. Specifically, I suggest that export intermediary performance can be analyzed from three underlying perspectives, namely, transaction costs, principal-agent relationships, and organizational resources and capabilities. Each of them is rooted in a strong analytical framework, and each partially solves the puzzle of export intermediary performance. Collectively, they will be used to derive an integrated model that answers our key question: What determines export intermediary performance?

TRANSACTION COSTS

A fundamental feature in international business is cross-border transactions, which are more costly, complex, and difficult than domestic transactions. Williamson, a guru on transaction cost theory, used a metaphor to define *transaction costs* (1985: 1–2):

In mechanical systems we look for frictions: Do the gears mesh, are the parts lubricated, is there needless slippage or other loss of energy? The economic counterpart of friction is transaction cost: Do the parties to the exchange operate harmoniously, or are there frequent misunderstandings and conflicts that lead to delays, breakdowns, and other malfunctions?

Just as all physical interfaces involve friction forces, all economic transactions entail costs. Among these, international transactions tend to incur higher costs due to the geographic and cultural separation between buyers and sellers located in different countries. As a result, transaction cost theory, with its focus on the attributes of economic transactions and the strategies employed to minimize the costs associated with these transactions, becomes a particularly relevant tool for our purposes.

First proposed by Coase (1937) and later articulated by Williamson (1975, 1985), transaction cost theory has become an influential paradigm in organizational economics, with extensions found in strategic management, marketing channels, and international business (Barney and Ouchi, 1986; Buckley and Casson, 1976; Hennart, 1982; Hill and Kim, 1988; Robins, 1987; Stern and Reve, 1980). Transaction costs include the costs of searching for the right transaction partner, negotiating the sales contract, monitoring transaction performance, as well as enforcing contract compliance (Williamson, 1975, 1985). The theory is concerned with how to organize efficient economic transactions with minimum costs (North, 1990; Toyne, 1989).

Since transaction costs are nontrivial, economic actors will try to employ appropriate strategies to minimize these costs by selecting the optimal mode of transaction (Klein, Crawford and Alchian, 1978; Williamson, 1975, 1985, 1991a, 1991b, 1993a, 1993b, 1996). Specifically, they can either (a) make (produce) goods or services in-house or (b) buy goods or services from the market, depending on which transaction mode entails lower costs and higher benefits. When the transaction costs of exchanges through the market (the "buy" option) are too high, firms will attempt to produce certain goods and services in-house (the "make" option); and vice versa (Masten, 1984, 1996; Masten, Meehan and Snyder, 1991). These transaction decisions, often called "make-or-buy" decisions, have been the focus of transaction cost theory (Monteverde and Teece, 1982; Walker and Weber, 1984, 1987). In a nutshell, the theory evaluates the relative costs of coordinating exchange via the *visible* hand of an organizational hierarchy (i.e., make), compared with the costs of coordinating exchange via the *invisible* hand of the market system (i.e., buy) (Coase, 1937).

Export transactions are inherently risky because export-related transaction costs are always higher than domestic transaction costs due to exporters' "liability of foreignness" in overseas markets (The hazard of doing business abroad is discussed in the recent work of Barkema, Bell, and Pennings [1996], Li [1995], Mitchell, Shaver, and Yeung [1994], Ricks [1993], and Zaheer [1995]). Since economic actors will attempt to minimize transaction costs, most institutional arrangements in organizing international business are believed to carry a transaction-cost-minimizing property (Hennart, 1982, 1989;

Hennart and Anderson, 1993; North, 1990).[1] The use of export intermediaries is no exception. Viewed from such a transaction cost lens, the role of export intermediaries is to help lower export-related transaction costs for their manufacturing clients, and, therefore, the performance of export intermediaries depends on how successful they are in lowering these costs. The diffusion of export intermediaries as an organizational form during the past 400 years, along with the acceleration of that diffusion process in the late twentieth century (see Chapter 3), testifies to the transaction-cost-minimizing property that such an organizational form brings to international transactions (Peng, 1994b, 1995b, 1996).

When exporting, manufacturers, especially small and internationally inexperienced ones, confront substantial export-related transaction costs. These costs stem from a great deal of risk, uncertainty, and complexity in foreign markets, heightened by many firms' lack of knowledge and experience (Johanson and Valhne, 1977). Moreover, geographic and cultural differences may lead to different interpretations of explicitly signed contracts, let alone implicit social contracts (Hofstede, 1980; Macneil, 1978). Facing these formidable export-related transaction costs, current and would-be exporters essentially have two strategic choices in the export channel decision: (a) direct export (establish integrated export channels in-house); or (b) indirect export (rely on export intermediaries to handle exports).[2]

As shown in Table 5.1, the manufacturer's channel choice decision rests on the comparison of the relative costs and benefits of each choice (Anderson, 1988; Rosenbloom, 1987; Stern and El-Ansary, 1992). Establishing in-house export channels and direct sales forces (i.e., the make option) gives the exporter better control over the distribution of its products. Direct sales forces are considered more willing to perform nonselling activities (e.g., paperwork, trade shows, services), push new products, and carry products whose selling cycle is relatively long (Basu, et al., 1985; Eisenhardt, 1988). Intermediaries, on the other hand, are considered unwilling to do anything without an immediate, certain, and concrete payoff (Anderson, 1985, 1988). But the option of setting up in-house export channels requires that the manufacturer overcome substantial export-related transaction costs when dealing with foreign markets directly. Moreover, the manufacturer needs to shoulder the additional overhead costs incurred when expanding organizational boundaries to establish integrated, in-house channels (Arrow, 1974). Many small, inexperienced exporters find the transaction costs of dealing directly with foreign markets to be too formidable to overcome, and are unwilling or unable to commit their limited resources to exports (Bilkey, 1978; Cavusgil, 1984a, 1984b; Ilinitch and Peng, 1993, 1994).

The option of using intermediaries, on the other hand, enables the manufacturer to avoid dealing directly with transaction uncertainties in unfamiliar settings. Moreover, by bundling product lines of several, noncompeting manufacturers, intermediaries can generate product synergy and economies of scale in selling that no single product line can provide (Lilien, 1979). Therefore, the use of intermediaries allows the manufacturer to minimize investment and operating costs in distribution channels (Anderson, 1985, 1988; Lilien, et al., 1992). However, such an option introduces agency costs, due to the inherent conflict of interest in such a principal-agent (manufacturer-agent) relationship (see the next section for more development of this point). Specifically, the manufacturer will have to delegate the export marketing job to intermediaries and will not be able to control all aspects of the overseas distribution of its products. As a result, the manufacturer will experience some "control loss" problems associated with the use of export intermediaries (Eisenhardt, 1988).

In the language of transaction cost analysis, the export channel choice decision is essentially a make-or-buy decision, and transaction

Table 5.1
The Make-or-Buy Decision in Export Channel Choice:
The Manufacturer's Perspective

Channel Decision	Make (Hierarchy)	Buy (Market)
Export Entry Mode	Direct export	Indirect export
Channel Choice	Integrated, in-house channels	Independent intermediaries
Benefits	Better control over distribution channels	Reduced export-related transaction costs in foreign markets
Costs	Increased export-related transaction costs and overhead costs	Increased agency costs

cost theory is "the currently accepted paradigm that guides the subject of forward integration in marketing channels" (Rangan, Corey and Cespedes, 1993: 455). Given the comparative nature of transaction cost theory (Williamson, 1975, 1985), the channel choice literature does not specify whether one choice is preferred over the other (Anderson, 1988). However, the theory does suggest that manufacturers will select a channel choice that minimizes transaction costs (Rangan, et al., 1993).

So far this analysis has been undertaken from the perspective of manufacturers that make channel choice decisions. At this point, a change in perspective is necessary in order to understand the determinants of export intermediary performance. Specifically, from the perspective of intermediaries, they will have to strive to present lower transaction cost solutions for the manufacturer in order to maximize their chances of being selected and, consequently, their chances for success. As a result, their performance depends on how well they can influence the manufacturer to select their services rather than choosing the direct export mode. In other words, the performance of intermediaries depends on increasing the odds of being selected by the manufacturer in the short run and being retained in the long run. Otherwise, the manufacturer can always attempt to switch to the direct export mode or quit exporting as a default option, both of which will depress the demand for export intermediary services.

In summary, if export intermediaries are viewed as a transaction-cost-minimizing device for manufacturers, then their performance determinants become clear. However, such a perspective alone does not fully capture the complexity surrounding the export intermediary performance question. In order to probe deeper into the determinants of these firms' performance, we also have to understand the nature of the relationship between manufacturers and intermediaries.

PRINCIPAL-AGENT RELATIONSHIPS

The relationship governing manufacturers and intermediaries is an "agency" relationship, which has been the focus of another major branch of organizational economics, agency theory (Jensen and Meckling, 1976). This theory is concerned with the problems that result from one party's (the principal) reliance on the other (the agent) to perform certain tasks. While the principal's and agent's interests overlap substantially, they also have an inherent conflict of interest. Stated alternatively, the division of labor and conflicting goals of the two parties may lead to a host of "agency problems"

(Alchian and Demsetz, 1972; Jensen and Meckling, 1976). Specifically, because the agent may not completely share the principal's goals and because the agent has better information about the details of the tasks (i.e., information asymmetry), the agent may have both the motivation and the opportunity to behave in a way that maximizes his or her own utility at the expense of the principal's. As a result, the principal has to incur *agency costs* associated with such a relationship (Eisenhardt, 1988, 1989a; Fama, 1980).

Agency theory predicts that the principal will attempt to employ incentives and threats to minimize agency costs. Since the agency relationship is a significant factor in almost all exchange transactions (Arrow, 1985; Holmstrom, 1989), the central concern is "how the principal can best motivate the agent to perform as the principal would, taking into account the difficulties in monitoring the agent's activities" (Sappington, 1991: 45).

The relationship between manufacturers and intermediaries embodies a classic principal-agent model (Bergen, et al., 1992). In this case, the two parties are cooperative and interdependent, yet rationally may pursue different and/or contradictory goals (Peng, 1996; Peng, Hill and Ilinitch, 1997). As agents, intermediaries perform an important economic function by acting as a link between domestic manufacturers and overseas buyers that otherwise would not have been connected (Cosimano, 1996). Such a function is critical in export transactions, which are inherently risky, uncertain, and complex. Initially, many manufacturers have very little choice but to rely on export intermediaries to enter overseas markets. Export intermediaries can calm manufacturers' fears about foreign markets by leveraging their knowledge about foreign markets and by demonstrating their efficiency in selling products abroad. In short, export intermediaries as agents help reduce the probability of unsuccessful trade and help their client firms enter export markets.

At the same time, because intermediaries are agents, they may not always behave in a way that is in the best interests of their client firms. Manufacturers may want to maximize export earnings with minimum costs, and intermediaries, on the other hand, may want to maximize their own earnings by extracting the highest possible fees from manufacturers. Such a conflict of interest is the heart of agency theory and perhaps is best described by Jensen and Meckling (1976: 308):

If both parties to the relationship are utility maximizers there is good reason to believe that the agent will not always act in the best interests of the principal. The principal can limit divergence from his interests by establishing appropriate incentives for the agent and by incurring monitoring costs designed to limit the aberrant activities of the agent. . . . However, it is generally impossible for the principal or the agent at zero cost to ensure that the agent will make optimal decisions from the principals' view point.

Specifically, since information about agent behavior and performance is costly (Stigler, 1961), manufacturers risk *adverse selection*, whereby intermediaries may misrepresent their qualifications and resources in order to secure the overseas distribution contract (Sappington, 1991; Sharma, 1997). Another source of agency costs is *moral hazard*, whereby intermediaries fail to exert sufficient effort on manufacturers' behalf in overseas markets (Brickley and Dark, 1987; Eisenhardt, 1988).

Although manufacturers as principals are naturally interested in minimizing these agency costs, they face a dilemma: Most small and inexperienced exporters often have to rely on intermediaries to enter export markets (Lafontaine, 1993; Lasser and Kerr, 1996). Then, how can they motivate export intermediaries to perform well? According to agency theory, intermediaries will be motivated to perform, if (a) manufacturers are able to monitor and verify the performance of intermediaries in order to attenuate the information asymmetry situation; or (b) intermediaries are provided with strong threats that deter their potential opportunism, and/or with incentives that are not in conflict with manufacturers' interests. Therefore, in addition to transaction cost determinants explicated in the previous section, export intermediary performance will also depend on whether manufacturers can properly structure the agency relationship in a way that motivates intermediaries to perform (Lafontaine, 1993; Sharma, 1997).

In terms of performance monitoring, principals can (a) specify in the export contract key decisions requiring the manufacturers' approval such as pricing and credit; (b) require periodic sales reports by product and market; and (c) include a termination clause enabling the manufacturers to break the export contract with intermediaries without cause with a reasonable amount of notice such as with 60 days' notice (Root, 1994). However, small, internationally inexperienced manufacturers typically are unable to effectively monitor export intermediaries, thus leading to widespread dissatisfaction with intermediary performance (Bello, et al., 1991; Haigh, 1994).

In terms of threats, when the agent is not performing satisfactorily, manufacturers as principals can threaten to (a) discontinue the current intermediary and select new agents; (b) stop using agents and perform the export tasks directly; and/or (c) quit exporting. The first threat is the most viable option, because there are many export intermediaries competing to win the export contract, and this competition serves to restrain the agent's potential opportunism (Perry, 1992). Many manufacturers maintain multiple intermediaries (Dutta, et al., 1995; Stern and El-Ansary, 1992). Some of them also use foreign-based import intermediaries in addition to—or instead of—domestically-based export intermediaries (Bello and Lohtia, 1995; Rosson and Ford, 1982). As a result, the competition among intermediaries serves as a limit to agency problems (Anderson, 1988).

The second threat is less viable for many small, inexperienced exporters. To stop using agents and perform the export tasks by themselves (i.e., "going direct to market") is essentially a threat to vertically integrate the export channel function (Majumdar and Ramaswamy, 1995). While in theory it is possible (Grossman and Hart, 1986), in practice it may require substantial resources and capabilities which are very costly to develop (Argyres, 1996; Masten, 1984, 1996; Masten, et al., 1991; Monteverde and Teece, 1982; Walker and Weber, 1984, 1987). Many small manufacturers are simply unwilling or unable to do that (Ilinitch and Peng, 1993, 1994). In other words, this threat may be a credible one for larger manufacturers. It is "simply irrelevant" for many smaller manufacturers that "cannot consider vertical integration as a feasible alternative" (Heide and John, 1988: 21).

The last relevant threat for many small manufacturers is simply to quit exporting. Indeed many do. At the outset of the 1990s, small manufacturers—defined by the Small Business Administration as firms having fewer than 500 employees—produced almost half of the gross national product, yet contributed only 10 percent of total U.S. exports (Small Business Administration, 1991). Despite the potentially competitive products they produce, many of them do not bother to export in fear of the hurdles associated with exporting, and many others quit exporting after some unsuccessful trial (Richardson and Rindal, 1995). This option does serve as a constraint since it depresses the demand for export intermediary services.

In addition to threats, manufacturers as principals can also offer a number of incentives that motivate intermediaries to work harder (Lafontaine, 1993). Geographical exclusivity is one of the incentives typically employed. When entering an export contract with manufacturers, most intermediaries would require some form of exclusivity, the minimum being exclusive export rights to at least one country. The most demanding intermediaries, which are also those with the best track record and hence the strongest bargaining power, would require worldwide exclusive rights (Brasch, 1978). Most manufacturers are willing to grant some form of exclusivity, since intermediaries' profits will depend on the development of the market(s) and they are likely to work harder. Another incentive scheme typically employed is to require intermediaries to take title to the goods. While principals attempt to shift their risk to agents, some intermediaries are willing to take on such a challenge, since, after they cover their costs, all the residual profits will go to the intermediaries. As a result, intermediaries, having taken title to the goods, have a stronger set of incentives to develop the export markets for these products.

In summary, viewed from a principal-agent perspective, the performance of export intermediaries as agents is determined by the threats and incentives provided by manufacturers as principals. Specifically, intermediaries must assure their client that the agency costs they bring to the relationship are less than the transaction cost savings they generate. Otherwise, if agency costs are too much, manufacturers may switch to other intermediaries, integrate the export distribution function by themselves, or simply quit exporting, thus wiping out the possibility for the intermediary to make a profit.

ORGANIZATIONAL RESOURCES AND CAPABILITIES

Both transaction cost theory and agency theory help us understand the nature of export transactions and manufacturer-intermediary relationships. They further suggest that an export intermediary's performance depends on whether it can help manufacturers lower export-related transaction costs and whether it can be properly motivated by manufacturers. However, these theories have very little to say about export intermediaries' *internal* resources and capabilities, since they only focus on intermediaries' *external* relationships with manufacturers. A growing number of researchers have argued that, instead of external factors, the resources and capabilities firms possess are the fundamental drivers of their performance (Barney, 1991, 1997; Conner, 1991; Teece, et al., 1997). Therefore, any inquiry into the performance determinants of export intermediaries will also have to examine their internal resources and capabilities.

Since the 1980s, the view that a firm's resources and capabilities determine its performance has been called the "resource-based view of the firm" (Wernerfelt, 1984; Barney, 1991). It has emerged as a distinct theory in the strategic management literature in recent years (Barney, 1997; Conner and Prahalad, 1996; Mahoney and Pandian, 1992; Prahalad and Hamel, 1994; Spender and Grant, 1996). The theory traces its origin to Penrose's (1959) early conceptualization of the firm as a collection of resources, such as physical, financial, human, and organizational resources. Over time, some resources are developed into capabilities that enable the firm to exploit economic opportunities (Nelson and Winter, 1982; Teece, et al., 1997). Also rooted in the tradition of Austrian economics (Schumpeter, 1942), this theory focuses on the firm's ability to discover, acquire, and develop resources and capabilities whose significance competitors have yet to realize (Casson, 1990; Jacobson, 1992; Kirzner, 1973, 1979). The heart of this theory lies in the entrepreneurial discovery of market opportunities and the buildup of resources and capabilities that take advantage of these opportunities ahead of competitors (Lieberman and Montgomery, 1988).

More formally, resources and capabilities refer to "strategically relevant financial, physical, individual, and organizational attributes of the firm" (Barney, 1997: 144). Although some authors tried to make a distinction among *"resources," "capabilities,"* and another closely related term *"core competencies"* (Stalk, Evans and Shulman, 1992), "it is likely that they will become badly blurred in practice" (Barney, 1997: 144). Moreover, it seems unlikely that a debate about the terminologies will be of much value to practitioners. As a result, following Barney (1997), the terms "resources" and "capabilities" are used interchangeably and often in parallel throughout this book.

According to resource-based theory, not every resource or capability will determine firm performance. Key to these strategically relevant resources and capabilities are their (a) value, (b) uniqueness, and (c) difficulty of imitation; only by possessing these will the firm be able to generate economic "rents" in the marketplace (Amit and Shoemaker, 1993). First, according to Barney (1997: 145), in order to be valuable, "Resources and capabilities must enable a firm to exploit environmental opportunities or neutralize environmental threats." He went on to suggest that "A firm's resources and capabilities are valuable if, and only if, they reduce a firm's costs or increase its revenues compared to what would have been the case if this firm did not possess those resources" (Barney, 1997: 147).

In addition to adding value to the firm, these resources and capabilities must also be unique and rare. Otherwise, if a firm merely possesses common resources and capabilities that all the competitors already have or can imitate, its competitive advantage will be easily competed away, and it will be difficult to achieve superior performance in the long run (Barney, 1991, 1997). In other words, there is a great deal of truth in the old saying that "If everyone can do it, you can't make money at it."

Finally, valuable and unique resources and capabilities must also be difficult for competitors to imitate if these abilities are to give a firm sustained competitive advantage. In other words, these resources and capabilities must be *imperfectly imitable* (Chi, 1994;

Lippman and Rumelt, 1982). A reason why a firm's resources and capabilities may be costly to copy is that competitors may have a hard time understanding the relationship between the resources and capabilities controlled by the firm and its competitive advantage. Stated alternatively, the relationship between a firm's resources and capabilities on one hand and its competitive advantage and resultant performance on the other hand may be *causally ambiguous* (Dierickx and Cool, 1989; Reed and DeFillippi, 1990). Moreover, "it may be that not just a few resources and capabilities enable a firm to gain a competitive advantage but that literally thousands of these organizational attributes, bundled together, generate these advantages" (Barney, 1997: 155).

In short, as an analytical lens, resource-based theory is highly relevant here in pursuing the question of what determines export intermediary performance. Compared with research in economics, strategic management research is more interested in firm performance (Rumelt, Schendel and Teece, 1994; Summer, et al., 1990). Compared with the two economic theories (transaction cost and agency theories), resource-based theory, which is firmly rooted in the strategic management literature, has a direct focus on the determinants of firm performance. Specifically, according to Barney (1997: 151), "Firms that possess and exploit costly-to-imitate, rare, and valuable resources in choosing and implementing their strategies may enjoy a period of sustained competitive advantage and above-normal economic performance."

The very existence of export intermediaries depends on their possession of valuable, rare, and hard-to-imitate resources and capabilities, such as knowledge about overseas markets, expertise in the export processes, and abilities to handle foreign negotiations. Otherwise, if these resources and capabilities can be easily acquired and imitated, then manufacturers will attempt to develop export capabilities in-house, thus diminishing the chances for export intermediaries to exist and succeed. Indeed, many large manufacturers have developed such capabilities and forced intermediaries to concentrate on small and midsize manufacturers that are unable to acquire these capabilities. Therefore, export intermediaries not only compete against each other in the race to discover new market opportunities and develop necessary resources and capabilities, but also compete against manufacturers that have the incentive to develop these abilities in-house. The best-performing intermediaries, therefore, will be the winners in this race for competitive advantage (Peng, 1996).

The resource-based perspective is insightful since it fundamentally shifts the analysis from being manufacturer-centered to being intermediary-centered. The two previous theories concentrate on the manufacturer, which is interested in minimizing export-related transaction costs and maximizing agent performance. Accordingly, intermediaries are viewed as relatively passive entities responding to manufacturers' channel choice decisions with negligible bargaining power to influence manufacturers. Moreover, agents are assumed to be largely homogeneous, with little differential in their resources and capabilities, except to the extent that their efforts may vary as a result of threats and incentives employed by principals (Levitt, 1995; Nelson, 1991). In fact, it may be these unrealistic assumptions that have led to the lack of research interests and efforts on export intermediaries; in other words, "if they don't count, why study them?" (Peng, 1996).

Resource-based theory challenges these assumptions by suggesting that intermediaries are heterogeneous, with a wide range of resources and capabilities. Existing research in channel choice has been criticized for its failure to appreciate that as small firms competing at the other end of the channel decisions, intermediaries also have their own competitive advantages and organizational capabilities that can influence manufacturers' decisions (Peng, et al., 1997). For example, the information asymmetry situation, which principals view negatively, may become a source of competitive advantage for agents (Nayyar, 1990). Viewed from such a perspective, export intermediaries are not passive, homogeneous agents merely responding to manufacturers' channel decisions. In contrast, many export intermediaries are entrepreneurial firms each possessing unique expertise in foreign markets and export processes that is sought after by manufacturers. Some even proactively search for small and reluctant exporters and bring their products abroad (Ilinitch and Peng, 1993, 1994). Overall, export intermediaries exhibit a considerable degree of diversity in their resources and capabilities, which may account for their performance differential.

In summary, if export intermediaries are viewed as firms consisting of a collection of resources and capabilities, then their performance will depend on the value, uniqueness, and imitation difficulty of these organizational attributes. Therefore, resource-based theory, in combination with transaction cost and agency theories, leads to an integrated model that will enable us to probe deeper into the previously unexplored question of export intermediary performance.

AN INTEGRATED MODEL

Each of the three theories introduced above partially solves the puzzle of export intermediary performance. Taken together, they paint a clear picture of the nature of the export intermediary firm which culminates in an integrated model, consisting of a definition, three assumptions, and three propositions. This model starts with a new definition of export intermediaries:

Definition: Export intermediaries are agents whose resources and capabilities help lower export-related transaction costs for their manufacturing clients (i.e., principals).

Informed by three strong analytical perspectives, this new definition of export intermediaries is certainly an improvement over the original definition given in Chapter 2. Furthermore, it enables us to spell out three assumptions that facilitate the generation of core propositions. Given the interdependent relationship between export-related transaction costs that manufacturers have to overcome and agency costs that intermediaries tend to bring, it is realistic to suggest:

Assumption 1: Manufacturers tend to use direct, integrated channels when export-related transaction costs are less than agency costs brought by export intermediaries.

Assumption 2: Manufacturers tend to use export intermediaries when export-related transaction costs are more than agency costs brought by export intermediaries.

In contrast to the assumptions held by transaction cost and agency theories, export intermediaries are not likely to be passive, waiting for manufacturers to select them. Instead:

Assumption 3: Export intermediaries have the incentive to improve their organizational resources and capabilities in order to increase the odds of being selected by manufacturers.

The new definition of export intermediaries and the three assumptions allow for the generation of three core propositions, which directly tackle the determinants of export intermediary performance. First, according to transaction cost theory, the performance of the export intermediary is directly related to its abilities to lower export-related transaction costs for its manufacturing clients. If it is unable to provide a lower transaction cost solution to manufacturers, there would be little rationale for its existence and poor prospects for good performance. To sum up:

Proposition 1: The greater its abilities to lower export-related transaction costs for manufacturers, the stronger the intermediary's performance.

Second, according to agency theory, the export intermediary will perform better if its performance is monitored and verified by its principals. However, manufacturers, especially small and internationally inexperienced ones, are usually unable to commit resources to effectively monitor and verify intermediary performance. This is a dilemma: Since monitoring performance is costly, if manufacturers know how to effectively monitor export intermediary performance, they may be able to export directly and may not need intermediaries.[3] The other way for manufacturers to motivate the intermediary to perform well is to impose threats that would deter opportunism, and/or provide incentives that achieve the alignment of interests between principals and agents. Thus:

Proposition 2: The more credible the threats imposed by manufacturers and/or the stronger the incentives provided by manufacturers, the stronger the export intermediary's performance.

In addition, according to resource-based theory, the performance of the export intermediary will depend on how valuable, unique, and difficult to imitate its resources and capabilities are. In other words, possession of these resources and capabilities will enable the intermediary to create and sustain competitive advantage, and the absence of these attributes will lead to poor performance. To state formally:

Proposition 3: The stronger the valuable, unique, and hard-to-imitate reources and capabilities possessed by the export intermediary, the stronger its performance.

Within this integrated model, the relationship among these three core propositions is interrelated, each tackling a particular aspect of export intermediary performance. In order to establish the validity of the model, the propositions need to be tested with empirical data. Otherwise, they remain as unsubstantiated theoretical statements or, simply, as "propositions." While propositions state the relations among entities and their attributes at a more abstract level, hypotheses, on the other hand, are more concrete statements of these relations that are more observable and hence testable (Bacharach, 1989). And it is the testing of research hypotheses that either supports or falsifies propositions and theories (Kuhn, 1970; Popper, 1972). Therefore, we need to "translate" propositions into hypotheses and then test these hypotheses.[4] Given the complexity surrounding the determinants of intermediary performance, such translation is a difficult undertaking. In fact, transaction cost, agency, and resource-based theories have been singled out as three of the most difficult-to-operationalize theories in strategy and organizational research (Godfrey and Hill, 1995).

Proposition 1, based on transaction cost theory, suggests a direct relationship between the export intermediary's transaction-cost-minimizing abilities and its performance. Then what are these abilities? To answer this question, we first need to define what transaction costs are. Due to their ubiquity in economic exchanges, transaction costs have been notoriously difficult to define and measure directly and accurately (Allen, 1991; Barzel, 1985; Godfrey and Hill, 1995).

Proposition 2 grows out of agency theory. It suggests a direct relationship between the threats and incentives on one hand and intermediary performance on the other hand. Since this study, like many other social science studies, does not take place in a controlled laboratory, it is hard to assess the degree of change on the part of intermediary performance based on changes in principals' threats and incentives. In other words, it will be difficult to know how the intermediary's performance will change once threat X or incentive Y is added or removed (Cook and Campbell, 1979).

Finally, Proposition 3, based on resource-based theory, challenges us to measure organizational resources and capabilities. Such a task has always been demanding, since many of the resources and capabilities that form the basis of a firm's competitive advantage are often intangible (Hall, 1992, 1993; Hansen and Wernerfelt, 1989; Itami, 1987; Reed and DeFillippi, 1990). If they are tangible, they become more visible to competitors and hence may become more imitable (Barney, 1991). Therefore, there is a paradox between those intangible resources and capabilities on one hand, and their observability and measurability on the other hand (Godfrey and Hill, 1995).

In summary, the integrated model, based on three underlying theories, suggests a new definition, three realistic assumptions, and three core propositions specifying the determinants of export intermediary performance. However, these propositions will have to be translated into hypotheses that can be subject to empirical testing. Such a task will be dealt with in the next section.

TESTABLE HYPOTHESES

The integrated model suggests that export intermediary performance is determined by the joint impact of transaction cost and agency cost minimizing, as well as the possession of valuable, unique, and hard-to-imitate resources and capabilities. Given the difficulties in isolating these constructs and the integrated nature of these relationships, it is necessary to treat these propositions as an interdependent set when translating them into testable hypotheses.

Specifically, according to Jensen and Meckling (1976) and Williamson (1975, 1985), both transaction costs and agency costs can be decomposed into three key components: (a) search costs; (b) negotiation costs; and (c) monitoring/enforcement costs. Focusing on these more manageable components of transaction costs and agency costs, as opposed to concentrating on these costs as a whole, will help ease the difficulty of translation. Moreover, abilities to minimize these costs can be regarded as important organizational resources and capabilities that determine export intermediary performance (Barney, 1991, 1997). Given these integrated relationships, I derive four testable hypotheses which posit that as long as the export intermediary has the resources and capabilities to help the manufacturer lower export-related transaction and agency costs along these three dimensions, its services will be sought, its survival viable, and its success likely (Figure 5.1). Each of these hypotheses will be developed in more detail below.

Search Cost Minimizing

Search costs typically involve the costs of acquiring knowledge through conducting export market research and planning (Green and Kohli, 1991; Walters, 1993). Acquiring such knowledge without external help would require significant time and resources, especially for small and midsize firms with little international experience. In distant, unfamiliar markets where publicly available market information is lacking and organizational forms are different (e.g., Eastern Europe and China), such search costs can be enormous and prohibitive (Luo and Chen, 1996; Peng, 1992, 1994a, 1997a, 1997b, 1997d). Yet knowledge about foreign markets is critical to export success (Gripsrud, 1990; Luo and Peng, 1998; Stross, 1990). Johanson and Valhne (1977: 28) posited that "there is a direct relation between [foreign] market knowledge and [foreign] market commitment." Overall, possession of such knowledge will enable the firm to deal with foreign customers with relative ease, while lack of such knowledge may retard the export expansion process.

The high costs of searching for knowledge about foreign markets and export processes have not only kept many would-be exporters from expanding internationally, but also may lead to an inadequate search prior to exporting, which may in turn increase the probability

Figure 5.1
Determinants of Export Intermediary Performance:
Mapping the Hypotheses

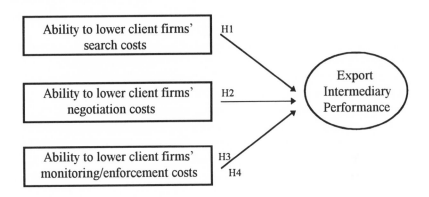

of export failure. This is where export intermediaries can help, by providing knowledge about foreign markets, experience with export processes, and familiarity with foreign languages and cultures. Compared with the high search costs associated with the option of direct export, the search costs of looking for a domestically based export intermediary may be much lower (Haigh, 1994; Peng, 1996).[5] In the case of the best export intermediaries, their superior knowledge and their ability to leverage this knowledge will result in lower search costs, thus providing much needed expertise to help remove the fear and uncertainty for the manufacturer (Denis and Depelteau, 1985). Therefore:

Hypothesis 1: The more knowledgeable it is about foreign markets and export processes, the more likely the export intermediary will be successful.

Negotiation Cost Minimizing

According to transaction cost and agency theories, negotiation costs not only include the costs of conducting international negotiations, but also include the costs of potential hazard when dealing with unfamiliar foreign negotiators (Fayerweather and Kapoor, 1976; Tung, 1982, 1988). Inexperienced exporters may find their lack of knowledge and experience in export markets compounded by their lack of understanding of, and sensitivity to, the intricacies of negotiations with customers from different cultural and economic backgrounds (Peng, 1997c; Pye, 1982; Weiss, 1993, 1994). As such, they may find export negotiations more complex, frustrating, and troublesome than domestic negotiations (Graham, 1983, 1987; Graham, Mintu and Rodgers, 1994; Salacuse, 1988). Even when trying to handle the negotiations directly, they may find themselves parties to bad deals, which significantly increase the probability of export failure (Adler, Brahm and Graham, 1992).

Given these drawbacks of direct export negotiations undertaken by small firms, export intermediaries can often lower negotiation costs because of their experience in negotiating such contracts, their networks and contacts overseas, and their ability to prevent and resolve misunderstanding due to language and cultural gaps. In other words, other things being equal, they help produce a better deal for the exporter, which reduces the probability of export failure. Therefore, by helping client firms lower negotiation costs, export intermediaries can increase their odds of being selected and retained. Thus:

Hypothesis 2: The greater its ability to undertake export-related negotiations, the more likely the export intermediary will be successful.

Monitoring/Enforcement Cost Minimizing

In addition to search and negotiation costs, export-related transaction and agency costs also include monitoring/enforcement costs that cannot be ignored. Once market research is completed and a sales contract negotiated, how well the contract is performed becomes an immediate concern. Nonperformance may result from foreign buyers' misunderstanding of contract specifics due to genuine cultural differences or from their deliberate opportunistic behavior (Williamson, 1975, 1985). As a result, the exporter dealing with foreign customers directly must be constantly on guard for such transaction hazards, the resolution of which can be costly (Bersani, 1992; *Far Eastern Economic Review*, 1994; Peng and Heath, 1996). Thus, export intermediaries that can help lower these costs will be sought.

The use of intermediaries, on the other hand, introduces potential agency costs into the manufacturer-intermediary relationship (Bergen, et al., 1992; Jensen and Meckling, 1976). As agents, intermediaries may behave in a way that is not always in the best interests of their principals, such as withholding critical information about the foreign markets and monopolizing the communication between the exporter and foreign buyer. If agency costs in this relationship are deemed to be too high, the exporter (i.e., principal) may opt to become the residual claimant by integrating the intermediary function and choosing the direct export mode (Grossman and Hart, 1986; Perry, 1990, 1992), or may decide to quit exporting at all. Thus, export intermediaries' chances of being selected and retained also depend on whether they can assure their client firms that the potential agency costs will be less than the monitoring/enforcement costs manufacturers would have incurred when engaging in direct export.

Since manufacturers, especially small and inexperienced ones, are usually unable to directly and effectively monitor export intermediary performance, they may decide not to do that (Bello, et al., 1991). Instead, they may use outcome-based contracts with intermediaries (Eisenhardt, 1988, 1989a). Specifically, they may require that intermediaries take title to the goods. Taking title to the goods by intermediaries solves a major agency problem inherent in the principal-agent relationship: It achieves the alignment of the interests of principals and agents (Bergen, et al., 1992; Jensen and Meckling, 1976). It provides the strongest incentive for intermediaries to work hard; otherwise, intermediaries will be stuck with the goods they have bought from manufacturers. Moreover, to the manufacturer, a seemingly complex export sale now becomes a relatively simple domestic sale to a U.S.-based intermediary, thus allowing for lower monitoring/enforcement costs (Peng, 1996). Therefore, manufacturers' needs to integrate the export distribution channel can be minimized, and overhead costs which would have incurred with regard to establishing integrated, in-house export channels are avoided (Grossman and Hart, 1986).

To intermediaries, manufacturers' preference of using outcome-based contracts requiring the possession of the title to the goods is a major challenge. Most export intermediaries in the United States are very small and unable to access the financing needed to take title to the goods. Traditionally, many of them were founded as export management companies (EMCs) which did not take title to the goods and only worked on commission. As manufacturers increasingly insist that intermediaries take title, the ability to take title to the goods becomes a part of the valuable, unique, and difficult-to-imitate resources and capabilities that may differentiate the successful intermediaries from less fortunate ones. Therefore:

Hypothesis 3: The better its ability to take title to the goods, the more likely the export intermediary will be successful.

In addition to the ability to take title, the choice of products that intermediaries specialize in will also have a bearing on their performance. They can choose to concentrate on complex, technology-intensive (high-tech) products or on commodity (low-tech) ones. The distribution of complex products requires a great deal of transaction-specific investment, such as specialized sales force training and postsale services (Williamson, 1975, 1985). Manufacturers need to closely monitor these activities to ensure that they are performed up to their standards and enforce these standards if necessary. Intermediaries are considered unwilling to invest in such training and services without an immediate, certain, and concrete payoff (Anderson, 1985, 1988; Basu, et al., 1985; Eisenhardt, 1988). In other words, the monitoring and enforcement costs of using intermediaries to distribute complex products may be too high. Therefore, manufacturers of complex products are more likely to use integrated channels to exercise greater control over distribution, thus leaving little room for intermediaries (Anderson and Coughlan 1987; Anderson and Schmittlein, 1984; Coughlan, 1985; Dutta, et al. 1995; Klein, Frazier and Roth, 1990; Klein and Roth, 1990; Majumdar and Ramaswamy 1995; Rangan, et al. 1993).

As a result, for intermediaries, specializing in complex, technology-intensive products may not appear to be a good strategy, since they face manufacturers' credible threats to integrate the channel function. Some opportunistic manufacturers may want to first use intermediaries to carry these complex products to "test the water" in foreign markets and may then phase out intermediaries (Root, 1994). As a result, intermediaries have a stronger set of incentives to specialize in commodity products, which may give them a better chance of being selected and retained over the long run. Therefore:

Hypothesis 4: The more willing it is to specialize in commodity products, the more likely the export intermediary will be successful.

In summary, I propose four hypotheses that can be used to assess the determinants of export intermediary performance. Derived from the three core propositions, these hypotheses focus on relationships that are more observable and hence testable.

DISCUSSION

Drawing on three underlying analytical perspectives, this chapter has outlined an integrated model of the determinants of export intermediary performance, which represents the first-ever attempt in the literature to tackle this important and unexplored question (summarized in Table 5.2). The central thesis in this model is that resources and capabilities to minimize export-related transaction costs for manufacturing clients while containing agency costs are the

Table 5.2
A Summary of the Integrated Model

Definition	Export intermediaries are agents whose resources and capabilities help lower export-related transaction costs for their manufacturing clients (i.e., principals).
Assumption 1	Manufacturers tend to use direct, integrated channels when export-related transaction costs are less than agency costs brought by export intermediaries.
Assumption 2	Manufacturers tend to use export intermediaries when export-related transaction costs are more than agency costs brought by export intermediaries.
Assumption 3	Export intermediaries have the incentive to improve their organizational resources and capabilities in order to improve the odds of being selected by manufacturers.
Proposition 1	The greater its abilities to lower export-related transaction costs for manufacturers, the stronger the export intermediary's performance.
Proposition 2	The more credible the threats imposed by manufacturers and/or the stronger the incentives provided by manufacturers, the stronger the export intermediary's performance.
Proposition 3	The stronger the valuable, unique, and hard-to-imitate resources and capabilities possessed by the export intermediary, the stronger its performance.
Hypothesis 1	The more knowledgeable it is about foreign markets and export processes, the more likely the export intermediary will be successful.
Hypothesis 2	The greater its ability to undertake export-related negotiations, the more likely the export intermediary will be successful.
Hypothesis 3	The better its ability to take title to the goods, the more likely the export intermediary will be successful.
Hypothesis 4	The more willing it is to specialize in commodity products, the more likely the export intermediary will be successful.

primary determinants of export intermediary performance. As manufacturers formulate make-or-buy decisions in export channel choices,
export intermediaries, which tend to be small service firms, stand at
the other end of such decisions. Under these circumstances, the best
strategy for intermediaries seems to be creating, acquiring, and
developing resources and capabilities that will lower export-related
transaction costs for their client firms on one hand and controlling
agency problems on the other hand, thus increasing the odds of being
selected and retained.[6] Moreover, the difference among export intermediaries' resources and capabilities along these dimensions will
account for a large part of their performance variance. If supported,
this model will be of enormous value to practitioners in search of
export intermediary services, operators of export intermediaries, and
government officials in charge of export promotion, as well as would-
be entrepreneurs interested in the export business.

In the scholarly literature, this model represents a conceptual
integration of three theoretical perspectives drawn upon research in
organizational economics and strategic management. Rooted in
organizational economics, transaction cost and agency theories are
manufacturer-centered, interested in specifying the decision criteria
for manufacturers. On the other hand, resource-based theory, grown
out of strategic management research, is more intermediary-orient-
ed, focusing on the importance of the internal resources and
capabilities that intermediaries possess. Given such tension between
these theories, some scholars argued that when studying organizational problems, researchers should focus on the firm, namely, the
export intermediary in this case, instead of its external relationships.
Some of them even suggested that importing economic models for
strategy and organizational research is "dangerous" (Perrow, 1986),
"risky romance" (Hirsch, Friedman and Koza, 1990), and "bad for
practice" (Ghoshal and Moran, 1996; see also Donaldson, 1985, 1990;
Zajac and Olsen, 1993). Despite such criticism, the view shared by a
large number of researchers is that cross-fertilization and integration
between economics and organizational research may lead to further
advancement in our understanding of firm behavior (Barney, 1990;
Camerer, 1985; Chiles and McMackin, 1996; Eisenhardt, 1989a;
Hansen and Wernerfelt, 1989; Hesterly and Zenger, 1993; Hill, 1990;
Mahoney and Pandian, 1992; Montgomery, Wernerfelt and Balakrishnan, 1989; Rumelt, et al., 1994).

I clearly share the view of the "integration" school. I believe that
when one studies complex problems such as the determinants of
export intermediary performance, it is important to harvest the best
available insights from multiple disciplines. Unfortunately, most
existing studies have a very strong disciplinary orientation. For

example, most transaction cost researchers approach the channel choice decision entirely from the manufacturer's perspective. Likewise, most agency theorists examine how principals such as manufacturers structure agency relationships in order to maximize agent performance. Not surprisingly, resource-based theorists have been championing the role of organizational resources and capabilities to the extent that they become the sole determinants of firm performance. This lack of interdisciplinary crossover is unfortunate, but one can hardly blame these disciplinary specialists.

As a management scholar housed in a business school, I take it upon myself in this chapter—as well as in this book—trying to bring down the disciplinary boundaries and build bridges across theoretical perspectives. I believe that multiple perspectives may lead to a model that is more rigorous, realistic, and testable. As reviewed in Chapter 4, previous work in the area of export intermediaries is sparse. Propositions and hypotheses specifying the determinants of export intermediary performance are noticeably absent in the literature. As a result, export intermediaries remain a group of firms whose performance has been surrounded by myth and misunderstanding (Peng and Ilinitch, 1997). In contrast, the integrated model that I have advanced in this chapter represents an exception in this literature. Equipped with propositions and hypotheses, this testable model is able to serve as a launching pad to directly investigate the determinants of export intermediary performance.

CONCLUSIONS

Being the first-ever attempt to investigate the determinants of export intermediary performance, the integrated model, which draws upon three major theoretical perspectives in organizational economics and strategic management, has made conceptual progress not only in the form of a new definition and three assumptions, but also in the form of three core propositions and four testable hypotheses. In order to establish the validity of the model, propositions will have to be examined and hypotheses tested. These are the challenges that will be dealt with in the next two chapters.

NOTES

1. The utmost manifestation of such a transaction-cost-minimizing property has been the rise of multinational enterprises (MNEs). The establishment of hierarchical links across countries through the presence of MNEs is considered an efficient way to reduce transaction costs for large

firms trading across borders (Buckley and Casson, 1976; Dunning, 1980, 1988, 1993; Hennart, 1982, 1989; Rugman, 1981).

2. I assume that for small, inexperienced exporters which tend to seek help from intermediaries, other modes of foreign market entry, such as licensing, establishing joint ventures, and engaging in foreign direct investment, are not feasible in the beginning. All these options involve a great deal of information gathering, followed by a lengthy negotiation process and an even more demanding implementation stage. Moreover, the firm needs to constantly safeguard its interests against opportunistic exploitation by the host firm abroad. All these entail substantial transaction costs which tend to discourage small exporters from undertaking such endeavors. This assumption is well supported by the stage theory of internationalization (O. Anderson, 1993; Johanson and Valhne, 1977; Leonidou and Katsikeas, 1996; Melin, 1992; Root, 1994). Small manufacturers that are internationally sophisticated do exist (Oviatt and McDougall, 1994, 1995). However, they are clearly the exception rather than the rule.

3. A small number of large manufacturers maintain dual distribution channels domestically (i.e., employing both reps and house accounts) in order to monitor and compare intermediary performance (Dutta, et al., 1995). Such dual distribution channels, however, are much less common in export markets. One of the reasons is that it is very expensive to maintain dual distribution channels for foreign markets.

4. For precise definitions of theories, assumptions, propositions, and hypotheses, as well as the relationship among these concepts in the research process, interested readers can consult Bacharach (1989), Cook and Campbell (1979), Kerlinger (1986), and Popper (1972).

5. While pursuing the indirect export mode, the exporter can also elect to use overseas-based intermediaries such as distributors and agents (Bello and Lohtia, 1995; Rosson and Ford, 1982). However, the search costs to look for these foreign-based intermediaries tend to be higher than the search costs to look for domestically-based intermediaries.

6. In theory, export intermediaries can undertake another strategy to protect their business and improve their performance, namely, a backward vertical integration strategy (Mahoney, 1992). This strategy will enable intermediaries to expand into the production and manufacturing function, thus stabilizing their supplies. While there is a large body of research on vertical integration strategy (Carlton, 1979; D'Aveni and Ilinitch, 1992; D'Aveni and Ravenscraft, 1994; Galbraith and Stiles, 1984; Harrigan, 1985; Klein, et al., 1978; Levi, 1985), it is not very relevant to U.S. export intermediaries. This is because export intermediaries in the United States are usually too small to be able to financially acquire manufacturers. Large Japanese trading companies (the *sogo shosha*), in contrast, have extensively employed this strategy, or threatened to employ it, when bargaining with manufacturers (Yoshihara, 1982). Given this book's focus on U.S. export intermediaries, this strategic option is not explored in depth here. However, it remains as an interesting area for future research.

CHAPTER 6

Explaining Export Intermediary Performance: Findings from Six Case Studies

Social scientists follow rules of scientific inquiry in their investigation, and the care they exert in their research methodologies ensures the objectivity, robustness, and generalizability of their results. In order to test the validity of the integrated model of export intermediary performance, a combination of qualitative and quantitative research methods, which is called a *hybrid methodology*, is employed. This chapter reports the findings from six case studies which emerged from the qualitative phase of the investigation. Chapter 7 highlights the findings from a large-sample mail survey using quantitative methods.

Given the use of a hybrid methodology, this chapter starts with a discussion of the choice of methods. Then the case studies are described and analyzed, followed by discussions and conclusions.

HYBRID METHODOLOGY

Social scientists have a number of tools in their repertoire, and the particular research methods chosen are guided by the research question at hand (Campbell, Daft and Hulin, 1982; Cook and Campbell, 1979; Kerlinger, 1986). Within the constraints of time, budget, and resources, methods that can best answer the key question will be chosen. Since the research question of this book explores the fundamental drivers of export intermediary performance, it is necessary to first collect performance data of the firms and then focus on the nature of their different abilities which influence their performance.

Since the vast majority of U.S. export intermediaries are small, privately held firms whose performance data are not publicly available, a methodology based on published archival sources is not feasible. Most existing research on the characteristics of these firms utilized a quantitative methodology using large-sample mail surveys in order to obtain proprietary information (Batra, 1991; Bello and Williamson, 1985a, 1985b; Brasch, 1978; Coopers and Lybrand, 1984; Hay Associates, 1977; Howard and Maskulka, 1988; U.S. Department of Commerce, 1990). With a relatively large sample size, ranging from 85 (Hay Associates, 1977) to 258 firms (Bello and Williamson, 1985a, 1985b), these studies were able to capture the basic contours of export intermediaries in the United States with a high degree of confidence. However, by aiming to capture the *typical* behavior from a large sample, coarse-grained statistical analyses such as these may lose the nuances and insights concerning *individual* firms' strategies, resources, and performance.

Qualitative field-based case studies of individual firms are able to circumvent the pitfalls of large-sample quantitative studies. Fine-grained case studies are able to capture the complexities of the relationship under study, thus allowing for new insights to emerge (Eisenhardt, 1989b; Glaser and Strauss, 1967; Miles and Huberman, 1984; Yin, 1989). On the other hand, case studies, especially single-site, single-firm ones, have been criticized for being less "objective" than large-sample analyses. Explanations and interpretations of qualitative data from case studies tend to be ad hoc, with relatively poor generalizability (Emerson, 1983; Popper, 1972). Few case studies have exploited opportunities to impose greater rigor on their analyses by incorporating testable hypotheses. Moreover, case studies are expensive and time-consuming to undertake, involving the negotiation with organizations to gain access, travel to research sites, and interaction with participants. As a result, case studies are vastly outnumbered by large-sample quantitative studies. For example, Perry's (1992) work, involving 35 on-site interviews, represented the only published research that has utilized qualitative, case study methods to approach this type of firm.

In short, coarse-grained, quantitative methods and fine-grained, qualitative methods are complementary to each other. Given the advantages and pitfalls of these two methods, a hybrid methodology combining the best of these methods seems to be an ideal choice. Because of the dynamics and complexity of the relationship under study, social scientists who have relied either on case studies or large-sample methodologies may have missed important aspects of the problem they studied. By merging both quantitative and qualitative methods, researchers can benefit from advantages of these two methods while minimizing the exposure to their pitfalls (Jick, 1979). Therefore, a hybrid methodology is employed in this study, involving two phases, namely, a qualitative one and a quantitative one. The end result, I believe, will be more objective, robust, and generalizable. This chapter reports the findings from the first phase of the hybrid methodology.

QUALITATIVE METHODS

Introduction

Qualitative methods are nonstatistical analyses of data. They are the primary means of undertaking case studies like those reported in this chapter. A case study is "a history of a past or current phenomenon, drawn from multiple sources of evidence. It can include data from direct observation and systematic interviewing as well as from public and private archives" (Leonard-Barton, 1995: 40). For our purposes, a case study is a close-up inquiry about an export intermediary's history, attributes, and performance.

The beauty and power of qualitative case studies have been noted by a large number of scholars. Not surprisingly, given their interests in fine-grained organizational issues, researchers in strategy, management, and marketing have been mostly interested in such a methodology (Bettis, 1991; Bonoma, 1992; Daft and Lewin, 1990; Eisenhardt, 1989b; Jacobson, 1992; Parkhe, 1993; Pettigrew, 1995; Rangan, et al., 1993; Van de Ven, 1992). Interestingly, some economists, despite their interest in large-sample statistical analyses, have also suggested that "it is almost imperative that case study techniques be combined with more formal empirical analysis" (Masten, et al., 1991: 3–4). In the organizational economics literature, Williamson's (1975, 1985) case studies of make-or-buy decisions have been followed by many other qualitative studies which make use of very detailed data (e.g., Argyres, 1996; Klein, et al., 1978; Masten, 1996; Rangan, et al., 1993). Moreover, a number of recent studies using qualitative methods have generated interesting results which might not have emerged had quantitative methods been used (e.g., Ilinitch and Peng, 1993, 1994; Peng, 1997a, 1997b).

Advantages

There are two primary advantages of qualitative case studies, when compared with quantitative methods. First, qualitative studies are the best approach to initiate a new line of inquiry in an area where there has been very little previous research (Glaser and

Strauss, 1967). The area of export intermediary performance represents such a setting which warrants the use of qualitative methods. Researchers using these methods are able to connect themselves with the details of the organization under study, interact with case study informants and interviewees, and make better sense of the relationships that they intend to uncover (Huber and Van de Ven, 1995; Pettigrew, 1995). In contrast, quantitative studies tend to measure quantifiable relationships based on an incremental extension of previous results or armchair, axiomatic deduction (Kuhn, 1970). When the research question is new and little is known about what to measure, plunging into quantitative studies may lead to "mindless" number crunching with little idea of what is being measured and why certain constructs are measured and others are not (Bettis, 1991). Qualitative studies can avoid these pitfalls (Briggs, 1986; Campbell, et al., 1982).

Second, qualitative studies are likely to generate empirically valid results because of the very methods these studies employ. The research process, especially for field-based case studies such as those reported in this chapter, is intimately tied with evidence so that it is very likely the results will be consistent with empirical observation (Glaser and Strauss, 1967; Yin, 1989). With meticulous attention to details and multiple viewpoints from different participants, case studies are likely to be more accessible and relevant to practitioners. In contrast, many quantitative studies have generated results that are obscure and difficult to interpret. While there are many factors behind the interpretability of the results, one possible reason is that some quantitative researchers have not understood the relationships under study well enough and they may have measured spurious relationships—again, the pitfalls of "mindless" number crunching and the large-sample mentality (Bettis, 1991). By seeking input from multiple participants with different perspectives, qualitative studies can help ensure that data do not come from spurious sources and that results mirror reality (Mintzberg, 1979).

In summary, qualitative methods are able to initiate research in a new area of inquiry with little prior work, and generate valid results with intimate connections to the empirical reality. As a result, this study started with a qualitative phase.

Analytical Approach

The fundamental purpose of qualitative studies is to uncover previously unknown or unclear relationships through rich, empirically based descriptions and observations. In order to generate novel insights, Eisenhardt (1989b: 536) suggested that qualitative studies should begin "as close as possible to the ideal of no theory under consideration and no hypothesis to test." However, she went on to admit that "it is impossible to achieve this ideal of clean theoretical slate" (1989b: 536). This observation has been corroborated by several other writers, such as Pettigrew (1995: 114), who suggested that "no qualitative researcher starts with his or her mind a blank, waiting for it to be filled with evidence." In this study, I did not start with a "blank." Instead, guided by the emerging integrated model, I was interested in knowing whether the model would make sense to practitioners in the field, and how to measure several constructs in a later, quantitative phase, such as "export knowledge" and "negotiation ability."

While quantitative studies call for random sampling, qualitative research seeks *theoretical* sampling, which refers to obtaining samples of populations, events, and activities guided by researchers' emerging theory or model (Glaser and Strauss, 1967). The emerging model suggested that there would be differences between more successful and less successful export intermediaries. Therefore, a multiple-case comparative sample, including both highly successful and unsuccessful ones, was sought. This was consistent with Pettigrew's (1995: 103) advice to "go for polar types." A single-site, single-firm case study is subject to limits in generalizability and potential biases, such as the representativeness of this single firm, exaggeration of the salience of the data, and observer biases (Leonard-Barton, 1995). Multiple cases, on the other hand, improve the validity of the results and help guard against observer biases (Yan and Gray, 1994; Yin, 1989). Moreover, I sought firms located in different regions to avoid the possibility that the determinants of export intermediary performance might be region-specific. In the end, a multiple-firm, multiple-site, comparative sample was obtained, involving six firms located in two states. Three of them were successful and the other three were less successful.

Analyzing data is the heart of qualitative studies, and it is "both the most difficult and the least codified part of the process" (Eisenhardt, 1989b: 539). Due to the relatively open-ended nature of data gathering, "over time, data mount astronomically and overload the information-processing capacity of even a trained mind" (Huber and Van de Ven, 1995: xiii). While "there are probably as many approaches as researchers," according to Eisenhardt (1989b: 540), "the overall idea is to become intimately familiar with each case as a stand-alone entity. This process allows the unique patterns of each case to emerge." After researchers analyze within-case data, it becomes possible to search for cross-case patterns (Miles and Huberman, 1984; Strauss, 1987; Yin, 1989). Cross-case search of the patterns forces researchers to go beyond initial impressions gained from each case, thus enhancing the probability of capturing novel findings.

In summary, the basic analytical approach of qualitative studies is the attempt to uncover previously unknown or unclear relationships. Since no statistical or quantitative techniques are employed to analyze the data, it is important to select cases that are "transparently observable" (Pettigrew, 1995: 102) through a purposive, theoretical sampling process. Once within-case data are analyzed, cross-case patterns should be searched.

Data Collection

Given the pitfalls of single-site, single-firm case studies and my interest in knowing what is behind both the success and failure of U.S. export intermediaries, six firms, including examples of success and failure, were selected for detailed case studies.[1] These comparative case studies took place in Seattle, Washington, and Honolulu, Hawaii, both of which are regional hub cities with a significant amount of export trade with the world marketplace in general, and the Asia-Pacific region in particular. The five case studies involving Seattle-based firms were completed in 1994. The last one, Hawaii Exports, was completed in 1995. All case studies involved two participants from the same firm, and two interviewers were present. Multiple interviews, postinterview phone calls, and the collection of company documents and sales materials were employed to gather data. In selecting the cases, I ensured that they were within the parameters of export intermediaries established in Chapter 2, namely, (a) located in the United States; (b) independent; and (c) engaged in export sales. Moreover, I limited the sample to intermediaries which primarily handled relatively simple, commodity-type (low-tech) exports such as apparels, foodstuffs, and pulp/paper, in order to minimize "extraneous variation" (Eisenhardt, 1989b) that might be derived from differences between simple and complex products.[2]

Table 6.1 summarizes the major characteristics of the six firms in the sample, whose names have been disguised. Three of them were successful by most standards (Asia Trade, Cascade Exports, and Hawaii Exports), and the other three were more or less unsuccessful (Bountiful Produce, Dragon International, and Evergreen Pacific). Each description below presents a historical background, an overview of the business, and an assessment of the firm's performance. Cross-case patterns from these qualitative data will be reported in the following section.

Table 6.1
A Summary of the Six Case Studies

Case Studies*	(1)**	(2)	(3)**	(4)	(5)	(6)**
Informants	2 (co-owners)	2 (managers)	2 (president & manager)	2 (co-owners)	2 (co-owners)	2 (co-owners)

Demographics

Personnel	5	8	40	3	2	28
Primary Exports	Food-stuffs	Agricultural products	Agricultural products	Scrap metal	Pulp and paper	Apparels
Founding	1992	1981	1947	1989	1994	1984
Top Three Markets (% of Total Exports to That Market)	Russia (80%) Taiwan (10%) China (5%)	Japan (50%) Canada (30%) Germany (10%)	Taiwan (40%) Korea (30%) Japan (15%)	China (75%) Taiwan (20%) Vietnam (5%)	N/A (Not yet)	Japan (100%)

Performance

Per Capita Sales (thousand)	$400	$150	$575	$333	0	$357
Sales Margin	—***	6%	21%	3%	N/A	15%
Sales (thousand)	$2,000	$1,200	$23,000	$1,000	0	$10,000
Self-Rated Success Measure (1–5 Scale, 1=Best)	1	3	1	4	4	1

* Case Studies: (1) Asia Trade; (2) Bountiful Produce; (3) Cascade Exports; (4) Dragon International; (5) Evergreen Pacific; and (6) Hawaii Exports.
** Successful firms.
*** Informants declined to provide this information.

SIX CASE STUDIES

Case Study I: Asia Trade

Asia Trade was founded in 1992 by a recent Russian immigrant and his American wife, the two co-owners who were interviewed. In 1985 they met in Beijing as Chinese language students sent from the opposite camps of the Cold War. Then they moved on to work in trading companies in Hong Kong and Taiwan, polishing their Chinese and accumulating experience in the export business. The end of the Cold War brought this couple to the United States to found the company, taking advantage of the newly opened markets in the Russian Far East, an area where the man was raised and has extensive connections.

The collapse of the former Soviet Union created chaos as well as opportunities (Peng, 1994a; Peng and Heath, 1996). As entrepreneurs, the young couple and their company had been "thriving on chaos" (Peters, 1987). Their principal market is the Russian Far East, a vastly untapped market ready for American products (Moxon, 1995). Focusing on the general food shortage there, they had been successfully bringing processed foodstuffs, such as canned foods, beverages, and flour, mostly sourced from the Pacific Northwest, to Vladivostock, the major city in the Russian Far East.

The business environment in the newly opened Russian markets has been harsh and tough, to say the least (Kvint, 1994), and the Far East region, the "Wild West" in Russia, is even worse. With tenacity, determination, and a bit of luck, Asia Trade carved out a niche for itself. Its sales were half a million dollars in 1992, their first year. The 1994 sales reached two million dollars, a quite remarkable figure given the firm's age and size. The co-owners attributed their success to their general knowledge about the Russian language and culture and their connections with key importers (Hypothesis 1), as well as their willingness to travel to Russia to conduct negotiations (Hypothesis 2). Moreover, they stressed their ability to take title to the goods that they exported (Hypothesis 3). In addition, they complained about the difficulties of obtaining trade-related financing from U.S. banks, and they said they often had to rely on "dubious" sources of financing from Russia in order to take title to the goods.

On a 1–5 scale, 1 being the most successful, the two co-owners rated their firm's performance as 1. While the co-owners declined to provide data on net export sales margin, which could be a more objective measure of performance, they did provide data on per capita export sales of their company, which reached $400,000 in 1994, the second highest in the six-firm sample. In addition to serving the Russian Far East market, where they sold 80 percent of their products, they also exported to Taiwan (10 percent) and China (5 percent). Overall, the Asia Trade case provides some support for the idea that an export intermediary capable of minimizing export-related transaction costs for U.S. manufacturers on multiple dimensions stands a good chance of becoming successful. As the Russian Far East markets have begun to open up, American producers naturally would like to enter. However, unfamiliarity and inexperience with these markets lead to high search, negotiation, and monitoring/enforcement costs. It is these distant, unfamiliar foreign markets that provide a maneuvering space for entrepreneurs at Asia Trade to thrive.

Case Study II: Bountiful Produce

Bountiful Produce also worked in the general area of exporting foodstuffs, mostly consisting of apples, strawberries, raspberries, and other produce. It was founded in 1981. In 1994, it employed a staff of eight people and its top three markets were Japan (50 percent of its total export sales), Canada (30 percent), and Germany (10 percent). Two of its export managers were interviewed.

After some initial difficulties in the early 1980s, the company's sales reached one million dollars in the mid-1980s, and they have remained at approximately that level since then. Attempts to improve sales from that level had not been very successful. According to the managers, the primary reason for flattened sales was the "glass ceiling" that Japanese distributors implicitly imposed on them. They believed that the Japanese let them in initially as a way to reduce the U.S. government pressure to open the Japanese market; once they were in Japan with a certain level of sales, they did not have much room for further expansion. Although Bountiful Produce had two employees who spoke fluent Japanese, the managers believed that their negotiation abilities were still limited and that their relationships with the Japanese buyers could be improved. Dealings with the Canadians and Europeans were much easier. Confirming the importance of taking title to the goods to the success of an export intermediary, the managers admitted that they tried whenever possible to secure financing in order to take title of the goods. However, they were only able to take title to 80 percent of their exports, working on commission for the rest of their sales.

On a 1–5 scale, with 1 being the most successful, these managers gave their company a 3. The firm's per capita export sales in 1994 reached $150,000, with a 6 percent margin of net export sales. The Bountiful Produce case illustrates what an "average" export intermediary can be. It does have some capabilities in minimizing the producers' export-related transaction costs, namely, its relative success in penetrating the key Japanese market (Hypothesis 1), its negotiation abilities (Hypothesis 2), and its willingness to take title to the goods whenever possible (Hypothesis 3). However, none of these capabilities is excellent or outstanding when compared with a more successful example such as Asia Trade. Bountiful Produce appears to be incapable of breaking or penetrating the perceived glass ceiling in its major market. As a result, its future prospects do not appear to be very promising, according to the managers.

Case Study III: Cascade Exports

The oldest firm in the sample, Cascade Exports, was founded in 1947 by two veterans from World War II. Currently employing 40 people, it was also the largest one in the sample, with 1994 sales reaching 23 million dollars. Working primarily in the area of exporting agricultural products to the Far East, it served markets in Taiwan, Korea, Japan, and a few other countries. Its president and export manager were interviewed.

The company initially used a "follow-the-military" strategy. The founders first served in the military and were stationed in Japan immediately after the end of World War II. Coming back home, they sensed that there would be a market for American agricultural products in Asia because so many homesick GIs were stationed there. They took advantage of their connections in the military and got themselves some government contracts to sell to the military. Over the years, as American influence expanded in the Far East and the standard of living increased in countries such as Japan, Korea, and Taiwan, their products not only became acceptable among U.S. military circles in these countries, but also gained popularity among the general public there. Therefore, even when the United States cut down its military forces stationed in the Far East, the demand for products that Cascade Exports carried, such as American beef, apples, and processed foods, continued and even rose in recent years.

During the past four and a half decades, the company experienced a great deal of ups and downs. However, its efforts persisted, and it took pains to work with American agricultural producers in order to provide the right kind of products to its customers. As East Asian economies boomed and became more affluent, customers there demanded many more differentiated and sophisticated products that catered to their needs. In the process, Cascade Exports accumulated an enormous amount of knowledge about such trends in consumer taste in the Far East, as well as a solid working relationship with distributors and importers there. Such expertise, in turn, became a source of the company's competitive advantage to attract U.S. manufacturers, which were more willing to let Cascade Exports handle their exports than to let other inexperienced intermediaries do the job. Moreover, from the beginning, Cascade Exports insisted on taking title to the goods, thus further simplifying the producers' problems.

On a 1–5 scale, the two interviewees gave Cascade Exports a 1, the highest performance rating. Its per capita sales ($575,000) and net export sales margin (21 percent) in 1994 corroborated the "subjective" 1–5 rating. Cascade Exports celebrated its fiftieth anniversary in 1997. Such longevity makes the company an interesting study of what a successful export intermediary can be. Taking advantage of decades of experience and expertise, it has the resources and capabilities to present lower transaction cost and agency cost solutions to agricultural exporters which face a great deal of uncertainty in foreign markets. Overall, the Cascade Exports case is an American success story that sets an example for other export intermediaries.

Case Study III: Dragon International

Dragon International was founded by a Hong Kong immigrant and his American partner in 1989. Their primary business was to export scrap metal products from salvage operations in the United States to the Far East, including China (75 percent of its total sales), Taiwan (20 percent), and Vietnam (5 percent). The two co-owners were interviewed.

The two co-owners previously worked in a steel company's export department for several years. Sensing the demand for scrap metal materials in booming Asian economies, they quit their jobs at the steel company and started their own business. They divided the work into two parts, with the Hong Kong immigrant mostly dealing with customers in Asia, and the American partner working with U.S. suppliers. Like many small businesses, their beginning was full of uncertainties and difficulties. After losing money during the first three years, they started to break even in the fourth year, and their sales in 1994 reached the one-million-dollar mark. On average, they took title to 50 percent of the goods they handled.

Overall, the co-owners were not satisfied with the performance of their company, giving it a 4 for their performance out of a 1–5 scale, with 1 being the best. Although Dragon International's per capita export sales reached a respectable $333,000, its export sales margin was only 3 percent in 1994. Its primary threat came from U.S.

producers that wanted to connect with buyers in Asia and switch to direct exporting once Dragon International paved the way. Their secondary threat was Asian importers who also wanted to contact the manufacturers directly for various reasons, such as inquiring about the technical specifications, and to bypass the intermediary. It appears that Dragon International, like Bountiful Produce, is just another "average" export intermediary. It has certain resources and capabilities to appeal to prospective U.S. manufacturers, such as its knowledge and connections with Asian buyers (Hypothesis 1), its abilities to negotiate deals (Hypothesis 2), and its propensity to take title to goods (Hypothesis 3). But these resources and capabilities appear to be barely over the threshold level to keep the company in business so far. As one co-owner told us, "We are not sure about whether we will still be in business for the next five years."

Case Study V: Evergreen Pacific

Founded in the first part of 1994, Evergreen Pacific was one of the youngest export intermediaries, essentially "a new kid on the block." The informants were two of its co-owners, who were born in China and went to school in the United States.

Their aim was to bring pulp and paper products from the Pacific Northwest to Asia, with an eye first on China and with Hong Kong and Taiwan on the horizon. However, the company had a rocky start, because the worldwide pulp and paper prices were on the rise in 1994, and manufacturers did not need much extra help from the intermediaries to sell their products. On the other hand, buyers in China pressed Evergreen Pacific to find U.S. pulp and paper manufacturers that were willing to sell below the current market prices, which were 40 percent higher than their 1993 level. In such a seller's market, established intermediaries with long-term relationships with manufacturers were able to secure their share of the business, but new intermediaries such as Evergreen Pacific had a hard time locating manufacturers willing to talk to them. I specifically inquired about whether their connections with the Chinese importers would be strong enough to allow them to take title to the goods, once they found an exporter. Their answer was that they did not have such financing sources, which further handicapped their potential to land a sale.

As of December 1994, when the two co-owners were interviewed, Evergreen Pacific had not registered any sales. As a result, they were unable to provide more objective performance data such as per capita export sales and the export sales margin. Using a more subjective self-rated measure of performance (a 1–5 scale, with 1 being the best), they gave their firm a 4, the lowest in the sample. Evergreen Pacific did perform a few consulting projects for several U.S. companies, providing information about the pulp and paper market in the Far East. Overall, the Evergreen Pacific case illustrates an export intermediary that is plagued by its lack of valuable resources and capabilities for manufacturers. Trying to explain the firm's lack of success provides several insights. First, the search costs in such an environment were already low, since foreign buyers came to the United States to present themselves and were eager to bid up the limited supply from U.S. producers at that time (Hypothesis 1). Likewise, the negotiation costs were low for the manufacturers too, since in such a seller's market they could take an upper hand in negotiations and dictate the terms (Hypothesis 2). Finally, Evergreen Pacific's inability to take title to the goods further decreased its chances of being selected (Hypothesis 3). Its timing to enter the pulp and paper industry at this particular time was unfortunate; it could have done better had the markets not been that strong for the producers.

Case Study VI: Hawaii Exports

The last case study is about a company located in Hawaii. In the 1990s, the economy of Hawaii is shouldered by three major industries—tourism, the military, and agriculture—and the state has hardly any significant manufacturing bases (*Market Facts Hawaii*, 1995). As a result, the export performance of the state is not impressive, and its export volume usually ranks close to the bottom of the list of all the fifty states. However, strong export potential exists for unique products such as tropical agriculture, apparel (Aloha wear), and crafts for which Hawaii is internationally known. During the 1990s, nearly two and a half million foreign visitors come to visit the state every year (the total tourist headcount was approximately six and a half million in 1994); among them, one and a half million routinely come from Japan (*Market Facts Hawaii*, 1995: 24). As the westernmost point of the United States and a crossroads for U.S.-Asia interaction, Hawaii "may well serve as a bellwether state" for Asia-bound exports (Hook and Czinkota, 1988: 52). In addition, Hawaii has an insular location. In order to achieve sufficient economies of scale for competitive production, local firms must frequently look beyond the islands for markets. Furthermore, due to Hawaii's distance from the mainland United States, selling to markets in the contiguous forty-eight states is not necessarily the easiest way to expand market reach; rather, the geographic proximity of other Asia Pacific countries may encourage exports (Hook and Czinkota, 1988;

Lee and Brasch, 1978). Finally, centuries of immigration have resulted in a local population that is significantly attuned to the cultures of
major Asian countries such as Japan, China, Taiwan, Korea, and the
Philippines, thus lowering cultural barriers between local producers
and their markets in Asia.

Hawaii Exports took advantage of the opportunities presented by
the dynamic business environment on the islands. It was founded in
1984 by two local entrepreneurs of Japanese descent, and it
currently employed 28 people. Its owners, who previously operated
two retail stores selling souvenirs to visitors in Waikiki, were familiar with retail customers from Japan. They noticed two interesting
trends. First, Japanese tourists loved to buy anything that was made
in Hawaii, whether it was macadamia nuts, Aloha shirts, or sun-
glasses. Second, business fluctuated on a seasonal basis, with
summer sales much higher than winter sales, which only had a short
peak around Christmas time. In other words, when the tourists were
gone, the retail business would go downhill. The owners then realiz-
ed that if they could export the same kind of Hawaii-made products
to countries such as Japan, their business would stabilize and not
experience the usual seasonal fluctuation.

With this powerful idea, they started to market their products to
Japan in 1986. They first asked Japanese tourists visiting their
stores to identify their particular tastes and interests in customer
surveys. Then they inquired about whether the tourists would like to
see these items available in Japan, and the response was overwhel-
mingly positive. One of the vacationers identified himself as a buyer
for a small trading company (the *senmon shosha*) and was interested
in the Aloha wear line that the store was carrying. Thus, the first
export order went to that small Japanese trading company based in
Osaka and the merchandise sold well. Given that nearly one percent
of the entire Japanese population is attracted to Hawaii every year,
the demand for and interest in Hawaii-style clothing can be
potentially substantial in Japan. The status-conscious Japanese tourists, upon their return, like to wear their Aloha wear and Hawaii-
flavored T-shirts as well as give these items as gifts to friends and
relatives, thereby further stirring up the interest in these products.
As a result, even people who cannot afford to spend their vacation in
Hawaii may sometimes want to buy Hawaii-style clothing just for the
fun of it or for the sake of keeping up with the Joneses (or the
Suzukis) who have been to the islands.

Upon the successful launch of the first export order, Hawaii Exports started to capitalize on the idea of capturing Japanese demand
at home. It printed a catalog of products with affordable shipping
costs and let tourists visiting its Waikiki stores take the catalog back

to Japan. It eventually launched direct catalog sales to Japan. Recently a lot of catalog houses on the U.S. mainland have started to do direct sales with Japan,[3] and Hawaii Exports is one of the very few in Hawaii that do this.

After the Gulf War and subsequent recession in 1990, continued economic troubles in Hawaii's two major markets—California and Japan—contributed to a significant loss of visitors (*Market Facts Hawaii*, 1995: 24). Nevertheless, Hawaii Exports continued to succeed, because its business no longer depended on visitors coming to the islands; instead, it could reach export customers in Japan who might be unable to come to Hawaii but still wanted to purchase some "minor indulgence" items such as an Aloha shirt. Hawaii Exports worked closely with local apparel producers that rely on them to enter the key Japanese markets. Many local store owners came to ask for help too, because tourists, even though they came to visit, were spending less now, and there was a huge surplus of unsold goods. Because of its continued operation of the Waikiki stores and the continuous cash flow from export catalog sales, Hawaii Exports was able to take title to 100 percent of the goods it carried.

With a 1994 sales volume approaching 10 million dollars, the two owners gave their firm a 1, the best possible rating, on a 1–5 scale on firm performance. Per capita export sales at Hawaii Exports reached $357,000, and its net export sales margin was 15 percent in 1994, both of which were excellent indicators of its performance. The future prospects of the firm appear to be strong. On the one hand, their store operations in Waikiki are expected to pick up as Japan and California recover from their recessions and send more visitors. On the other hand, there is a lot more business that can be done in Japan, and the firm is also keeping an eye on China, Hong Kong, Korea, and Taiwan as potential new markets.

Summary

These six case studies provide a wealth of information about the diversity of export intermediary firms. Having provided a brief description of these six cases *individually,* I will highlight the key findings *across* these six cases in the next section.

FINDINGS ACROSS THE SIX CASES

The case studies were designed to unpack some of the complexities surrounding the determinants of export intermediary performance in a fine-grained fashion. Specifically, I was interested in (a) what factors entrepreneurs and operators of export intermediaries thought were important to export intermediary performance, and (b) what factors actually contributed to firm performance.

Lowering Client Firms' Search Costs

Across the six cases, several dimensions of the ability to lower client firms' export-related search costs were identified (see Table 6.2). First, principals' experience in exporting has been identified by all informants as an important predictor of performance. The measure was the number of years in this business, including the time working for other export-related businesses. In the case of Cascade Exports, their principals averaged forty years of experience, thus presenting a significant competitive advantage. One of its owners commented:

Since we have been in this business for such a long time, we have pretty much seen all the ups and downs in the [export] marketplace. We know how

Table 6.2
Ability to Lower Client Firms'
Export-Related Search Costs

Case Studies*	(1)**	(2)	(3)**	(4)	(5)	(6)**
Principals' Export Experience	7 years	12 years	40 years	8 years	2 years	12 years
Foreign Language Proficiency	Russian Chinese	Japanese German	Japanese Chinese Korean	Chinese Vietnamese	Chinese	Japanese
Number and % of Foreign-born Personnel	3 (60%)	2 (25%)	4 (10%)	1 (33%)	2 (100%)	7 (25%)
*Number and % of Personnel Who Lived/ Studied Abroad****	5 (100%)	6 (75%)	20 (50%)	2 (67%)	2 (100%)	20 (71%)

* Case Studies: (1) Asia Trade; (2) Bountiful Produce; (3) Cascade Exports; (4) Dragon International; (5) Evergreen Pacific; and (6) Hawaii Exports.
** Successful firms.
*** Including the number and percentage of foreign-born personnel above.

to find export customers and persuade our clients to stay in the export business despite the market fluctuations. Over time, our experience gives us a reputation that is widely known.

Such an experience, in turn, gives companies such as Cascade Exports a great deal of knowledge about the particular markets it serves (i.e., Japan, Taiwan, and Korea). In all these markets, customers value long-term relationships built over a period of time. Since a history of prior relations among organizations has an important effect on the nature of future relations (Gulati, 1995; Heide and Miner, 1992; Levinthal and Fichman, 1988), Cascade Exports is able to leverage such knowledge and relationships to help its manufacturing client firms lower their search costs. In contrast, the two principals at Evergreen Pacific, which is the least successful firm in the sample, barely had two years of experience before opening their own company. Their lack of experience places them at a disadvantage, especially when competing against established firms such as Cascade Exports.

Another important dimension that was identified by all the informants is proficiency in the language spoken in the target markets. While many foreign business people speak some English, the ability to speak the target language shortens the distance between the two parties and overcomes some of the initial cultural barriers. Consistent with the findings of studies on ethnic entrepreneurs (Aldrich and Waldinger, 1990; Borjas, 1990; Waldinger, Aldrich and Ward, 1990), several principals/managers were found to be immigrants. These entrepreneurs have not only brought their culture and language talents to this country, but also possessed important connections with their home countries (e.g., China, Hong Kong, and Russia) which can be especially helpful in international trade.

Moreover, I found that export intermediaries tend to draw foreign language talents from two primary pools of people: (a) foreign-born immigrants and (b) Americans who have studied foreign languages and culture. As Table 6.2 indicates for each firm, I measured the percentage of foreign-born personnel and the percentage of personnel who had lived or worked abroad. While the percentage of foreign-born personnel ranges from 10 percent at the relatively large Cascade Exports to 100 percent at the tiny Evergreen Pacific, the percentage of personnel who had lived or worked abroad (including both immigrants and native-born Americans) shows a more consistent pattern, in that all firms have at least 50 percent of personnel with such experience.

Overall, experience in exporting, as well as knowledge and expertise in foreign languages and cultures accumulated from experience abroad, gives some intermediaries distinctive competency to find the right customers and markets for their manufacturing clients, thus lowering a manufacturer's export-related search costs. All successful intermediaries exhibit an entrepreneurial drive that differentiates them from the less successful one. For example, in the case of Hawaii Exports, which started with retail operations in Waikiki catering to tourists, the owners did not want to be solely dependent on tourist sales. Instead, they formulated a "chase-the-tourists-back-home" strategy. According to an owner:

Although we are dependent on tourists, that does not mean we can only wait here for tourists to come to visit our stores. If we follow tourists back to their home, then we can reach a much larger market and create more stable demand.

The relentless search for new markets and the abilities to capitalize on these opportunities appear to be a part of the important resources and capabilities that provide firms that possess them with a significant competitive advantage. This is especially true in newly opened markets such as Russia. Listen to the owner of Asia Trade, which specializes in trading with the Russian Far East:

While Americans and other Westerners have flocked to Moscow and St. Petersburg, very few have ever visited Vladivostock [the major city of the Russian Far East], which was off limits to foreigners only a few years ago. Yet the market there is huge and underserved. This creates a tremendous opportunity. But you've got to know the people there and become their friends in order to make a deal. Otherwise they just don't trust you and won't buy your products. Some American firms have noticed such an opportunity, but they have no idea whom to talk to in Vladivostock even though they may know some people to talk to in Moscow. This is definitely an area we can help because we've known some key people there for a long time and, basically, know whom to talk to.

In summary, Hypothesis 1 seems to be supported by qualitative data from these case studies. Specifically, knowledge about foreign markets and export processes appears to be a major source of competitive advantage for successful intermediaries.

Lowering Client Firms' Negotiation Costs

International negotiations presented a significant challenge to many exporters, especially small, inexperienced ones. As a result, intermediaries' abilities to reduce the risk and uncertainty associated with such negotiations will be sought after by client firms. The case data point to two factors that lead to lower negotiation costs: (a) frequency of handling negotiations on behalf of clients, and (b) negotiation skills (see Table 6.3).

Three firms in the sample, Asia Trade, Dragon International, and Hawaii Exports, always handle negotiations on behalf of their clients, while others sometimes do that and sometimes just pass information leads to their clients to aid negotiations. Handling export negotiations establishes the presence of the export intermediary, thus allowing for deeper participation in the client firm's export business. Merely passing information limits the room for the intermediary to maneuver between the two parties. In the words of a manager at Bountiful Produce:

We wish we could always participate in the negotiations, if not totally in control of such negotiations. In that way, we can ensure that the two parties [the foreign buyer and the domestic client] appreciate our contributions to the particular transaction. Otherwise, once we supplied certain information our client firm wanted, we usually don't hear from them anymore. As a result, we run the risk of being forgotten.

Concurring such remarks, an owner of Dragon International explained that:

Table 6.3
Ability to Lower Client Firms'
Export-Related Negotiation Costs

Case Studies*	(1)**	(2)	(3)**	(4)	(5)	(6)**
Frequency of Handling Negotiations on Behalf of Clients	Always	Some-times	Some-times	Always	Some-times	Always
Location of Negotiations	Always abroad	Mostly in the U.S.	Half abroad, half in the U.S.	Always abroad	Mostly in the U.S.	Mostly in the U.S.
Self-Reported Negotiation Skills (1–5 Scale, 1=Best)	1	2	1	1	2	1

* Case Studies: (1) Asia Trade; (2) Bountiful Produce; (3) Cascade Exports; (4) Dragon International; (5) Evergreen Pacific; and (6) Hawaii Exports.
** Successful firms.

If possible, we always insist on handling the negotiations on behalf of our clients. We know from time to time that they want to bypass us, and, believe me, most of them will do so once their export sales reach a certain level. So we can only make a living during their initial stages of exporting. Handling negotiations is one way we can add value to the entire process. If during their early stage in exporting, we have already given up this value-adding step, then what can we do in the future as they become more experienced in exporting by themselves?

Not surprisingly, all informants regarded negotiation skills as a highly important competency in this business and were quite confident about their negotiation skills. Even in the case of Evergreen Pacific, a start-up firm established in 1994, its own negotiation skills were also rated quite high. One owner at Evergreen Pacific, which so far has not registered any sale, told me that:

Negotiation skills are definitely a major competitive weapon in this business. Because we are a very young company. Some manufacturing firms didn't believe in our abilities and only wanted us to provide some information leads about the pulp and paper market in Hong Kong and China. Once we convinced some clients that we could do a good job to handle their negotiations for them, we wanted to make sure that the negotiations go well since we wanted to prove ourselves. Unfortunately none of the negotiations so far has been successful. But I don't think it was because our negotiation skills were not good enough. The negotiations actually went quite well, but our clients couldn't accept the quite reasonable terms we negotiated for them.

Our informants seem to have split opinions in terms of where the negotiations should be held. While Asia Trade and Dragon International always conducted negotiations abroad, others took a more liberal stand, avoiding any fixed locations. As a result, the location of export negotiations does not seem to matter. A manager at Cascade Exports stressed that:

This is a two-way business. You don't want to travel to the other guy's city all the time, but he also doesn't want to always come to your place. So the simplest solution is to reciprocate the location of annual sales negotiations, one year in Seattle, and the next year in Taipei, and so on and so forth.

In summary, the frequency of handling negotiations on behalf of the clients and the intermediary's negotiation skills combine to lower the client firms' export-related negotiation costs. If the intermediary is not perceived by the client as presenting a low negotiation costs alternative, then the intermediary will not be able to be deeply involved in the negotiation process, thus limiting its performance potential. Consistent with Hypothesis 2, negotiation abilities do appear to be an important part of intermediaries' resources and capabilities, one that has an impact on their performance.

Lowering Client Firms' Monitoring/Enforcement Costs

Export-related monitoring/enforcement costs also figure prominently in the manufacturer's export channel decision. Such costs can be substantial and become a source of frustration that deters the manufacturer's further export expansion. Successful export intermediaries can lower such costs for their client firms, thus encouraging more export sales. However, the presence of agency costs makes this principal-agent (manufacturer-intermediary) relationship more complex. Therefore, how do intermediaries lower export-related monitoring/enforcement costs for their clients, while assuring the clients that agency costs are within acceptable bounds?

Consistent with Hypothesis 3, the case data suggest that the principal way to solve this paradox is to take title to the goods, instead of working on commission. As Table 6.4 shows, the three most successful firms in our sample, Asia Trade, Cascade Exports, and Hawaii Exports, all take title to 100 percent of the goods. Bountiful Produce and Dragon International take title to between 50 to 80 percent of the goods. Evergreen Pacific, the least successful firm in our sample, has never taken title to any goods since its inception.

The importance of taking title to the goods has been stressed many times by our informants. For example, according to an owner of Hawaii Exports:

Whether a trading company can take title to the goods exported often differentiates a successful trading company from a less successful one. There are many small manufacturers out there that don't want to bother with the complexities involved with exports. Even when they are marginally interested in finding an export market, they only want to find a trader who can handle the export process for them. Better yet, they would like to find a trader to buy their products and then resell them. For the trader, this is a tremendous opportunity, if he can take title to the goods. By taking title, the trader basically has the entire export business of those small firms for himself.

While the ability to take title to the goods can be translated into a competitive advantage for an intermediary, the inability to do so, on the other hand, would severely handicap an intermediary. An owner at Evergreen Pacific admitted that:

Table 6.4
Ability to Lower Client Firms'
Export-Related Monitoring/Enforcement Costs

*Case Studies**	(1)**	(2)	(3)**	(4)	(5)	(6)**
Frequency of Taking *Title to Goods*	100%	80%	100%	50%	0%	100%

* Case Studies: (1) Asia Trade; (2) Bountiful Produce; (3) Cascade Exports; (4) Dragon International; (5) Evergreen Pacific; and (6) Hawaii Exports.
** Successful firms.

Our lack of resources to take title to the goods is a key factor behind our lack of success so far. Many exporters would like to dump their products and risks on to the trading company. Once they heard you couldn't buy goods from them but could only work for them on a commission, they became suspicious. This is especially true for a young company such as ours with a very short history and very low visibility.

These findings provide strong support for Hypothesis 3. It is also consistent with the evolutionary pattern of export intermediaries in the United States. In recent decades, the distinction between commission-based export management companies (EMCs) and title-taking export trading companies (ETCs) has become increasingly blurred, as more and more intermediaries, even traditional EMCs, have started to take title to the goods (Batra, 1991; Brasch, 1978; U.S. Department of Commerce, 1990). For manufacturers, transferring title to intermediaries minimizes the need to monitor and verify agent performance, since intermediaries have very strong incentives to sell these goods. In other words, taking title minimizes agency costs for manufacturers, thus becoming a preferred mode of contract structure with intermediaries. As a result, the performance-enhancing implication of such a behavior to reduce transaction costs and agency costs is clear.

Summary

Overall, the findings across the six cases suggested a direct, positive relationship between the abilities to lower client firms' export-related transaction costs and agency costs on one hand, and the intermediary's performance on the other hand. Specifically, three hypotheses (1, 2, and 3) received strong support from qualitative data generated from the case studies. Hypothesis 4 was by design not tested with the case study sample. Since only export intermediaries dealing with commodity-type products were included in the sample, the case studies were unable to either support or refute this hypothesis, which posits a direct relationship between the intermediary's willingness to specialize in commodity products and its performance. Overall, the three key hypotheses of the integrated model have been supported by the case study results.

DISCUSSION

While the integrated model of export intermediary performance articulated in Chapter 5 brings three underlying theoretical perspectives to bear on a research question that has rarely been attempted before, it was not clear whether the propositions and hypotheses would make sense to entrepreneurs and operators of export intermediaries in the real world. As a response to the call for more field-based case studies before attempting large-sample quantitative manipulation (e.g., Bettis, 1991; Daft and Lewin, 1990; Godfrey and Hill, 1995; Pettigrew, 1995; Van de Ven, 1992), six case studies were designed to provide a microscopic view of what is behind the success and failure of export intermediaries in the United States. Case study participants largely supported the logic and rationale of the core propositions and hypotheses. Moreover, the findings shed considerable light on complex, unobservable constructs such as "knowledge of foreign markets" and "negotiation ability." Of course, to argue that the six case studies "prove" the integrated model would be far fetched. Nevertheless, they greatly increase the confidence in the explanatory power of this model. In addition, given that the six sampled firms were located in different states and yet exhibited similar attributes of the determinants of their performance, the findings are able to provide some triangulation in support of the integrated model.

In addition to generating qualitative support for the integrated model, the case studies also allow for an integration among transaction cost, agency, and resource-based theories. Viewed from a resource-based perspective, each of the transaction-cost- and agency-cost-minimizing abilities specified in the hypotheses can be conceptualized as an intangible, firm-specific resource, contributing to the success or failure of these firms (Barney, 1991, 1997; Hall, 1992, 1993). The heterogeneity of resources among export intermediaries, as evident in the case findings and other studies (e.g., Brasch, 1978;

Perry, 1992; Root, 1994), seems to account for a large part of their performance variance.

Moreover, these intangible resources and capabilities appear to be valuable, unique, and hard-to-imitate, thus giving firms that possess them competitive advantages. Since intimate knowledge about certain foreign markets and export processes takes a long time to develop and better negotiation skills might take even longer to mature, over time, such knowledge and skills may become a strategic asset (Amit and Shoemaker, 1993; Dierickx and Cool, 1989). For example, principals of Cascade Exports have accumulated on average forty years of experience in the export business. These hard-to-imitate attributes give the firm a strong reputation that helps draw client firms. The combination of superb knowledge and negotiation skills with the ability to take title to the goods might be rarer, given the difficulties of securing trade financing in the United States. As a result, firms that have these resources such as Asia Trade, Cascade Exports, and Hawaii Exports are in a position to sustain competitive advantage in the fierce competition for export intermediary services (Day and Wensley, 1988; Hunt and Morgan, 1995). In other words, these intangible resources and capabilities may be regarded as key success factors for export intermediaries (Cavusgil and Kirpalani, 1993; Hall, 1992, 1993). It is important to note that some of the more commonly available resources, such as foreign language proficiency, may be qualifiers, but by themselves are not real key success factors. However, a firm's bundling of many of these resources together in a value-adding way, as exemplified by Asia Trade, Cascade Exports, and Hawaii Exports, is highly unusual, thus giving rise to the firm's "combinative capabilities" that underlie its competitive advantage (Kogut and Zander, 1992).

As the analytical underpinning of the integrated model, transaction cost and agency theories have a major strength in their clear specification of the economic relationship between manufacturers and intermediaries. On the other hand, Ghoshal and Moran (1996), Hirsch, et al. (1990), Perrow (1986), and Zajac and Olsen (1993) have criticized these theories for being excessively narrow, focusing only on the principal's point of view. Although these criticisms may be extreme, they do suggest a need "to expand to a richer and more complex range of contexts" using complementary theories (Eisenhardt, 1989a: 71).

While transaction cost and agency theories have been criticized for being too narrow, resource-based theory has been criticized for being too broad (Collis, 1994; Porter, 1991). According to Conner (1991: 145), "at some level, everything in the firm becomes a resource and hence resources lose explanatory power." Often these resources cannot be clearly described, let alone accurately observed, defined, and measured (Barney, 1991, 1997; Godfrey and Hill, 1995; Reed and DeFillippi, 1990). Miller and Shamsie (1996: 519) suggested that "although it has generated a great deal of conceptualizing, the resource-based view is just beginning to occasion systematic empirical study." They moved on to argue that unless these ideas can generate testable hypotheses, they may only be called a "view" but not a "theory."

Delineating the differences between transaction cost and resource-based theories, Conner (1991: 143) wrote that "the resource-based approach embraces the (positive) value-creating potential of the firm . . . rather than avoidance of the (negative) effect of opportunism [of the transaction cost perspective]." Mahoney and Pandian (1992: 370) suggested that "the resource-based theory is linked to transaction cost theory because resource combinations are influenced by transaction cost economizing." "Transaction costs surely influence the accumulation of resources," according to Foss, Knudsen and Montgomery (1995: 14), who went on to observe that "there has been very little systematic work on the precise relations between the resource approaches on the one hand and transaction costs on the other." Similarly, Zajac and Olsen (1993) argued that the single-firm, cost minimization emphasis of transaction cost theory needs to be complemented by a resource-based perspective emphasizing joint value creation between transaction partners. Overall the consensus among many researchers seems to be that "a fruitful area for further theory development may be exploration of situations in which integration decisions can be expected to depend on one or the other of these circumstances, or a combination" (Conner, 1991: 143).

Here in the case of export intermediaries, such an empirical setting has been identified in which transaction cost, agency, and resource-based theories combine to suggest a more refined and comprehensive model of firm performance. Rather than providing separate explanations of firm performance, factors brought into play by resource-based theory may be regarded as antecedents or preconditions to the abilities to minimize transaction costs and agency costs. Another way to interpret the findings is that we might view transaction cost and agency theories as providing the context in which firms' resources and capabilities are embedded. As a result, the integrated model is able to bring these three theories together in a coherent way to bear on a previously unsolved problem, namely, the determinants of export intermediary performance.

CONCLUSIONS

Qualitative case studies are an ideal launching pad to initiate a new area of research. As the first phase of a hybrid methodology, six case studies have been used to investigate the integrated model of export intermediary performance. The qualitative findings support key hypotheses of the model. Specifically, as hypothesized, the performance of firms in our sample seems to be driven by the acquisition and possession of transaction-cost- and agency-cost-minimizing abilities which can be regarded as intangible resources and capabilities. Overall, the integrated model of export intermediary performance is found to be able to explain a great deal of what is behind the success and failure of the six sampled export intermediaries.

Compared with many single-site, single-firm case studies, the six-case design provides a higher degree of confidence in the results. However, six firms are not that many. Time, budget, and resource constraints do not allow for studying a large sample of firms with the fine-grained case study method. Given the anecdotal nature of the data and the small size of the sample, it is not certain whether these findings are merely ad hoc explanations that work well with this small group of firms, or are robust and generalizable to many other export intermediaries. For example, I claim in the paragraph above that the case findings explain "a great deal" of the determinants of export intermediary performance. But it is not clear exactly how much is explained by these results. While some explanatory factors of firm performance, such as principals' experience and ability to take title to the goods, differ among successful and unsuccessful intermediaries, other factors, such as foreign language proficiency and negotiation skills, are present in all firms in the sample. In other words, these results do not allow us to reach a *definitive* answer to the key question concerning the determinants of export intermediary performance; instead, they provide a *tentative* answer that seems to make sense with this small sample of six firms. By design, the fine-grained, case study method is unable to provide a definitive answer with generalizability. Such a challenge will be dealt with in the next chapter using quantitative methods.

NOTES

1. Appendix 1 contains more details of case selection, data collection and analyses. A more technical description can be found in Peng (1996).

2. As a result, the case studies were unable to examine Hypothesis 4, namely, the impact of specialization in commodity versus complex products

on export intermediary performance. This hypothesis was investigated by quantitative methods reported in Chapter 7.

3. Because Japan's many-layered retail distribution system jacks up retail prices, many American catalog houses have found that they could beat the Japanese retail stores on price, even after additional mailing and shipping costs are included. Moreover, international mailing and shipping costs are not that much. According to an article in the *Business Week* (1995b: 64), "it costs less to mail across the sea than across Tokyo." The same article also describes the little known export success of U.S. catalog houses such as Hawaii Exports.

CHAPTER 7

Explaining Export Intermediary Performance: Findings from a Mail Survey

Chapter 5 outlines an integrated model of the determinants of export intermediary performance, with a new definition, three assumptions, three propositions, and four hypotheses. A hybrid methodology is employed to test this model using both qualitative and quantitative methods. Chapter 6 reports findings from six case studies, which are the first phase of the hybrid methodology. As an exploratory step, these findings are able to support the integrated model in a qualitative way. However, how strong the support is remains unknown. Field-based case studies tend to be "an *interpretive* enterprise" (Emerson, 1983: vii, original emphasis), whose results are anecdotal, tentative, and hence unquantifiable. As a result, case study findings have usually been regarded as a first step toward providing a more quantifiable and hence more concrete answer to research questions.

As the second part of the hybrid methodology, this chapter confronts the challenge of providing a more definitive answer to the question of what determines export intermediary performance. Specifically, it reports the findings of a large-sample mail survey using quantitative methods. To the best of my knowledge, there has been no published, large-sample research on export intermediary performance. Therefore, this part of the study represents the first of its kind and makes a number of unique contributions to the literature.

The chapter highlights the quantitative methods employed, followed by a description of the sample characteristics and variable selections. Then I move on to report the findings. Discussions and conclusions follow.

QUANTITATIVE METHODS

Introduction

The primary quantitative methods employed here are multiple regression analyses, a technique widely used in social science research. "Regression" means statistical relations between two variables, such as X and Y (Neter, Wasserman and Kutner, 1989: 26). One of these two variables, say Y, is called a "dependent variable," whose value, by definition, depends on the other variable, the "independent variable," or X in this case. In other words, changes in Y can be *explained* by changes in X. In social science research, the dependent variable is usually the outcome of a complex set of relations, instead of just one independent variable. Therefore, a regression model containing only one independent variable is often too imprecise to be useful. A more sophisticated approach is to use a number of independent variables, such as X_1, X_2 . . . X_n, to explain one dependent variable, Y—hence the term "multiple regression." In our integrated model, the dependent variable is the performance of export intermediaries. Because there are a number of independent variables influencing the performance of these firms, such as transaction costs, agency costs, and firm resources and capabilities, multiple regression analyses have to be employed in order to adequately explain the determinants of export intermediary performance.

Advantages

There are three primary advantages of quantitative methods, when compared with qualitative methods. The fundamental advantage is the ability to simultaneously take into account the effect of many factors (i.e., independent variables) on an outcome of interest (i.e., dependent variable) to researchers and practitioners, and to deal with a large number of observations. This helps guard against constructing ad hoc explanations, which are an inherent limitation of small-sample case studies. As tentative answers to research questions, ad hoc explanations may work well with a relatively small sample, but these are seldom sufficient once a large sample is examined by quantitative methods.

The second advantage of quantitative methods is their ability to clearly demonstrate the hypothesized relationship. Such a link, or its absence, can be found by multiple regression analyses, which associate changes in the independent variable by one unit with changes in the dependent variable by a certain *coefficient*. The coefficients generated by regression analyses provide two pieces of information.

The first concerns the direction of the association, namely, whether the association is positive or negative. Positive associations mean that the two variables move in the same direction. If an independent variable, such as the age of the owner, is found to be positively related to export intermediary performance, then that variable is said to boost firm performance. Negative associations, on the other hand, indicate that the two variables move in the opposite direction. If another variable, such as the age of the firm, is negatively related to performance, then that variable is regarded as a constraint to the success of the firm. The second piece of information involves the strength of the associations. Whether positive or negative, the magnitude of the associations denotes how closely the movement of one variable follows the movement of another one. Indeed, to ascertain if there is any meaningful and significant relationship between two variables, researchers determine whether there is at least a less than 5 percent chance that an association is accidental or spurious. Otherwise, if that criterion is not met, the association may be purely by chance, such as the often-joked-about correlation between weather changes and stock market fluctuations.

The third notable strength of quantitative methods is their ability to explain typical behavior, instead of aberrations, outliers, or exceptions. To determine whether a relationship between two variables is systematic or merely isolated in time or place demands the examination of a large number of cases, which a limited number of case studies are incapable of.[1] Multiple regression analyses come in handy for this purpose because of their ability to handle a large number of cases.

In summary, quantitative methods are able to simultaneously deal with a large number of variables, to clearly demonstrate hypothesized relationships, and to investigate a large number of cases. These strengths contrast sharply with the weaknesses of qualitative methods, characterized by their small sample sizes and less-than-objective interpretation of data. Therefore, quantitative methods can greatly complement qualitative methods, and their combination is likely to enable us to probe deeper into the research question (Jick, 1979).

Analytical Approach

The fundamental purpose of quantitative research is to test a theory or a model in order to see whether the theory or model holds with a large sample of observations. However, theories and models, expressed in the form of propositions, are usually too general to be directly testable (Bacharach, 1989). Therefore, the primary analytical approach is to simplify the theory or model into a set of independent and dependent variables that can be examined by multiple regression analyses.[2] This simplification process is called hypothesis specification, or in laymen's terms "translation." In Chapter 5, I "translated" three core propositions of the integrated model of export intermediary performance into four testable hypotheses (see Table 5.2 for a summary). Obviously, a hypothesis cannot incorporate too many variables. The selection of a small and manageable set of variables for hypothesis testing must be guided either by theory or by practice (Bacharach, 1989). In this case, the derivation of hypotheses was guided by three underlying theories (i.e., transaction cost, agency, and resource-based theories) and by my previous participation and observation of export intermediary activities. Through the six case studies reported in Chapter 6, I further examined these hypotheses in a qualitative way in order to ensure that they did not contradict with the ideas and practices of entrepreneurs and operators of export intermediaries.

Once a theory or model has been translated into hypotheses, it becomes possible to test these hypotheses. The question of concern then becomes, Given that this is the way we hypothesize about the determinants of export intermediary performance, how likely is it that a large sample of intermediaries will behave as hypothesized? A hypothesis will be rejected if statistical analyses do not yield results consistent with the hypothesized relationship, and/or if it fails to meet a conventionally set criterion for acceptance, such as the 5 percent significance level. Otherwise, the hypothesis will be accepted.

Like other theories and models in social science research, the integrated model of export intermediary performance rests on the fundamental assumption that firms are "rational" in the sense that they maximize their preferences to the degree permitted by the constraints that they face. In the present case, this rationality assumption has been specified in three more detailed assumptions, which indicate (a) the condition under which manufacturers are likely to use direct, integrated channels; (b) the condition under which manufacturers are likely to use export intermediaries; and (c) the incentive of export intermediaries to maximize their performance (see Table 5.2 for a summary). These conditions are *assumed* and not tested. That is, if quantitative results contradict our hypotheses, we do not give up these assumptions; instead, we reject the hypotheses. Critics may argue that some of these assumptions are not realistic. For example, it is widely known that many small business owners do not maximize their profits. Since most export intermediaries in the United States are small firms, some owners and principals may choose to remain inactive for personal reasons. While acknowledging their existence, social scientists generally regard these cases as "irrational" exceptions or outliers and continue to hold the rationality assumptions which are believed to be applicable in a majority of cases. These assumptions are necessary because, arguably, they are indispensable to social science research; otherwise, it will be very difficult to make predictions about the relationship between two variables in a hypothesis (Friedman, 1953).

In summary, the basic analytical approach is to hypothesize the performance of export intermediaries as a function of four determinants specified in the four hypotheses. Given the assumption that firms—both manufacturers and intermediaries—are rational actors interested in maximizing their profits and minimizing costs, these hypotheses can be tested for their validity.

Data Collection

All variables used in the quantitative phase of the study came from a large-sample mail survey. Given the fact that the six case studies took place in only two states and that my interest was in knowing what is behind the success and failure of the entire population of U.S.-based export intermediaries, it was necessary to undertake a nationwide survey. As a result, a *random* sample of 1,046 export intermediaries located in forty-nine states and the District of Columbia was targeted.[3] These firms were selected from the "Trading Companies" section of the 1994 edition of the *Export Yellow Pages* published by the U.S. Department of Commerce, which was routinely used by practitioners. The vast majority of contact persons listed in the directory were owners, principals, and managers who were believed to have better information about their firms' performance and capabilities. A four-page survey questionnaire was constructed with the aid of the case study findings and multiple pretests. The mail survey was executed in 1995, with two rounds of mailings. The "total design method" (Dillman, 1978) was strictly followed in order to maximize the response rate and to encourage accurate answers.[4]

Out of a total of 1,046 surveys sent out, 131 were returned because of incorrect addresses or expired mail-forwarding orders. Therefore, the effective sample was reduced to 915. Among these, 195 surveys were returned from thirty-eight states and the District of Columbia, thus yielding a response rate of 21.31 percent (195/915).[5] This response rate compared very favorably with those obtained by other similar studies, ranging from 15.4 percent in Batra (1991) to 29.6 percent in Hay Associates (1977).

Export intermediaries in California (140), New York (94), and Florida (93) led the number of firms sampled in each state. Among 195 respondents, firms in California (29), Florida (22), and New York (14) led the way. In terms of the response rate from firms in different states, export intermediaries in Idaho (100 percent), Colorado (50 percent), and Rhode Island (50 percent) led the way. Since failed firms might be less willing or likely to respond (i.e., surveys sent to firms that went out of business were returned by the postal service), it was possible that the respondents included more successful firms. A number of statistical tests were employed to determine whether there was any regional or demographic bias among the respondents (i.e., whether firms in certain regions or with certain demographic attributes were more likely to respond) (Armstrong and Overton, 1977).[6] None of these tests detected any significant bias, thus suggesting that the sample was representative of the population of export intermediaries in the United States during the time of the study.

In short, 1,046 export intermediaries were randomly drawn to participate in a nationwide mail survey. The survey yielded a respectable sample of 195 respondent firms, which could be considered as unbiased representatives of the entire population of export intermediaries in this country.

SAMPLE CHARACTERISTICS

This section contains demographic information about the 195 respondent firms, which formed the basis of data used in regression analyses reported in the next section. Since these firms represented a random and unbiased sample, this information can be regarded as a state-of-the-art "snapshot" of the population of export intermediaries in the United States in the 1990s.

Respondents and Their Firms

The overwhelming majority of respondents (84 percent) were owners and principals, who were in the best position to provide accurate information about their firms (Table 7.1). Given the confusion between the terms "export management company" (EMC) and "export trading company" (ETC), respondents were asked how they would characterize their business. One-third of them described their firms as export trading companies, followed by nearly one-quarter as export/import intermediaries, and nearly one-fifth as export management companies. These statistics indicate a trend that U.S. export in-

Table 7.1
Respondents and Their Firms

	Response Number	Percentage
(a) Respondents' positions		
Owner	130	66.67%
Principal	33	16.92%
Manager	15	7.69%
Salesperson	3	1.54%
Other*	12	6.15%
No response	2	1.03%
Total	195	100.00%
(b) How respondents described their firms		
Export trading company	68	34.87%
Export/import intermediary	48	24.62%
Export management company	37	18.97%
Export intermediary	30	15.39%
Manufacturer's representative	5	2.56%
Other	5	2.56%
No response	2	1.03%
Total	195	100.00%

* Including four presidents, two CEOs, one partner, one vice president for international operations, one international marketing director, one chief administrative officer, and two unidentified.

termediary firms have gradually moved away from their traditional export management role to engage in more export trading as well as import trading.

Firm Size, Age, and Markets

The survey results confirm what many familiar with the industry have long thought to be true: U.S. export intermediaries are generally small. As shown in Table 7.2, more than half of the respondent firms had fewer than five people involved in the operations, and less than 10 percent had more than twenty-five people. The mean size of the respondent firms was 6.77 individuals, including both principals/

Table 7.2
The Size and Age of Respondent Firms

	Response Number	Percentage
(a) Size measured by the number of people involved*		
1–4	101	51.79%
5–9	32	16.41%
10–24	23	11.79%
25–49	7	3.60%
50 and over	10	5.13%
No response	22	11.28%
Total	195	100.00%
(b) Size measured by total export sales		
Less than $500,000	55	28.21%
$500,000–1 million	19	9.74%
$1–4.99 million	42	21.53%
$5–9.99 million	16	8.21%
Over $10 million	18	9.23%
No response	45	23.08%
Total	195	100.00%
(c) Firm age		
Less than 5 years	63	32.31%
6–10 years	51	26.15%
11–20 years	42	21.54%
21 and over**	39	20.00%
Total	195	100.00%

* Including both principals and employees.
** The oldest firm in the sample was founded in 1915.

owners/managers and employees, with a standard deviation of 3.41. In terms of sales, close to 40 percent indicated total export sales of less than $1 million in 1994, and less than 10 percent reported total export sales of more than $10 million. Among various categories of small businesses (i.e., companies with fewer than 500 employees) defined by the Small Business Administration (1989: 18), the typical export intermediary would be classified as a "very small" business, which is the smallest category, defined as having fewer than twenty employees. It is not an exaggeration to say that the typical export intermediary would be a "dwarf among the dwarfs."

Notwithstanding the relatively small size of the respondent firms, one out of every five of them had a history of more than twenty years, and another one-fifth of the respondent firms had been in business for eleven to twenty years. The oldest firm in the sample was founded in 1915. On the other hand, about one-third of them started their business during the past five years (Table 7.2).

In terms of the markets, Table 7.3 shows that one-third of the respondents identified Asia Pacific as their top market, followed by over one-fifth who indicated Latin America as their top market. Over 10 percent of the respondents rated Middle East/Africa as their top market. Another 10 percent of them ranked West Europe as their top

Table 7.3
Top Markets and Regional Expertise of Respondent Firms

	Response Number	Percentage
(a) Top markets		
Asia Pacific	65	33.33%
Latin America	45	23.08%
USA (for imports)	22	11.28%
Middle East/Africa	21	10.77%
West Europe	20	10.26%
East Europe/former Soviet Union	10	5.13%
Canada	4	2.05%
No response	8	4.10%
Total	195	100.00%
(b) Regional expertise		
Asia Pacific	61	23.46%
No regional focus	55	21.15%
Latin America	45	17.31%
Middle East/Africa	39	15.00%
West Europe	28	10.77%
East Europe/former Soviet Union	14	5.38%
Other	11	4.23%
Canada	7	2.70%
Total	260*	100.00%

* Including expertise in multiple regions by one firm.

market. Taken together, East Europe/Commonwealth of Independent States (the former Soviet Union) and Canada were regarded as top markets by less than 10 percent of the respondents (Table 7.3).

Firm Expertise and Experience

All together, the 195 respondents indicated their regional expertise on 260 occasions, including the mention of "no regional focus" (Table 7.3). Consistent with the importance of the Asia Pacific markets, close to one-quarter of them specialized in that region. The second largest group, over 20 percent of them, maintained no particular regional focus. Another 17 and 15 percent of them indicated that

Table 7.4
Foreign Language Expertise of Respondent Firms

Foreign Languages	Response Number	Percentage
(a) Language spoken by personnel at the firm		
Spanish	94	24.10%
French	80	20.51%
Other languages*	52	13.33%
German	47	12.05%
None	29	7.44%
Japanese	28	7.18%
Chinese	23	5.90%
Russian	20	5.13%
Arabic	17	4.36%
Total	390**	100.00%
(b) Percentage of personnel capable of more than one foreign language		
0	68	34.87%
1–24%	24	12.31%
25–49%	21	10.77%
50–74%	39	20.00%
75–100%	43	22.05%
Total	195	100.00%

* Languages other than those listed here.
** Including expertise in multiple languages in one firm.

they specialized in Latin America and Middle East/Africa, respectively. West Europe and East Europe/the former Soviet Union commanded less attention (11 and 5 percent, respectively), and only 2.70 percent of the respondents indicated that they specialized in exporting to Canada.

In terms of where such regional expertise came from, language capabilities of the respondent firms were assessed. The results were impressive (Table 7.4). An overwhelming majority (over 90 percent) of the respondents had in-house foreign language expertise. Approximately two-thirds of the firms had personnel with expertise in more than one language. More significantly, in over one-fifth of them, over 75 percent of the people working there were capable of more than one foreign language.

When the respondents' place of birth was asked, 40 percent of them indicated that they were immigrants born outside the United States (Table 7.5). All together, forty-one countries were represented. Two-thirds of the respondent firms had foreign-born personnel working for them. In over one-fifth of these firms, more than 75 percent of

Table 7.5
Place of Birth of the Personnel in Respondent Firms

	Response Number	Percentage
(a) Respondents' place of birth		
USA	115	58.97%
Foreign country*	78	40.00%
No response	2	1.03%
Total	195	100.00%
(b) Percentage of foreign-born personnel at the firm		
0	68	34.87%
1–24%	24	12.31%
25–49%	21	10.77%
50–74%	39	20.00%
75–100%	43	22.05%
Total	195	100.00%

* Forty-one countries (West Europe: Twenty-seven; Asia: Twenty; Middle East/Africa: Thirteen; Latin American: Twelve; East Europe/the former Soviet Union: Four; and Canada: Two).

the people working there were born abroad. These statistics clearly indicate that immigrants are very active in facilitating U.S. exports.

In terms of the experience of the respondents, most of them were very experienced in the export business, with over half of them having over ten years of experience (Table 7.6). Among this more experienced group, a significant portion of them, nearly 30 percent, had in excess of twenty years of experience in exporting. Given the relatively senior-level position the respondents held, their experience might be more extensive than that of other people in these firms. However, when the average experience of the top three decision makers in these firms was also assessed, the results were equally impressive, with close to half of these people having more than ten years of experience (Table 7.6).

The respondents also had strong abilities in handling sales negotiations, with more than half of them claiming to have "better than average" ability, among whom nearly one-quarter of the respondents indicated "very strong" ability (Table 7.7). Nearly half of them were also frequently involved in sales negotiations.

The respondents' ability to take title to the goods was less clear cut (Table 7.8). While 23 percent of them indicated a very strong willingness to take title to the goods compared with their top three competitors, only 13 percent strongly agreed that they had the finan-

Table 7.6
Respondent Firms' Experience in the Export Business

	Response Number	Percentage
(a) Respondents' own export experience		
0–5 years	56	28.72%
6–10 years	36	18.46%
11–20 years	45	23.08%
More than 20 years	58	29.74%
Total	195	100.00%
(b) The average export experience of the top three decision makers		
0–5 years	55	28.21%
6–10 years	44	22.56%
11–20 years	58	29.74%
More than 20 years	38	19.49%
Total	195	100.00%

cial ability to do that. On the other hand, over 20 percent of them were unwilling to take title to the goods. This unwillingness could be attributed to their lack of ability to secure financing: Over 30 percent of them indicated that they had less than average ability to obtain financing in order to take title to the goods. This result is not surprising, given the well-known difficulties of obtaining trade-related financing in the United States.

Client Firms and Typical Products

Close to half of the client firms that the respondents served were those that were either uninterested in exporting or occasional exporters (Table 7.9). It is clear that export intermediaries were helping these internationally inexperienced firms, most of which were small and midsize ones, enter export markets. In addition, 23 and 16 percent of their client firms were established exporters and globalized firms, respectively, suggesting that intermediaries were also find-

Table 7.7
Respondent Firms' Negotiation Ability

	Response Number	Percentage
(a) Negotiation ability		
Very little	6	3.08%
Less than average	10	5.13%
Average	41	21.03%
Better than average	59	30.26%
Very strong	48	24.62%
No response	31	15.90%
Total	195	100.00%
(b) Frequency of handling sales negotiations		
Very infrequent	8	4.10%
Less than average	19	9.74%
Average	43	22.05%
More than average	47	24.11%
Very frequent	46	23.59%
No response	32	16.41%
Total	195	100.00%

Table 7.8
Respondent Firms' Ability to Take Title to the Goods

	Response Number	Percentage
(a) Willingness to take title to the goods		
Very little	20	10.26%
Less than average	24	12.31%
Average	52	26.67%
Better than average	27	13.84%
Very strong	45	23.08%
No response	27	13.84%
Total	195	100.00%
(b) Ability to take title to the goods		
Very little	35	17.95%
Less than average	26	13.33%
Average	55	28.21%
Better than average	28	14.36%
Very strong	25	12.82%
No response	26	13.33%
Total	195	100.00%

ing a niche to provide services to these larger and more experienced exporters.

In terms of the type of products they handled, a wide variety of Standard Industrial Classifications (SICs) could be found, with little indication of concentration on any particular industry (Table 7.9). Most of the respondents were very experienced in handling their typical products, with 40 percent of them indicating their experience was "better than average" and one-quarter of them having "very extensive" experience (Table 7.10). Overall, one-third of them exported commodity products only, and over 20 percent exported 100 percent value-added products or service products. A large number of them, nearly 40 percent, exported a mixture of commodity and value-added products (Table 7.11).

Firm Performance

Since the heart of this study is the determinants of export intermediary performance, I sought multiple measures of performance (as

Table 7.9
Type of Client Firms and Products

	Response Number	Percentage
(a) Type of client firms		
Uninterested in exporting	31	15.90%
Occasional exporter	64	32.82%
Established exporter	44	22.56%
Globalized firm	32	16.41%
Other	15	7.69%
No response	9	4.62%
Total	195	100.00%
(b) Type of products		
SIC 35*	51	10.02%
SIC 36**	46	9.04%
SIC 20***	45	8.84%
SIC 38****	30	5.89%
SIC 34*****	28	5.50%
Non-top-five SIC codes	304	59.72%
No response	5	0.99%
Total	509******	100.00%

* Industrial machinery and equipment.
** Electronics and allied products.
*** Food and kindred products.
**** Instruments and allied products.
***** Fabricated metal products.
****** Including firms handling multiple SIC products.

shown in Table 7.12). In terms of export sales during 1994, 28 percent sold less than $100,000 worth of goods on a per capita basis, and over one-third achieved per capita export sales between $100,000 and $249,000. Only a handful (5 percent) reported per capita export sales in excess of $500,000.

In terms of net export sales margins, nearly three-quarters of the respondents reported their margins to be less than 25 percent, among which nearly 40 percent of them were within 11 to 25 percent. Only 15 percent of them achieved net sales margins in excess of 25 percent, and one firm reported a "supernormal" margin of over 100 percent.

Table 7.10

Respondent Firms' Experience in Handling Typical Products

	Response Number	Percentage
Very little	8	4.10%
Less than average	13	6.67%
Average	38	19.49%
Better than average	82	42.05%
Very extensive	47	24.10%
No response	7	3.59%
Total	195	100.00%

Table 7.11

Type of Exports Handled by Respondent Firms

	Response Number	Percentage
100% commodity products	63	32.31%
100% value-added products	24	12.31%
Mix of commodity and value-added	73	37.43%
100% service exports (e.g., consulting)	16	8.20%
No exports (100% imports)	2	1.03%
No response	17	8.72%
Total	195	100.00%

When asked for a subjective assessment of their overall performance on a 1–5 scale vis-à-vis their top three competitors, one-third of them believed that they were more or less on a par with others, one-quarter of them moderately agreed that their performance was better, and over 10 percent of them strongly agreed that they were more successful. On the other hand, about 15 percent of them admitted that their performance was below that of their competitors.

Summary

The demographic profiles of the respondent firms are consistent with those obtained from earlier studies (e.g., Batra, 1991; Bello and Williamson, 1985a, 1985b; Brasch, 1978; Coopers and Lybrand, 1984;

Table 7.12
Performance of Respondent Firms

	Response Number	Percentage
(a) Measured by per capita export sales		
Less than $100,000	54	27.70%
$100,000–249,000	72	36.92%
$250,000–499,000	39	20.00%
$500,000 and more	10	5.13%
No response	20	10.25%
Total	195	100.00%
(b) Measured by net export sales margin		
Under 1%	7	3.59%
1–10%	61	31.28%
11–25%	77	39.49%
26–50%	18	9.23%
51–100%	13	6.67%
Over 100%	1	0.51%
No response	18	9.23%
Total	195	100.00%
(c) Measured by agreement with the statement: "Compared		
with your top three competitors, your firm is more successful overall."		
Strongly disagree	11	5.64%
Moderately disagree	18	9.23%
Neutral	67	34.36%
Moderately agree	49	25.13%
Strongly agree	22	11.28%
No response	28	14.36%
Total	195	100.00%

Hay Associates, 1977; Howard and Maskulka, 1988; Perry, 1992; U.S. Department of Commerce, 1990). Export intermediary firms in the United States in the 1990s are typically small-sized, but highly experienced enterprises operated by entrepreneurs with strong backgrounds in foreign culture and markets. According to the integrated model, their expertise, experience, and capabilities will help explain a large part of their performance.

VARIABLES

All variables used in multiple regression analyses came from the returned surveys. This section briefly introduces dependent, independent, and control variables that were used in the statistical tests.

Dependent Variables

Export performance is the key dependent variable in this study. However, "there is no uniform definition of export performance in the literature" (Cavusgil and Zou, 1994: 4). Export performance measures can be economic (i.e., sales and profitability) or strategic (i.e., goal attainment) in nature. Previous research (Boyd, Dess and Rasheed, 1993; Cavusgil and Zou, 1994; Dess and Robinson, 1984; Zaheer, 1995) suggested that, in the absence of archival data, self-reported measures are acceptable and are often equally reliable when researchers take care to ensure data reliability. Similar to the practice used for the six case studies, multiple self-reported items in the survey were used to triangulate this important variable.

First, I sought information on per capita export sales as a relatively objective measure. Per capita export sales could be regarded as a measure of overall organizational productivity. Compared with total sales, per capita export sales controlled for differences between large and small firms, thus making the performance of these firms more comparable (Hill and Snell, 1989). Otherwise, if the performance measure were total sales, obviously larger firms would have a higher level of total sales, which might not be an indicator of good performance by itself. Second, information on intermediaries' net export sales margin was requested. As a profitability measure, net export sales margin reflected a firm's efficiency. Similar to the first measure, this measure was also an objective one.

In addition, I followed Cavusgil and Zou (1994) and Zaheer (1995) to ask respondents to rate their own performance, on a 1–5 scale, in comparison with the top three competitors they identified. This measure was more subjective, depending on the respondents' aspiration levels. Given the lack of prior research on export intermediary performance, I was unable to assign weights to these different performance measures. Therefore, I did not attempt to create a composite measure of firm performance as Cavusgil and Zou (1994) did. Instead, three performance measures were used as different dependent variables in regression analyses (Mosakowski, 1991).

I sought information on these performance measures for the two most recent years (1993–94), for which respondents were believed to have the best recall at the time of the survey (1995). Given the inherent fluctuation of the global marketplace, a one-year snapshot might not be an accurate reflection of overall firm performance. Therefore, I averaged performance over this two-year period in order to smooth out temporal fluctuations. However, 29 firms had to be deleted from the sample, since these firms had been founded after 1993 and, as a result, did not have complete data for their perfor-mance over the two-year period (1993–94). Therefore, the final sample for regression analyses was reduced to 166 firms founded in or before 1993, whose performance data were available for the two-year period (1993–94).[7]

In summary, three measures of export intermediary performance were obtained from the returned surveys as dependent variables for regression analyses. Two of them were more objective, namely, per capita export sales and net export sales margin. The last one was more subjective, involving the ranking of a firm's performance on a 1–5 scale in comparison with the top three competitors.

Independent Variables

Highlighted by the four hypotheses, four major independent variables were included in the study. Hypothesis 1 focused on inter-mediaries' knowledge of foreign markets and export processes. A multidimensional approach was employed to develop a scale to approximate this variable. I sought information on (a) the export experience of key decision makers; (b) experience in foreign cultures and environments as measured by place of birth, language abilities, and travel frequency; and (c) experience in the particular product industry. These measures were adapted from previous research reported by Anderson and Coughlan (1987) and Cavusgil and Zou (1994).

The second independent variable, negotiation ability in Hypothesis 2, was decomposed into two key dimensions. Extending the work of Graham (1987), Tung (1988), and Weiss (1994), I asked respondents to indicate on a 1–5 scale (a) whether they possess better negotiation ability and (b) whether they handle negotiations on behalf of the clients more often, when compared with their top three competitors.

To operationalize Hypothesis 3, I asked respondents to compare themselves with the firm's top three competitors, indicating (a) whether the firm is more willing to take title to the goods and (b) whether it has better financial abilities to do so. Similar to previous measures, this variable took the form of a 1–5 scale.

Finally, for Hypothesis 4, I used a 5-point scale developed by Anderson and Coughlan (1987) to approximate (a) the amount of training manufacturers give to the intermediary; (b) the amount of training the intermediary provides its overseas customers; and (c) the amount of postsale service provided. The rationale was that the more complex the products, the stronger the need for presale training and postsale services. For commodity products, these service requirements would be minimal (Anderson and Coughlan, 1987).

In summary, four independent variables were hypothesized to have a direct impact on export intermediary performance. In other words, they would be the determinants of these firms' performance, if the hypotheses were supported. More details of these variables can be found in the appendix (see Table A.6).

Control Variables

Firm size and age have been widely reported to have an impact on firm performance (Hannan and Freeman, 1989; Mintzberg, 1989; Mosakowski, 1991; Zaheer, 1995). Therefore, it was important to control these variables in order to ensure that the results were not biased due to differences in firm size and age. I first controlled for firm size measured by (a) the number of people employed by the firm; (b) the number of people involved in exporting; and (c) total export sales during 1993–94. I then controlled for firm age by asking the founding year of the business.

Summary

This section has briefly described the operationalization of various dependent, independent, and control variables. Length limitations necessitate the abbreviation of this description. More details of the entire data collection and variable operationalization process can be found in the appendix.

FINDINGS FROM HYPOTHESIS TESTS

The amount of information reported by the 195 respondents was huge. Even the amount of information provided by the 166 respondents whose performance data were complete for the most recent two-year period (1993–94) was tremendous. A method called factor analysis was employed to transform such a large amount of information into a small set of dependent, independent, and control variables.[8] Once such a transformation was completed, it became possible to formally test the four hypotheses. Specifically, the direction and strength of coefficients in each hypothesis were examined to determine whether a hypothesis was accepted or rejected.

Since three different dependent variables were used as proxies for export intermediary performance, in essence each hypothesis was tested three times. Therefore, how each hypothesis performed could be examined from multiple perspectives, thus allowing for a triangulation of the results. The results of each of these tests are reported below.

Test I: Determinants of Per Capita Export Sales

Table 7.13 contains the results of the first test using per capita export sales as the dependent variable. According to the hypotheses, the directions of the four coefficients should be positive in order to support the hypotheses (the first column of Table 7.13). As indicated in the second column of Table 7.13, all four coefficients did show positive signs as hypothesized.

Having coefficients showing the same sign as hypothesized was encouraging, but the sign in itself did not lead to the conclusion that

Table 7.13
Hypothesis Test I:
Per Capita Export Sales as Firm Performance

Independent and Control Variables	Expected Sign	Coefficient	t-value
(a) Independent variables			
Hypothesis 1: Export knowledge	(+)	0.191	3.59**
Hypothesis 2: Negotiation ability	(+)	0.291	2.38*
Hypothesis 3: Ability to take title	(+)	0.207	5.31***
Hypothesis 4: Product specialization	(+)	0.310	2.56**
(b) Control variables			
Control 1: Firm size		0.088	1.04
Control 2: Firm age		0.193	0.92
N		166	
Adjusted R^2		0.511	
F-value		4.71***	

* $p < 0.05$
** $p < 0.01$
*** $p < 0.001$

the hypotheses were supported. Since the results of statistical analyses were always probabilistic, maybe the four independent variables and the dependent variable just happened to be moving in the same direction. To prove beyond doubt that the four independent variables—export knowledge, negotiation ability, ability to take title, and willingness to specialize in commodity products—indeed determined export intermediary performance as represented by per capita export sales, it was necessary to examine the *t*-values, reported in the third column in Table 7.13. The larger these values are, the more significant the associations between independent and dependent variables are. For our purposes, the more significant the *t*-values, the better.

In this case, all *t*-values were significant. Among the four *t*-values generated, the one generated by the ability to take title to goods (Hypothesis 3) was the most significant, with a less than 0.1 percent chance that such an association between this particular independent variable and the dependent variable was accidental or spurious. In other words, we could almost be certain that these two variables behaved as hypothesized. The other two coefficients, export knowledge (Hypothesis 1) and willingness to specialize in commodity products (Hypothesis 4), were significant at 1 percent. In comparison, the one generated by negotiation ability (Hypothesis 2) was the least significant—albeit still above the threshold for acceptance. Specifically, there was a less than 5 percent chance that such an association would be spurious. Since any association between independent and dependent variables would have a 50–50 chance of moving in the same direction, normally any association that has a more than 5 percent chance to be a spurious correlation would be regarded as unacceptable in social science research. As a result, in the interest of maintaining rigor and robustness of the results, researchers would reject any hypothesis whose *t*-value is not significant at least at the 5 percent level. In this case, I was able to accept all the four hypotheses, not only because their coefficients were in the same direction as hypothesized, but also because their *t*-values were all significant at least at the 5 percent level.

In summary, using per capita export sales as the dependent variable to approximate export intermediary performance, I found significant support for the four hypotheses. Among these, Hypotheses 3 and 2 received the strongest and weakest support, respectively. Overall, the four independent variables and the two control variables were able to explain over 50 percent of the variance of the data, as shown by the adjusted R^2. As a result, the integrated model passed the first quantitative test.

Test II: Determinants of Net Export Sales Margin

For the integrated model of export intermediary performance to establish its validity, passing the statistical test once was not enough. Only repeated passing of multiple tests would give us adequate confidence in the model. In the second test, net export sales margin was used as the dependent variable to approximate firm performance (Table 7.14).

Again, the signs of the four coefficients were first examined. It was found that as hypothesized, the direction of these coefficients for all four hypotheses was positive. Then I moved on to investigate the t-values. In this case, t-values for the coefficients generated by two independent variables, ability to take title (Hypothesis 3) and willingness to specialize in commodity products (Hypothesis 4), were the most significant, at the 0.1 percent level. The t-value for the coefficient generated by export knowledge (Hypothesis 1) was also significant, indicating that there was less than 1 percent chance that

Table 7.14
Hypothesis Test II:
Net Export Sales Margin as Firm Performance

Independent and Control Variables	Expected Sign	Coeffi- cient	t-value
(a) Independent variables			
Hypothesis 1: Export knowledge	(+)	0.314	6.58**
Hypothesis 2: Negotiation ability	(+)	0.251	1.04
Hypothesis 3: Ability to take title	(+)	0.302	4.47***
Hypothesis 4: Product specialization	(+)	0.431	3.51***
(b) Control variables			
Control 1: Firm size		0.113	0.61
Control 2: Firm age		0.202	3.33**
N		166	
Adjusted R^2		0.438	
F-value		2.26**	

* $p < 0.05$
** $p < 0.01$
*** $p < 0.001$

such an association would be spurious. As a result, Hypotheses 1, 3, and 4 were accepted.

However, Hypothesis 2, the impact of negotiation ability on firm performance, was rejected. Specifically, although the direction of the coefficient was the same as hypothesized, the strength of the association between this particular independent variable and the dependent variable was not strong enough. There was a more than 5 percent chance that such an association would be accidental or spurious. As a result, this hypothesis had to be rejected.

In summary, in the second test, three out of four hypotheses were accepted with a high degree of confidence. One hypothesis was rejected. But overall, even with the rejection of one hypothesis, the model was able to explain nearly 44 percent of the variance in the data (adjusted R^2). Therefore, the integrated model also passed the second test.

Test III: Determinants of Self-Reported Performance

The first two tests were concerned with how the four hypotheses behaved using two objective measures of performance. The third and final test attempted to investigate whether the data would support the hypotheses when a subjective measure of performance was used. This measure was provided by respondents on a 1–5 scale, 1 being the best, to indicate the performance of their firms when compared with close competitors. The results of this test are reported in Table 7.15.

Again, the direction of the coefficients generated by the four independent variables was positive as hypothesized. In addition, the strength of the coefficients was examined. In this case, three coefficients, namely, export knowledge (Hypothesis 1), ability to take title (Hypothesis 3), and willingness to specialize in commodity products (Hypothesis 4), were all significant at the 0.1 percent level, thus enabling us to accept these hypotheses with a high degree of confidence.

Similar to the findings in the second test, Hypothesis 2 had to be rejected, because the coefficient, although in the same direction as hypothesized, was not significant enough. In other words, it would be risky to accept this hypothesis, given the more than 5 percent chance that the association between negotiation ability and self-reported performance would be accidental or spurious.

Overall, as shown by the adjusted R^2, the model was able to explain nearly 60 percent of the variance in the data, the highest in all three tests. Despite the lack of support for Hypothesis 2, the other

Table 7.15
Hypothesis Test III:
Self-Reported Indicator as Firm Performance

Independent and Control Variables	Expected Sign	Coefficient	t-value
(a) Independent variables			
Hypothesis 1: Export knowledge	(+)	0.556	4.77***
Hypothesis 2: Negotiation ability	(+)	0.176	0.89
Hypothesis 3: Ability to take title	(+)	0.672	7.53***
Hypothesis 4: Product specialization	(+)	0.413	5.08***
(b) Control variables			
Control 1: Firm size		0.045	1.36
Control 2: Firm age		0.131	0.91
N		166	
Adjusted R^2		0.581	
F-value		6.01***	

* $p < 0.05$
** $p < 0.01$
*** $p < 0.001$

three hypotheses again were accepted. In short, the integrated model again passed the third statistical test.

Summary

Using 166 firms drawn from a random sample of 195 firms, three statistical tests were run to investigate the rigor of the integrated model of export intermediary performance, which consists of four hypotheses. In essence, the hypotheses were tested on twelve occasions (four hypotheses each with three dependent variables). As shown in Table 7.16, on ten of these occasions, the hypotheses were accepted with a high degree of confidence, and on two of these occasions, one hypothesis was rejected. Overall, the integrated model performed reasonably well, passing these three tests and capturing over 40 to 60 percent of the variance of the data in these tests.

Table 7.16
Determinants of Export Intermediary Performance:
A Summary of Hypothesis Tests

Tests Using Different Dependent Variables as Firm Performance	Results
Hypothesis 1: Knowledge of foreign markets and export processes	
Test I: Per capita export sales	Supported**
Test II: Net export sales margin	Supported**
Test III: Self-reported performance	Supported***
Hypothesis 2: Negotiation ability	
Test I: Per capita export sales	Supported*
Test II: Net export sales margin	Not Supported
Test III: Self-reported performance	Not Supported
Hypothesis 3: Ability to take title to the goods	
Test I: Per capita export sales	Supported***
Test II: Net export sales margin	Supported***
Test III: Self-reported performance	Supported***
Hypothesis 4: Specialization in commodity products	
Test I: Per capita export sales	Supported**
Test II: Net export sales margin	Supported***
Test III: Self-reported performance	Supported***

* $p < 0.05$
** $p < 0.01$
*** $p < 0.001$

DISCUSSION

The integrated model presented in Chapter 5 and the anecdotal evidence gathered from the six case studies reported in Chapter 6 suggest that the intermediary's resources and capabilities to lower export-related transaction costs and agency costs will, to a large extent, determine its performance. Quantitative results in regression analyses reported in this chapter provide objective and robust evidence in support of this model. Of the four hypotheses, three (Hypotheses 1, 3, and 4) are strongly supported in three tests using different dependent variables, and Hypothesis 2 also receives mild support in one of the three tests.

These quantitative findings provide the first set of empirical insights about the determinants of export intermediary performance in the United States. Previous research in this area has either ignored the role of export intermediaries or failed to directly confront the intermediary performance question. Although there were several survey studies of these firms, none of these studies was able to specify a model of the determinants of these firms' performance. More specifically, no proposition or hypothesis was advanced. As a result, what determines the performance of export intermediaries has remained an unanswered question, despite its importance (Peng and Ilinitch, 1997). Equipped with the rigorous derivation of an integrated model drawing upon three underlying theories and aided by the qualitative findings of the six case studies, the quantitative phase of the study employed a mail survey that obtained a random, unbiased, and large sample representing a state-of-the-art "snapshot" of the entire population of these firms. Moreover, for the first time, hypotheses predicting the determinants of export intermediary performance were tested and supported, thus providing a definitive answer to the intermediary performance question.

These quantitative findings make three important contributions. First, these findings paint a clear picture of the demographic profiles of the sampled U.S. export intermediaries in the 1990s. While previous studies provided such information in earlier decades, none has updated these studies in the 1990s. Given the turbulence in the global economy, what was true about U.S. export intermediaries in the 1980s or earlier may not be correct about these firms in the 1990s and beyond. The most recent empirical study, by Perry (1992), employed a qualitative methodology involving thirty-five interviews, which were unable to provide generalizable information about the population of export intermediaries in the United States due to the small sample size and nonrandom selection of cases. The information re-ported in this chapter should prove to be useful to export intermediary operators interested in comparing their firms with other firms in the industry, to manufacturing company managers in search of export intermediary services, and to government officials in charge of export promotion, as well as to would-be entrepreneurs interested in entering the export business (Stroh, 1996, 1997).[9]

The second important contribution of these findings is the rigorously tested answer to the question, What determines export intermediary performance? As stressed repeatedly throughout this book, this is an important question that, surprisingly, has not been answered. Answering this question, the findings suggest that critical resources and capabilities differentiating a successful intermediary from an unsuccessful one include (a) the amount of knowledge about foreign markets and export processes; (b) the ability to skillfully conduct export negotiations; (c) the ability to secure financing in order to take title to the goods; and (d) the willingness to resist the temptation to specialize in attractive, complex (high-tech) products and to focus on less glamorous, commodity-based (low-tech) products. Each of these abilities takes years to develop, and the combination of all these capabilities is a rare event that might never be accomplished by many struggling firms. Some of the findings are *counter-intuitive,* such as the importance of specializing in low-tech commodity products.

The third and final contribution these quantitative findings make is scholarly. They empirically demonstrate the power of a genuine integration of three theoretical perspectives, namely, transaction cost, agency, and resource-based theories. Rooted in different intellectual traditions, these theories have different orientations and emphasis: transaction cost and agency theories focus on manufacturers as principals on the one hand, and resource-based theory is interested in intermediaries on the other hand. Despite numerous calls to integrate different theories, scholars are just beginning to engage in systematic investigation of the hard-to-tackle problems of bringing these theories together. One reason these three theories are hardly seen together in any studies is that they represent three of the most difficult-to-operationalize theories in organizational research (Godfrey and Hill, 1995). Transaction costs usually defy definition, agency costs are often hard to detect, and resources and capabilities, such as knowledge and expertise, by definition, are intangible and hence unmeasurable. This study suggests an innovative approach to bringing these three theories together in a coherent way and represents cutting-edge research on firm performance.

Having introduced the contributions, I believe it is also important to note their three major weaknesses. First, by design, quantitative methods are coarse-grained in that they are unable to provide fine-grained information about individual firms. The findings here paint a picture about the typical determinants of export intermediary performance. Since the results are probabilistic, it is possible that some firms may not possess certain resources and capabilities that are found to be important and may yet attain strong performance. For example, firm A may not be interested in taking title to the goods and firm B may specialize in high-tech products. In contrast to the hypotheses, both may enjoy superb performance. The quantitative findings are unable to explain these cases, except by labeling them as outliers. Nor can my findings explain the role of luck. What the findings do provide is a statistical prediction of how likely it is that firm C will be successful given the possession, or the lack, of certain critical resources and capabilities. Anticipating this weakness of quantitative methods, in phase one of the study I conducted six qualitative case studies to probe deeper into the dynamics of these firms which might have been missed by quantitative methods.

Another weakness associated with the findings is that they are based on cross-sectional data obtained at one point in time. An ideal research design would be to access longitudinal, multi-time-period data sets (Peng, 1997b). Unfortunately, the very nature of survey research makes it extremely difficult to assemble such large-sample, multi-time-period data sets. In the mail survey, I did attempt to obtain more longitudinal data, such as asking the respondents to indicate their firm size and export performance in multiple years. However, the results are not totally satisfactory, since I had to reduce the sample size from 195 to 166 in order to use performance data averaged over a two-year period (1993–94). The sample size would be further reduced to 129 if average performance over a three-year period were used (1992–94). In survey research, the reported data might be inaccurate beyond the most recent two or three years.

Moreover, the analytical approach I employed was reductionist. I assumed that it was possible to decompose elements of transaction costs and agency costs into three constituent parts, namely, search costs, negotiation costs, and monitoring/enforcement costs. The hypotheses, consequently, tested the strengths of the resources and capabilities in lowering these costs. Advocates of the systems approach have argued that the reductionist approach may not be able to capture the true determinants of firm performance, since one ability is very likely to affect the other and abilities have to be studied in a holistic way (Drazin and Van de Ven, 1985). However, potential problems associated with operationalizing the systems approach in such an exploratory inquiry rendered the reductionist approach the only method of choice in this study.

Finally, the quantitative findings are vulnerable to all the standard criticisms leveled at survey research, such as nonresponse bias, ambiguous memory, and social desirability effects (i.e., poor performers are not likely to respond, or if they do, they tend to paint a "rosy" picture in returned surveys) (Tomaskovic-Devey, Leiter and Thompson, 1994). In fact, the lack of strong support for Hypothesis 2, the role of negotiation ability, may be attributed to these problems. During the case study phase, it was found that even for firms with lackluster performance, their managers still rated their negotiation skills highly (see Table 6.3). In the survey results, it might be true that respondents, especially those with fewer capabilities, overrated their negotiation abilities, thereby blurring the distinction between successful and unsuccessful firms. Although informed by the literature, the measures used to capture the firms' negotiation ability were largely experimental. While considerable care was taken in constructing and testing the measures, survey data are by their very nature imperfect and may not fully capture all aspects of the phenomenon under investigation. Also, the data reduction strategy, while necessary in order to reduce a large number of variables to a manageable proportion, may have compounded any noise in the data, which may have lessened the support for Hypothesis 2.

In summary, the quantitative findings reported in this chapter contribute to the literature in three important ways. First, they provide an update about the demographic profiles of U.S. export intermediaries in the 1990s. Second, for the first time, they provide a definitive answer to the question, What determines the performance of export intermediaries? Finally, they represent cutting-edge research on firm performance by drawing on three difficult-to-operationalize theories. In addition, a number of weaknesses are addressed, including the coarse-grained nature of quantitative methods, the pitfalls associated with survey research, the limitations of the reductionist approach, and the reasons behind the lack of strong support for Hypothesis 2.

CONCLUSIONS

Continuing from Chapter 6, which reported the findings from six qualitative case studies, this chapter has reported the key findings from the quantitative phase of the hybrid methodology. Employing a nationwide, large-sample mail survey, this part of the study first obtained the demographic profiles of the 195 respondent firms, then tested the robustness of the integrated model of export intermediary performance using a subset of 166 respondents whose performance was available for a two-year period. The findings move one step beyond all existing studies in that a model focusing on the determinants of these firms' performance has been formulated, tested, and supported on a large-sample basis in a statistically significant way.

Previous empirical studies in this area had little guidance from theory, reported only the demographic profiles of these firms, and largely left the performance issue unexplored. In contrast, the study reported in this book is guided by a strong theoretical model with a complete set of definitions, assumptions, propositions, and hypotheses from the start, uses a qualitative approach to enrich the understanding of the phenomenon of interest, and presents quantitative findings in support of the model based on a large-sample survey. Therefore, this study represents the first of its kind among studies of U.S. export intermediary firms, and provides a concrete answer to the previously unexplored question of the determinants of export intermediary performance.

Especially during the second phase of the study reported in this chapter, the tentative answer to the intermediary performance question found in the six case studies can be replaced by a more definitive answer supported by quantitative evidence based on a large sample of firms. In conclusion, given the care exerted in the construction and administration of the mail survey, the quantitative results reported in this chapter are objective, robust, and generalizable.

NOTES

1. Case studies, on the other hand, are good at examining exceptional cases. For example, the six case studies reported in Chapter 6 investigated both highly successful and unsuccessful export intermediaries.

2. The appendix contains more details of regression models and statistical analyses. A more technical description can be found in Peng (1996).

3. The random selection process did not generate any export intermediary located in the state of Delaware.

4. The appendix contains more details of the total design method employed in the execution of the mail survey. A more technical description can be found in Peng (1996).

5. Surveys sent to the two firms sampled in Vermont were returned because of bad addresses. In addition, there were ten states from which no response was received. Out of a total of 915 firms randomly sampled, there were only twenty-two firms sampled in these ten no-response states. None of these ten states—Alaska, Mississippi, Montana, Nebraska, Nevada, North Dakota, South Dakota, Tennessee, West Virginia, and Wyoming—and Vermont appeared to be a major exporting state. As a result, the omission of export intermediaries located in these eleven states was judged to be insignificant for the results of the study.

6. The appendix contains more details of these tests of data integrity and reliability. A more technical description can be found in Peng (1996).

7. I also sought to obtain performance data from the respondents for the three most recent years (1992–94). Another set of multiple regression analyses was run using firm performance averaged over this three-year period. The results were very similar to those using performance data averaged over the two-year (1993–94) period. The only difference was that the final sample had to be reduced to 129 firms when three years (1992–94) of performance were used, since 66 firms were founded after 1992 and, as a result, did not have complete performance data for the three-year period (1992–94). Since results from a larger sample of 166 firms would be stronger than those from 129 firms, this chapter reports findings from regression analyses using the 166-firm sample with a two-year averaged performance. The findings from the 129-firm sample can be found in Peng (1996).

8. The appendix contains more details of factor analyses employed in the study. A more technical description can be found in Peng (1996).

9. The usefulness of these findings was confirmed by Mr. Leslie Stroh, publisher of *The Exporter Magazine,* during our phone conversations. Interested readers can see his editorials in the May 1996 and June 1997 issues of *The Exporter Magazine* highlighting preliminary findings of my study (Stroh, 1996, 1997).

CHAPTER 8

Conclusions

Trading across borders, export intermediaries have historically helped shape a great deal of the landscape of the global economy. In this process, their fortunes rise and fall. This pattern is certainly applicable to U.S. export intermediaries, whose predecessors, dubbed Yankee traders, were among the founding fathers of the American economy. However, during much of this century, their role has been gradually eclipsed by large manufacturers' direct exports and foreign investment. In the last two decades, as the nation confronts persistent trade deficit problems, export intermediaries have been found to be one of the hidden assets that this nation has in its arsenal to combat trade deficit problems and regain economic prominence.

Research reported in this book was motivated by a desire to know more about what determines the performance of export intermediaries (Chapter 1). Given the historical and contemporary importance of export intermediaries as a unique organizational form specializing in export trade, one ought to find numerous studies on this topic (Chapters 2 and 3). Surprisingly, previous research in both the trade and scholarly literature has largely overlooked this issue (Chapter 4). Therefore, an effort was made in Chapter 5 to derive an integrated model of export intermediary performance. This model was then empirically examined by a hybrid methodology combining qualitative and quantitative methods (Chapters 6 and 7). The findings shed considerable light on how export intermediaries can trade across borders and win.

This chapter first summarizes the major findings, followed by a discussion of the study's practical and scholarly contributions as well as its weaknesses. A number of managerial, policy, and research implications are then highlighted.

SUMMARY OF THE STUDY

Given the paucity of previous research, I drew upon transaction cost, agency, and resource-based theories to formulate and test an integrated model of the determinants of export intermediary performance. The model is rigorous in its derivation and comprehensive in its complete set of a definition, assumptions, propositions, and hypotheses. The model assumes that when making channel choice decisions, manufacturers are interested in minimizing export-related transaction costs as well as potential agency costs brought by intermediaries. It further assumes that intermediaries have the incentive to improve their organizational resources and capabilities in order to improve the odds of being selected by manufacturers. Based on these assumptions, the integrated model posits that the performance of export intermediaries is contingent upon their resources and capabilities to lower their client firms' export-related transaction costs and agency costs. From three core propositions, resources and capabilities are further decomposed into three constituent parts able to lower search, negotiation, and monitoring/enforcement costs for their client firms. From this model, I developed four testable hypotheses, which state that knowledge about foreign markets and export processes (Hypothesis 1), negotiation ability (Hypothesis 2), ability to take title to the goods (Hypothesis 3), and willingness to specialize in commodity products (Hypothesis 4) are all positively related to firm performance (see Table 5.2).

Given the exploratory nature of this inquiry, it was deemed necessary to employ a hybrid methodology combining qualitative and quantitative methods. Fine-grained, qualitative case studies are usually the first step to initiate a new line of research. However, their findings tend to be ad hoc and less generalizable due to the small sample size. On the other hand, coarse-grained quantitative studies using large samples are able to generate robust results. But critics have argued against mindless number crunching by quantitative researchers without detailed knowledge of the organizations that they study. Given the benefits and pitfalls of these different methods, a combined, hybrid methodology was expected to obtain the benefits of the two methods while minimizing the exposure to their limitations. The results, accordingly, would be more objective, robust, and generalizable.

The first phase of the hybrid methodology built on six qualitative field-based case studies of export intermediaries in Seattle and Honolulu. I attempted to unpack some of the complexities surrounding the determinants of export intermediary performance. The qualitative data supported the main thrust of the model and provided input that was later consolidated in the quantitative phase.

The second phase was a large-sample quantitative study based on a nationwide mail survey. A questionnaire was sent to a random sample of 1,046 export intermediaries in forty-nine states, of which 195 returned the survey. The hypotheses were then statistically tested and strongly supported, with the exception of Hypothesis 2, which received mild support. As a whole, the integrated model passed all three statistical tests, thus indicating its validity.

Representing a first-ever empirical attempt on this topic, this book provides a wealth of information about what is behind the success and failure of U.S. export intermediaries. Aided by rigorous derivation of the model and careful attention to the methodology, this study is able to provide a concrete answer to the research question and makes a number of unique contributions to the literature, which I turn to in the next two sections.

PRACTICAL CONTRIBUTIONS

An obvious contribution this book makes is improved knowledge about U.S. export intermediary firms, especially about their performance. While practitioners active in the export business are naturally interested in what is behind the success and failure of export intermediaries, research that is solely driven by theoretical considerations will probably be of little value to them. On the other hand, research that lacks theoretical depth probably cannot probe deeper into this complex question. This was reflected in several survey studies reporting demographical profiles of these firms (e.g., Batra, 1991; Bello and Williamson, 1985a, 1985b; Brasch, 1978; Coopers and Lybrand, 1984; Howard and Maskulka, 1988; U.S. Department of Commerce, 1990). Typically driven by a fact-finding, instead of theory-testing, mission, their research design was usually not influenced by any strong theoretical basis. As a result, none of them was able to rigorously examine the determinants of export intermediary performance. Perry's (1990) model of export intermediary evolution might be an exception in this largely atheoretical literature. However, she neither generated testable hypotheses nor engaged in formal statistical testing; instead, she used an exclusively qualitative method by interviewing thirty-five export intermediary managers and then claimed to find support for her model (Perry, 1992). Overall, no meaningful model, proposition, or hypothesis on export intermediary performance has been reported by this literature.

Since "nothing is so practical as a good theory" (Van de Ven, 1989: 486; Barney, 1997: vii), I focused on the practical problem of export intermediary performance by generating an integrated model drawing upon three underlying economic, organizational, and strategic theories. The end result has been the first-ever set of empirical insights that solve the intermediary performance puzzle in a definitive way. Specifically, an export intermediary's performance has been found to be significantly related to its resources and capabilities to lower export-related transaction costs and agency costs for its manufacturing clients. In terms of the three major types of transaction and agency costs, I have found strong support for the perspective that abilities to lower search costs and monitoring/enforcement costs are positively related to intermediary performance (Hypotheses 1, 3, and 4). The ability to lower client firms' export-related negotiation costs was also found to be positively related to firm performance; but this hypothesis received only mild, not conclusive, support (Hypothesis 2). Support for the overall model must be tempered by this fact.

While the research reported in this book was interested in exploring the fundamental determinants of export intermediary performance, it was *not* designed to investigate the magnitude of success and failure in this industry. However, the data generated can be used to help assess the distribution of successful and unsuccessful firms. As in many other industries, the number of truly successful firms may be very small. For example, in 1994, only 5 percent of the respondent firms employed more than fifty people, less than 10 percent achieved sales over $10 million, and 7 percent had net export sales margins in excess of 50 percent. In other words, firms such as Cascade Exports and Hawaii Exports are exceptions rather than the rule. On the other hand, this industry seems to be populated by a large number of "average" firms and a substantial number of unsuccessful ones, such as Bountiful Produce, Dragon International, and Evergreen Pacific. As a result, a tremendous number of exits as well as entries must be happening in this industry. Supporting this observation, one bit of interesting data not directly used in the calculations is that approximately one-eighth of the firms surveyed in 1995, 131 out of a 1,046-firm sample, were no longer at the addresses they listed in the 1994 edition of the *Export Yellow Pages* published by the Department of Commerce. While some might have moved to better or similar locations, it is safe to say that many of them had gone out of business.

Overall, this book fills an important gap in our understanding of this potentially important but rarely studied sector of the economy. It is not surprising that the export community has shown a strong interest in the findings of the study (Stroh, 1996, 1997).

SCHOLARLY CONTRIBUTIONS

While this study was motivated by the practical interest in improved understanding of U.S. export intermediary performance, it also draws upon the scholarly literature and, in turn, makes a number of contributions to that literature. Specifically, it points out new research directions in transaction cost, agency, and resource-based theories, as well as work on marketing channels, international business, and small business and entrepreneurship.

Contributions to Transaction Cost Theory

Inspired by Williamson's (1975, 1985) work, a considerable number of studies in transaction cost theory have focused on how firms make make-or-buy decisions, specifically how manufacturers decide whether to make certain components in-house or source them from outside suppliers (e.g., Argyres, 1996; Masten, 1984, 1996; Masten, et al., 1991; Monteverde and Teece, 1982; Mosakowski, 1991; Walker and Weber, 1984, 1987). However, none of these studies explored the determinants of the performance of the supplier, which is at the other end of these make-or-buy decisions. This study takes the manufacturer's decisions as a point of departure and twists the point of view from that of the manufacturer to that of the supplier, with the export intermediary being the supplier of export marketing services.

Research from the intermediary's perspective can help establish a critical yet untested theoretical link in transaction cost theory. One of the central tenets of the theory is that firms with the best transaction-cost-economizing abilities will choose the most appropriate governance structure, through make-or-buy decisions, and, consequently, attain the highest performance (Williamson, 1975, 1985). Direct tests of this proposition, however, are problematic because the performance of those governance structures that are not chosen is unobservable and, therefore, unmeasurable (Godfrey and Hill, 1995; Mosakowski, 1991). In other words, once the make option is selected, the costs and benefits of the buy option become very difficult to obtain; and vice versa (Masten, et al., 1991). Existing work has circumvented this problem by examining the effects of exchange attributes on governance choices rather than performance (Masten, 1996; Shelanski and Klein, 1995). In a nutshell, researchers have focused on Link 1 in Figure 8.1, and the central claim of the theory, namely, the performance-enhancing effects of the firm's transaction-cost-economizing behavior (Link 2), is *assumed* and remains *untested* (Poppo and Zenger, 1995: 42; Peng, 1996, 1997c).

Figure 8.1
Transaction Cost Economizing and Firm Performance:
Focusing on the Make-or-Buy Decision

Most make-or-buy studies have been conducted in a component manufacturing context. A further problem is that, as Walker and Weber (1984: 387, added emphasis) noted, in such a context, "in general, the effect of transaction costs on make-or-buy decisions was *substantially overshadowed* by comparative production costs." Similar to the unobservable nature of transaction costs associated with the unchosen governance choice, "production cost differences between the market and in-house operations cannot always be assessed directly" (Walker and Weber, 1984: 376). Since manufacturers are believed to simultaneously minimize both production and transaction costs when reaching make-or-buy decisions (Monteverde and Teece, 1982), the inability to *independently* compare the production and transaction cost differences has further contributed toward the inconclusiveness of existing research. Walker and Weber's (1987: 594, added emphasis) follow-up study, which tested the interactive effects of these two sets of costs, still led to the conclusion that "the influence of comparative production costs on make-or-buy decisions is *significant.*"

It seems ironic that these studies designed to capture the significant effects of transaction costs ended up testifying to the importance of production costs. Although "the results of this growing body of work [are] . . . reasonably consistent" (Joskow, 1991: 81), the failure to empirically establish Link 2 in Figure 8.1, namely, the relationship between transaction cost economizing and firm performance, has become sources of criticisms by Ghoshal and Moran (1996), Hirsch, et al. (1990), and Perrow (1986). While advocates of this theory proclaimed that it represents a part of the "impending revolution" in organizational research (Hesterly, Liebeskind and Zenger, 1990; Jensen, 1983), critics countered by suggesting that belief in the transaction cost logic may be "acts of faith, or perhaps of piety" (Simon, 1991: 27).

As a result, the theory will benefit from new tests that can demonstrate the linkage between firms' transaction-cost-economizing and their performance. The challenge calls for an empirical context in which transaction cost economizing is the primary motive for integration decisions and the hard-to-tangle interactive effect from production costs can be minimized. I believe that export channel decisions represent such a setting. The export channel choice decision of whether to rely on in-house channels or to enlist outside intermediaries represents a classic make-or-buy decision which involves little production costs.[1]

Given the mutual dependence of the exporter and the intermediary (Heide and Miner, 1992; Pfeffer and Salancik, 1978), if the intermediary's performance is satisfactory to the exporter, then the latter's performance will also be enhanced. Otherwise, the exporter can always switch to the "make" mode by establishing in-house direct export channels (see Figure 8.2). Therefore, if we can establish that the performance of the export intermediary is dependent upon its abilities to lower export-related transaction costs for the manufacturing exporter, then we can plausibly claim that it is the exporter's transaction-cost-minimizing behavior (i.e., the selection of the appropriate buy mode in channel choice through the use of intermediaries) that has led to its export performance that is better than the outcome of the make mode (i.e., establishing integrated, in-house export distribution channels). In other words, it is possible to *directly* test the transaction cost determinants of export intermediary performance, and such tests can also allow us to at least *indirectly* establish Link 2 in Figure 8.1.

The empirical tests reported in this book have done just that (Peng, 1996, 1997c). Granted that these are still not direct tests since I only focus on one of the two governance modes (i.e., buy export intermediary services) and the performance of the make mode (i.e., direct export through in-house channels) is not measurable. However, I believe that this approach allows us to establish a stronger inference about Link 2 in Figure 8.1, instead of simply assuming such a relationship. In other words, while this study does not directly establish such a link, it nevertheless is one step closer to filling this theoretically important but empirically untested gap.

Moreover, this study represents a new way of empirically tapping the elusive construct of transaction costs (Allen, 1991; Barzel, 1985; North, 1985). While direct measurement of such unobservable constructs is by definition impossible (Godfrey and Hill, 1995), I have decomposed the total notion of transaction costs into three principal components—namely, search costs, negotiation costs and monitoring/enforcement costs—according to the theory spelled out by Williamson (1975, 1985). Furthermore, I have used four proxies to model the abilities of export intermediaries to lower these different sets of export-related transaction costs. Focusing on a group of service firms

Figure 8.2
The Performance of Export Intermediaries:
A Test of the Previously Untested Link 2 in Figure 8.1

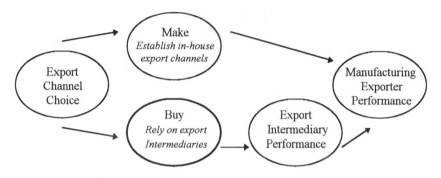

that do not have to shoulder significant production costs and that primarily work in the area to lower their clients' export-related transaction costs, I have found significant support for transaction cost theory, thus shedding new light on how to undertake the difficult task of empirical research in this area (Peng, 1997c).

In summary, this book contributes to transaction cost research by focusing on the other end of make-or-buy decisions. Using the case of export intermediaries, the study sheds considerable light on the theoretically important but empirically untested relationship between transaction cost economizing and firm performance. Moreover, it also represents a new approach to undertaking empirical work in this area.

Contributions to Agency Theory

Agency theory has also become a major paradigm in organizational research in recent years (Eisenhardt, 1989a; Levinthal, 1988). Influenced by the insights of Alchian and Demsetz (1972), Jensen and Meckling (1976), and Tirole (1986), to date most research in this area has focused on *intraorganizational* principal-agent relationships characterized by goal conflict and incomplete information. In other words, these are agency relationships within the organization or the firm, such as incentive contracts (Baker, 1992), job design (Holmstrom and Milgrom, 1991), and corporate governance (Jensen, 1987, 1989). For example, a great deal of work has been done in the area of corporate governance, namely, how stockholders as principals can come up with better threats and incentives that will prevent top managers acting as agents from behaving in a way that is at odd with principals' interests (Hill and Snell, 1989; Hoskisson and Turk, 1990; Jensen, 1987, 1989). The key threats are the board of directors and the market for corporate control, which pose constraints to agency problems (Fama, 1980; Jensen and Ruback, 1983). The compensation of top managers, on the other hand, has been regarded as a major incentive device that, when properly stipulated and carefully implemented, can help align the interests of principals and agents (Jensen and Murphy, 1990; Tosi and Gomez-Mejia, 1989). This stream of research has also examined the compensation of other employees as intraorganizational agents, such as faculty members in universities (Gomez-Mejia and Balkin, 1992) and sales forces in retailing (Basu, et al., 1985; Eisenhardt, 1988).

While insightful, this body of research has been criticized for two constraining assumptions. First, the existing work assumes a principal-centered model in that principals make all the decisions while agents are passive entities responding to these decisions (Hirsch, et al., 1990; Perrow, 1986). Second, agents are assumed to be relatively homogeneous without much differential in their capabilities, except to the extent that their efforts may vary as a result of threats and incentives employed by principals (Levitt, 1995; Nelson, 1991). These assumptions are more defensible in intraorganizational settings, since principals do have more power to make most key decisions and agents have nondiversified, organization-specific human capital invested in the employment relationship (Fama, 1980). However, these assumptions will have to be relaxed when agent performance in *interorganizational* relationships is concerned. In these settings, agents have more autonomy because they are not subject to bureaucratic controls and hierarchical monitoring by principals as in intraorganizational settings. Moreover, agents may be more heterogeneous than is assumed by traditional intraorganizational principal-agent models (Levitt, 1995; Nelson, 1991; Sharma, 1997).

This study contributes to the agency theory literature by focusing on the performance of agents in an interorganizational setting. Its hallmark is the departure from the usual viewpoint of the principal (Assumptions 1 and 2). I approach the issue from the viewpoint of the agent by specifying its behavioral preferences in Assumption 3. Once the constraining assumptions about agent behavior in intraorganizational research have been relaxed, it becomes very clear that as interorganizational agents, export intermediaries are not passive entities waiting for manufacturers to structure the relationship. Instead, many intermediaries are entrepreneurial firms actively influencing the odds of being selected and retained by manufacturers. Some of them even proactively go out to *recruit* principals, which tend to be reluctant small and midsize manufacturers not sure about how they can get their feet wet in export markets (Ilinitch and Peng, 1993, 1994).

Among the limited amount of agency theory research in inter-organizational settings, almost all studies took the principal's perspective, investigating how they make integration decisions (Anderson and Coughlan, 1987; Dutta, et al., 1995; Lafontaine, 1993; Lasser and Kerr, 1996; Majumdar and Ramaswamy, 1995). Very little has been done from the agent's perspective. Since the principal-agent relationship is a two-way relationship with mutual interdependence (Heide and Miner, 1992; Pfeffer and Salancik, 1978), focusing on one side and ignoring the other side will only, at best, uncover one side of the story. Therefore, it is necessary to bring the agent's perspective in order to enrich our understanding of this phenomenon. To the best of my knowledge, this study is among the first empirical attempts to study agent performance in an interorganizational setting from the agent's perspective. The results shed considerable light on how agents can actively build up their resources and capabilities to influence the principals' decisions.

While this new perspective is important, it is also worth noting that it is intended to complement—but not to replace—the existing perspective, which is principal- or manufacturer-centered. The derivation of the integrated model takes this complex, two-way relationship into account. Basically, the principals' perspective has been taken as our point of departure (Assumptions 1 and 2). As a result, it is also hypothesized that excessive agency costs will lead manufacturers to select direct, integrated channels instead of using intermediaries. In other words, while manufacturers' decisions do not make agents entirely passive or dependent, principals do place some very significant constraints on the maneuverability of the agents.

In summary, this study contributes to agency theory by focusing on agent performance in an interorganizational setting. Moreover, it departs from the convention of focusing exclusively on the principal and approaches the issue from the agent's perspective. The end result has been robust findings of the determinants of agent performance in this empirical context.

Contributions to Resource-Based Theory

While both transaction cost and agency theories are insightful, they have generally taken a manufacturer- or principal-centered perspective. Resource-based theory complements these two theories by adopting an intermediary-centered perspective. Specifically, this theory focuses on the intermediaries' particular resources and capabilities that give rise to their competitive advantage.

Economics, strategy, and organizational researchers are interested in the fundamental question that was first raised by Coase (1937): What is the nature of the firm? Each of these three theories suggests a different view of the firm: Transaction cost theory argues that the firm is a transaction cost minimizer, and agency theory projects the firm as an agency cost minimizer (Conner, 1991). In comparison, resource-based theory articulates a view of the firm as a value-adding mechanism which acquires, develops, and deploys valuable, unique, and hard-to-imitate resources and capabilities (Barney, 1991, 1997; Kogut and Zander, 1992; Mahoney and Pandian, 1992; Zajac and Olsen, 1993). More recent writings have further advanced the view of the firm as a collection of knowledge which takes on a path-dependent and tacit nature (Conner and Prahalad, 1996; Spender and Grant, 1996; Teece, et al., 1997). However, resource-based theorists have considerable difficulties in specifying what exactly resources and capabilities consist of, especially when these abilities are knowledge-based (Collis, 1994). "The dilemma for management is that, for the same reasons that competitors cannot replicate the firm's knowledge, so the firm itself may not understand it well enough to exploit it effectively" (Spender and Grant, 1996: 8). Critics have argued that such a paradox has led the theory to become a tautology: Since everything that a firm has can potentially become a resource or capability, the theory then can explain virtually everything, or nothing at all, about firm performance (Porter, 1991).

Despite the difficulties of undertaking concrete work in this area, a small but expanding empirical literature has been accumulating (Miller and Shamsie, 1996). This study contributes to this literature by empirically demonstrating the contribution of export intermediaries' resources and capabilities to their performance. Arguably, all four resources and capabilities tested in the hypotheses—knowledge about foreign markets and export processes (Hypothesis 1), negotiation ability (Hypothesis 2), ability to take title (Hypothesis 3), and willingness to specialize in commodity products (Hypothesis 4)—are firm-specific contributors to organizational performance. Of special interest to resource-based theorists are knowledge about foreign markets and export processes and negotiation ability. Both of these abilities take a long time to acquire and develop, and they are of a tacit and intangible nature that cannot be easily imitated by competitors in the export intermediary sector or by manufacturers interested in integrating the export channel function. Firms such as Asia Trade, Cascade Exports, and Hawaii Exports are leveraging these resources and capabilities; in other words, they are "trading" these resources and capabilities for rents (Amit and Shoemaker, 1993). Trading of these imperfectly imitable and imperfectly mobile resources and capabilities has always been difficult (Chi, 1994). And they are the sources of agency problems for manufacturers. If intermediaries attempt to extract rents that are deemed to be too high, then the costs of using these agents would outweigh the transaction cost savings they bring (Assumption 1).

The study also contributes to the empirical literature on resource-based theory by showcasing how this emerging theory, which is relatively weak when standing on its own due to the lack of definitions and empirical precedents, can come together with more established theories such as transaction cost and agency theories. This is different from the position of writers such as Conner and Prahalad (1996) and Kogut and Zander (1992). Kogut and Zander (1992: 396), for example, argued that transaction cost theory "is an insufficient vehicle by which to examine organizational capability." In contrast, the integrated model of export intermediary performance suggests that it is through the context—or the "vehicle"—of transaction-cost-minimizing as well as agency-cost-minimizing that resources and capabilities can add value to help improve firm performance. Since practically everything an intermediary possesses may be regarded as a resource or capability, resource-based theory by itself has been silent on which ones will determine firm performance. When resource-based theory is complemented by transaction cost and agency theories, it becomes clear which resources and capabilities are the critical ones providing value-added to intermediaries and their clients (Peng, et al., 1997; Peng and Ilinitch, 1995).

In summary, the study contributes to resource-based theory by empirically demonstrating the impact of valuable, unique, and hard-to-imitate resources and capabilities on firm performance. Moreover, the study also suggests an innovative way to advance empirical research in this area by integrating it with other theoretical perspectives.

Contributions to Marketing Channel Research

Like economics, strategy, and organizational scholars who study manufacturing firms, marketing researchers tend to focus on manufacturers' channel choice decisions, specifically whether to establish in-house distribution channels or rely on outside intermediaries (Anderson, 1985, 1988; Anderson and Coughlan, 1987; Anderson and Schmittlein, 1984; Aulakh and Kotabe, 1997; Campa and Guillen, 1995; Coughlan, 1985; John and Weitz, 1988; Klein, et al., 1990; Klein and Roth, 1990; Lilien, 1979; Rangan, et al., 1993). Again, such a one-sided emphasis on manufacturers overlooks the role of smaller intermediaries (Denis, 1990; Peng and Ilinitch, 1997). There is very little research on how intermediaries, at the other end of the distribution channel decisions, can improve their performance. This book fills an important gap in the marketing channel literature by introducing and testing a model of export intermediary performance. Given the importance of channel choice in marketing strategy (Kotler, 1983; Lilien, et al., 1992; Ronsenbloom, 1987; Stern and El-Ansary, 1992), such a model has a strong bearing on the overall channel performance.

Contributions to International Business Research

This book also makes a contribution to the international business literature, especially the stream of research on entry modes. Entry mode research has been a favorite topic for international business researchers (Aaby and Slater, 1989; Anderson and Gatignon, 1986; Cavusgil, 1984a, 1984b; Cavusgil and Zhou, 1994; Hennart, 1982, 1989; Hill and Kim, 1988; Hill, et al., 1990; Ilinitch and Peng, 1993, 1994; Root, 1994; Woodcock, Beamish and Makino, 1994). However, the emphasis, just like its counterparts in other areas of research, has always been the manufacturers' foreign market entry modes and has left one important link (i.e., the export intermediary) largely unexplored (Denis, 1990; Peng and Ilinitch, 1997). In contrast, this book recognizes the potential role export intermediaries may play. As a result, it contributes to the international business literature by focusing on a specific entry choice (indirect exports through intermediaries) from an underexplored perspective, namely, not from that of the exporter but from that of the intermediary. The implications of the intermediary's performance are profound, since a successful intermediary may help the exporter achieve a quantum jump in export expansion and an unsuccessful one may lead the exporter to nowhere (Haigh, 1994; Ilinitch and Peng, 1993, 1994).

Contributions to Small Business and Entrepreneurship Research

Research in small business and entrepreneurship has long been criticized for its lack of theoretical and empirical rigor (Cooper and Dunkelberg, 1987; Ireland and Van Auken, 1987; Keats and Bracker, 1988). Since much of the existing research focuses on larger firms, the theories and concepts generalized from such research are very difficult to apply in a small business context. Here in this book, I explicitly focus on a group of small businesses. While recognizing the interdependence between these small firms and their larger client firms in manufacturing, I have deductively derived and empirically tested the performance determinants of these firms by drawing on three underlying theories, thus introducing a strong theoretical model into small business/entrepreneurship research.

Summary

Overall, this book contributes to the scholarly literature in multiple ways. Theoretically, it enriches the three theories (i.e., transaction cost, agency, and resource-based theories) in organizational economics and strategic management by adopting a different perspective. Topically, it enhances research in marketing channels, international business, and small business and entrepreneurship.

WEAKNESSES

As in all other studies, research reported in this book also has several weaknesses that must be acknowledged. First, with regard to the integrated model, the resources and capabilities are the result of some antecedent variables or constructs. Although the case studies were designed to unpack some of these antecedents, I was mostly interested in these firms' *existing* abilities. In other words, the model that I formulated and tested is static and cross-sectional. Such an approach makes it difficult to capture how firms develop their resources and capabilities over time. Perhaps future longitudinal case studies and/or dynamic quantitative modeling will help solve this problem (Peng, 1997b).

Second, in terms of the performance of these firms, in both the qualitative and quantitative phases of the study, I exclusively relied on information supplied by owners, principals, and managers at export intermediaries whose recollection might be biased, subjective, and, hence, inaccurate (Huber and Power, 1985; Schwenk, 1985). Although Boyd, et al. (1993), Cavusgil and Zou (1994), Dess and Robinson (1984), and Zaheer (1995) reported that, in the absence of objective archival data, self-reported measures constitute an acceptable substitute, perhaps a better design would be also to survey their client firms and then to triangulate the accounts from both sides (Podsakoff and Organ, 1986; Haigh, 1994). However, this would be extremely difficult to achieve. Even during case studies, when informants were interviewed on site, they showed reluctance to reveal their clients for understandable reasons. Therefore, if the mail survey had asked the respondents to identify their client firms, the response rate might have been much lower.

Third, the study, especially the findings generated from the mail survey, is vulnerable to all the standard criticisms leveled at studies that use survey data, concerning social desirability effects, common method variance, inherent ambiguity, and nonresponse bias. However, given the lack of archival data sources, survey data are the only way to test the hypotheses for a large sample of firms; case studies, at best, can only provide anecdotal evidence. Moreover, I was careful in constructing the survey, consulting with academic experts and export practitioners, as well as case study informants. I pilot-tested the questionnaire with a small sample before settling on a final design. Moreover, upon receiving the returned surveys, I undertook a number of tests, which found no noticeable bias.[2] Therefore, I am as confident as is possible that the mail survey measured what it was designed to measure.

Fourth, although considerable care was given in constructing the measures in the mail survey, there is still room for improvement. While all case study informants agreed that negotiation ability was a critical capability for successful intermediaries, only one of the three formal tests of Hypothesis 2 was accepted; the hypothesis did not pass the other two tests. The failure to find strong support for Hypothesis 2 seems to lie in the failure of the negotiation ability construct to differentiate successful firms from unsuccessful ones.

Fifth, the study paid more attention to intermediaries' relationships with domestic manufacturers than to their relationships with overseas customers. Although it is evident that variables such as export knowledge and negotiation ability are important in intermediaries' dealings with overseas customers, such relationships have not been directly investigated. Given that an exploratory study such as this one could not model relationships that are too complex and that there already is a large body of international marketing literature on how to deal with export customers (see Aulakh and Kotabe, 1993; Leonidou and Katsikeas, 1996 for state-of-the-art reviews), I deliberately limited my attention to the often neglected manufacturer-intermediary relationship. Future research capable of simultaneously investigating the three-way relationship among manufacturers, intermediaries, and overseas customers will certainly be more desirable.

Finally, although the integrated model draws on three major theories, it is by no means comprehensive. Conceptually, it can benefit from at least three additional dimensions. The first is to account for repeated dealings between intermediaries and their clients and customers (Goffman, 1969). The current model allows for only a single round of transactions between the players. A more dynamic one derived from *game theory* can further specify these relationships more realistically by allowing for multiple rounds of transactions (Axelrod, 1984; Kreps, 1991; Kreps, et al., 1982). Firms' reputation and trustworthiness, which have not been modeled here, will become much more important in multiple-round transactions (Chiles and McMackin, 1996; Heide and Miner, 1992; Hill, 1990; Williamson, 1993a). The second area is the social dynamics permeating these firms and their operators. Since most intermediaries are small, the interpersonal relationships that their principals and managers cultivate with clients and customers may play a major part in determining firm performance (Gulati, 1995; Levinthal and Fichman, 1988; Ring and Van de Ven, 1994; Seabright, Levinthal and Fichman, 1992). In other words, drawing from *social exchange theory*, one can argue that the performance of export intermediaries is deeply embedded in the quality of the social networks of their principals and managers (Cook, et al., 1983; Granovetter, 1985; Peng and Luo, 1997). The third additional dimension is *"hybrid" modes* of transactions such as strategic alliances, joint ventures, and co-marketing arrangements that are "neither markets nor hierarchies" (Heide, 1992; Hennart, 1993; Powell, 1990; Williamson, 1991b). Given the recent interest in these hybrid forms, it seems likely that the ability to manage these relationships will also have an impact on firm performance (Contractor and Lorange, 1988; Peng and Shenkar, 1997). In short, the current model can benefit from a more in-depth economic analysis using game theory, a more fine-grained sociological analysis drawing on social exchange theory, and a more fine-tuned interorganizational inquiry focusing on hybrid modes of governance structure.

In summary, this study does contain a number of weaknesses, such as (a) the static nature of the integrated model; (b) the single source of potentially biased data; (c) the pitfalls of relying on the survey method; (d) the lack of success of certain measures in the survey; (e) the lack of attention to intermediaries' dealings with overseas customers; and (f) the inability to incorporate more relevant dimensions in the model. Given that this book represents an exploratory approach in a research territory which has hardly been covered, these weaknesses are inevitable. However, these limitations must be taken into account when interpreting and generalizing the findings.

MANAGERIAL, POLICY, AND RESEARCH IMPLICATIONS

Managerial Implications

For practitioners working in export intermediaries and would-be entrepreneurs interested in starting their own companies, this book contains profound implications. It calls for better understanding of the determinants of export intermediary performance, as well as deeper appreciation of the manufacturers' transaction-cost-based and agency-cost-based criteria in channel decisions. The high failure rate among these firms (Haigh, 1994) indicates that knowledge about the determinants of their performance may not yet be common among practitioners working in this industry. While the *perceived* entry barrier to this industry is low, the *actual* barrier to success is quite prohibitive, considering, for example, the importance of the ability to take title to the goods. Therefore, would-be entrepreneurs interested in opening their own export intermediaries may want to assess whether they already possess or are able to acquire the critical resources and capabilities that have been found in this study to be determinants of export intermediary performance.

First, do they have adequate knowledge and skills in the export business as well as in the product industry? It is relatively easy to start a small trading company, jumping on the recent international trade bandwagon. However, prior research and this book have shown that export-related knowledge and skills take a long time to accumulate, and export intermediaries founded by principals who do not possess a wealth of knowledge and experience in this business tend to have a rocky start and a difficult time when the market fluctuates.

Second, do they have the ability to take title to the goods? Many export intermediaries were founded on the premise that they could survive and prosper by working on commission. This may have been true during the heyday of export management companies (EMCs). But not anymore. Recently, as more intermediaries have begun to take title to the goods from their clients, manufacturers have become increasingly in favor of such intermediaries. As a result, intermediaries without such an ability face a severe competitive disadvantage.

Third, are they willing to specialize in less glamorous, mature, commodity products? Given the recent advances in various high-tech industries such as computers and telecommunications, as well as the glamour and prestige associated with these new products that are reportedly destined to rule the future, intermediaries may be tempted to enter these industries and attempt to bring these new products abroad. Indeed, Perry (1992: 153) suggested that "high-tech products are good prospects" for export intermediaries. However, such thinking has been refuted by voluminous research from the manufacturer's perspective, as well as research reported in this book which takes the intermediary's perspective. All these studies suggest that specializing in those high-tech products may not be the optimal strategy for the export intermediary. In these complex, technology-intensive industries and product areas, manufacturers have a greater propensity to use integrated, in-house distribution channels to enter foreign markets (Anderson and Coughlan, 1987; Rangan, et al., 1993; Williamson, 1975, 1985). As a result, export intermediaries are advised to specialize in those relatively mature, commodity products which require little sales force training and postsale services so as to maximize their probability of being selected and retained, thus maximizing their earnings and profits.

Fourth, do they have strong negotiation ability? While no definitive conclusion can be drawn about the importance of negotiation ability based on the quantitative results, qualitative findings generated from case studies do suggest that negotiation ability is an important component of the repertoire of successful export intermediaries (Lax and Sebenius, 1986). Therefore, individuals without strong negotiation ability may be advised to think twice before starting their own trading companies.

Overall, export intermediaries have a tremendous challenge in carving out a niche for themselves, given "the inhospitable trading environment and the growing sophistication and demands of domestic manufacturers and foreign buyers alike" (Perry, 1992: 154). They need to possess or develop valuable, unique, and hard-to-imitate resources and capabilities manifested in these dimensions in order to be successful.

In addition to these implications pertaining to practitioners working in export intermediaries, a number of research-based guidelines can also help managers at small and midsize manufacturers in search of export intermediary services. For manufacturers that know little about foreign markets and cannot afford their own export department, the findings suggest that the odds for developing a mutually beneficial relationship can be quite high if they are careful in selecting appropriate intermediaries. Specifically, they should look for intermediaries operated by entrepreneurs with substantial experience in exporting, with proven negotiation skills, with the ability to take title, and with the willingness to specialize in commodity products. In screening prospective export intermediaries, manufacturing company managers should select intermediaries specializing in their industry and having expertise in particular foreign markets that are of interest. To avoid potential agency problems (especially adverse selection and moral hazard problems), manufacturing managers should also solicit leads on the performance of prospective intermediaries from former clients and banks. Once a particular candidate has been selected, it is advisable to set revenue goals for target markets. Given the time it takes to develop a new export market, a two- or three-year contract with suitable cancellation clauses should be considered. For manufacturers, the ideal candidates are those intermediaries that are receptive to the idea of taking title to the goods.

The findings also have important implications for banks and other financial institutions. Given the importance of taking title to the goods to export intermediary performance and the fact that most U.S. export intermediaries lack such an ability, banks can lend more help in this regard. Instead of directly entering the export business with limited success,[3] banks could provide more export financing so that more intermediaries are able to take title to the goods. Given the rising demand for U.S. exports in many overseas markets, loans to export intermediaries may prove to be a lucrative business for more and more banks. Of course, care must be taken in making sure that only intermediaries with a proven track record or good potential to become successful will receive such loans.

Public Policy Implications

From a public policy perspective, the contributions of export intermediaries are valuable and should be encouraged to grow, given the importance of export expansion for this country (Richardson and Rindal, 1995). Unfortunately, congressional efforts in stimulating the growth of these firms through the enactment of the Export Trading Company Act (ETC Act) of 1982 were largely ineffective since the act did not address the real needs of export intermediaries. Because most U.S. firms in this industry are small, it is not realistic to expect them to emerge on the order of large general trading companies (the *sogo shosha*) from Japan. The small trading companies from Japan (the *senmon shosha*) may be a more suitable model for emulation (Sarathy, 1985). Offering antitrust waiver certificates, as envisioned by the ETC Act, has proven to be a moot point, or a "non-event" (Perry, 1992: 154), for these small intermediaries, which by and large have not been bothered by antitrust concerns.

Export intermediaries' more pressing concerns seem to lie in the area of obtaining export financing. Therefore, perhaps new legislation can be introduced to mandate that federal agencies such as the Export-Import Bank (Ex-Im Bank) pay particular attention to the needs of these firms. Currently, over 80 percent of the loans and services from the Ex-Im Bank are provided to small businesses employing fewer than 500 people. But as the profiles of export intermediaries obtained in the study show, the vast majority of export intermediaries are a lot smaller than this definition of small businesses. Most of them belong to the smallest category, namely, very small businesses with fewer than twenty employees. It is unclear how effective the Ex-Im Bank is in helping these "dwarfs among the dwarfs." Given the importance of taking title to the goods, it is critical for export intermediaries to secure export financing, and it is imperative that agencies such as the Ex-Im Bank lend their help. For example, until recently, accounts receivable for sales had been excluded as collateral for Ex-Im Bank loans because they were held by the foreign entity. Starting in April 1996, the Ex-Im Bank may now customize certain loan-structuring requirements on a case-by-case basis, allowing loan applicants such as export intermediaries to use accounts receivable as collateral. For intermediaries struggling to obtain export financing, this is certainly encouraging. However, many of them still may not be able to obtain such loans since another hurdle is that the U.S. exporter, such as the intermediary, must have a foreign subsidiary capable of collecting the accounts receivable (*The Exporter Magazine*, 1996). Given the small size of most U.S. export intermediaries, many of them will not be able to have foreign subsidiaries. But they will still need financing assistance. Therefore, it will be necessary to remove more of these hurdles.

Second, since the vast majority of U.S. export intermediaries are small firms, small business assistance organizations at the federal and state levels, such as the Small Business Administration (SBA), should pay more attention to the needs and wants of this type of small business, instead of focusing only on small manufacturing firms (Goodnow and Goodnow, 1990; Kotabe and Czinkota, 1992; Seringhaus, 1986). Given the persistence of the U.S. trade deficit and the increased integration of the domestic and international economy, other federal and state agencies should join the efforts of the Commerce Department to promote more U.S. exports. Assistance from organizations such as the SBA may prove to be critical, since the SBA can guarantee loans for small businesses and export intermediaries certainly can benefit from such help.

The final public policy implication one can draw from this study is with regard to immigration policy. Whenever a recession hits this country, immigrants tend to be the social group that receives much of the blame. The recent economic downturn has worsened such sentiments. However, this book clearly shows that immigrants are at the forefront of expanding U.S. exports. Immigrants from forty-one countries in Africa, Asia, Europe, Latin America, and the Middle East made up 40 percent of the 195 respondents to the nationwide mail survey (see Table 7.5). Moreover, among these 195 respondent firms, two-thirds have foreign-born personnel working for them. At one-fifth of these firms, more than 75 percent of the people working there are immigrants. These findings are consistent with the results of studies on ethnic entrepreneurship (Aldrich and Waldinger, 1990; Borjas, 1990; Waldinger, et al., 1990). Using the 1980 census data,

Borjas (1990: 164), for example, reported that "immigrants are slightly more likely to be self-employed than natives. The immigrant self-employment rate is 12 percent, while that of natives is 11 percent." It is obvious that given their background, experience and interest, immigrants have a comparative advantage in operating export intermediaries. Similar to Borjas's (1990: 163) findings, data generated from this study do not suggest that immigrant entrepreneurs are more successful than their U.S.-born counterparts. But the fact remains that they are working hard to leverage their knowledge and expertise about various foreign cultures and markets in order to bring American products and services abroad. Therefore, during this era of increased global competition, curtailing immigration in order to boost U.S. competitiveness seems to be a policy destined to backfire.

In summary, this book not only suggests important implications that are helpful to practitioners working in and/or working with export intermediaries, but also generates a number of public policy implications for other related organizations, such as the Ex-Im Bank, federal and state agencies in charge of export promotion, and immigrant and legislative circles interested in knowing more about the role of immigrant entrepreneurs in the economy.

Research Implications

This book also suggests a number of important implications for future research. First, it calls for more attention to firms competing at the neglected side of make-or-buy decisions. Currently, a lot is known about manufacturers' decision criteria in make-or-buy decisions such as whether to source in-house or externally, whether to use integrated or independent sales forces, and whether to engage in direct or indirect exports in order to enter foreign markets. While research from the manufacturers' perspective seems to have saturated, very little is known about how firms standing at the other end of these decisions may respond to them and improve their performance. Many firms in such a position are small businesses that do not have strong bargaining power when dealing with the larger manufacturers; nevertheless, they usually possess highly specialized and competitive resources and capabilities (Chen and Hambrick, 1995; Peng, et al., 1997; Sharma, 1997). Manufacturers usually have an incentive to work with these specialized small firms as agents in order to achieve common goals. Therefore, improved knowledge about how these smaller firms operate, compete, and perform will break new ground in transaction cost, principal-agent, and resource-based research.

Second, since this book is only the first study that explicitly focuses on the performance of U.S. export intermediaries, much more work remains to be done to overcome its weaknesses. Methodologically, longitudinal case studies to track the birth, growth, decline, and death of these firms will be a viable approach that moves beyond the existing static model (see Peng, 1997b for examples in a different context). Although difficult, future research should also attempt to survey the client firms of export intermediaries in order to triangulate the performance measure under investigation (Haigh, 1994). While the survey method may still be used, further refinement on the measures that performed weakly in this study will be necessary.

Third, conceptual refinements can be made to improve the integrated model, especially in the area of drawing upon other relevant underlying theories in social science research. Among these, game theory from economics and social exchange theory from sociology appear to be very promising. A game theoretic model will enable the expanded model to account for multiple rounds of transactions (Axelrod, 1984). A social exchange model, on the other hand, can focus on the cooperative aspects of the social, interpersonal and interorganizational relationships in which export intermediaries are embedded (Granovetter, 1985). In addition, an interorganizational model can examine how export intermediaries collaborate with their manufacturing clients and overseas customers in strategic alliances, joint ventures, and co-marketing arrangements, while maintaining intermediaries' own competitive advantage at the same time (Contractor and Lorange, 1988; Peng and Shenkar, 1997; Powell, 1990).

Fourth, comparative research embracing a multinational triangulation design should be undertaken to further our understanding of export intermediary performance beyond the borders of the United States (Peng, 1994b, 1995b; Peng and Peterson, 1994). It will be interesting to compare the performance determinants of U.S. export intermediaries versus, for example, those of small Japanese trading companies (the *senmon shosha*) (Sarathy, 1985), Korean general trading companies (Cho, 1984, 1987), or Chinese foreign trade corporations (Lardy, 1992; MacBean, 1996). Since national and corporate culture certainly impacts on firm behavior and performance (Hofstede, 1980, 1994; Porter, 1990), the integrated model that has been developed and tested in this book will probably have to incorporate culture-specific variables and hypotheses in order to be successfully tested in a different setting. Only through such repeated testing across a wide variety of countries can we legitimately claim that the integrated model corresponds to reality on a global basis (Boyacigiller and Adler, 1991; Peng and Peterson, 1994).

Finally, while this book focuses on export intermediaries, future research does not necessarily have to be confined to this relatively narrow empirical domain. Conceptually, many service firms, such as banks, investment firms, auto dealerships, and travel agencies, to name a few, are all intermediaries connecting producers and customers. Therefore, it remains to be seen how their performance is determined by resources and capabilities which minimize transaction costs and agency costs for their customers (*Business Week*, 1996). Similar to export intermediaries, these service firms do not engage in a significant amount of manufacturing production; therefore, the determinants of their performance will not be clouded by the interactive effects from production costs, such as those reported by Walker and Weber (1984, 1987). As a result, these service intermediaries provide *purer* settings for transaction cost and principal-agent research. Moreover, compared with their manufacturing counterparts, these service firms better embody the view of the firm as a collection of intangible, knowledge-based resources and capabilities, thus enabling them to be fertile grounds for resource-based studies. Some of these firms, such as banks, may have better and more accessible archival data about their performance. It will be interesting to extend the integrated model formulated and tested in this book into these different empirical settings to test its validity.

In summary, future work can take a number of directions to extend the research reported in this book. The most fruitful areas seem to lie in the continued effort to integrate transaction cost, agency, and resource-based theories, and to bring them to bear on a traditionally neglected end in make-or-buy research, namely, firm strategy and performance at the side opposite the manufacturers. Further refined studies of U.S. export intermediaries as well as comparative studies that embrace a multinational triangulation design will contribute toward improved understanding of this particular type of organization on a worldwide basis. Moreover, beyond the scope of this book, this new research agenda can be extended to study other intermediary firms.

COMPETING FOR THE FUTURE—AND WINNING

Since larger firms in the United States as well as in much of the industrial world are under increasing pressure to downsize, outsource, and restructure, smaller firms are now the primary generator of economic growth and the largest employer of the labor force. Therefore, increased attention to these small businesses is more important and relevant as we approach the next millennium. Moreover, during this "postindustrial" era, service industries now contribute more to the economy than manufacturing industries do. If scholarly research is to remain relevant in the rapidly evolving global economy (Hambrick, 1994; Pfeffer, 1993), then perhaps more research emphasis should be placed on those small service firms that compete at the other end of manufacturers' make-or-buy decisions.

This book has investigated a particular type of small service firms, namely, export intermediary firms in the United States, and developed, tested, and supported an integrated model of the fundamental determinants of their performance. Future research in this area of inquiry will not only help us advance the scholarly knowledge about these firms and their strategy, structure, and organization, but will also contribute to the performance of these firms which are becoming increasingly important in global competition.

What does the future hold for export intermediary firms on a worldwide basis in general, and in the United States in particular? The answer to this question lies in what core competencies and competitive advantages export intermediaries can find for themselves in a world of heightened competitiveness, lowered trade barriers, and improved communications. With very little exaggeration, *The Economist* (1995: 56) reported that these firms' "core competence over the years has been their customers' ignorance (of 'abroad' and its funny ways)." As their customers become more sophisticated and look for true value-added, export intermediaries must be able to deliver that in order to remain successful. Therefore, they must continuously acquire, develop, and deploy resources and capabilities that are valuable, unique, and hard-to-imitate. In the future, an export intermediary's abilities to exploit these resources and capabilities to lower client firms' transaction costs and agency costs will likely be the key factor that separates the winners from the mere survivors in international trade.

NOTES

1. There may be some additional production costs involved if the manufacturer needs to adapt or tailor its products for foreign markets. But for small and midsize manufacturers that usually rely on export intermediaries to enter foreign markets, these additional production costs can be considered minimal, except in the area of additional labeling and packaging which tend to be insignificant (Ilinitch and Peng, 1993, 1994). If these production costs are substantial, the results of the study will encounter severe interactive effects from production-cost-minimizing considerations as found by Walker and Weber (1984, 1987).

2. The appendix contains more details of these tests of data integrity and reliability. A more technical description can be found in Peng (1996).

3. Following the passage of the Export Trading Company Act of 1982, some U.S. banks announced that they would enter export trade by forming export trading companies. However, such attempts were largely unsuccessful, and most banks soon lost interest (Christensen, 1989). Financial markets even reacted negatively to U.S. banks' announcement about engaging in export trade due to banks' perceived lack of expertise in that area (Kryzanowski and Ursel, 1993).

Appendix: Research Methodology

This appendix is provided for readers interested in the research process that has resulted in this book (see Peng, 1996 for more details). My interest in export intermediary performance grew out of a previous project on export performance (Ilinitch and Peng, 1993, 1994). Attempting to uncover what was behind the quantum leap in export involvement among some very small manufacturers with little or no international experience, I came to realize the important role of export intermediaries in facilitating exports among these firms. This book builds on that foundation.

DEFINING THE PROBLEM

Although I had worked for several export intermediary firms in a consulting capacity before, I did not pay much attention to the performance of these firms. Rather, like most scholars in the field, I was interested in the performance of manufacturing exporters. When I began research for this book, the initial stage was somewhat loosely structured. In addition to the eighteen interviews with manufacturing exporters I participated in when working on the previous project, I first attended three trade shows and two export seminars and visited four trade-related government offices, including the Oregon Department of Agriculture, the Port of Seattle, the Small Business Administration, and the Washington State Department of Trade and Economic Development. Then I attempted to interview as many export intermediary operators as possible, ranging from a Japanese expatriate manager at a major *sogo shosha* in Seattle to over thirty intermediary managers in six cities (Boston, Dallas, Honolulu, Portland [Oregon], Santa Fe [New Mexico], and Seattle). Most of these were informal interviews, and some of them were on the phone. In addition, I requested information from the Export Trading Company Affairs Office of the U.S. Department of Commerce in Washington, DC.

During these preliminary interviews, I was struck by two findings. First, although export intermediaries could play a potentially important role in facilitating more exports and helping the nation combat its trade deficit problems, nobody seemed to have examined what determined their performance. Compared with the voluminous research on the export strategy, behavior, and performance of manufacturers, the literature on export intermediaries was sparse (Peng and Ilinitch, 1997). Within this limited literature, work on U.S. export intermediary performance was virtually nonexistent, although there was some research on worldwide intermediary development in general (Amine, 1987; Cho, 1987; Kim, 1986), and on Japanese trading companies in particular (Kotabe, 1984; Kojima and Ozawa, 1984; Sarathy, 1985; Yoshihara, 1982; Young, 1978). While there were a small number of survey studies describing the demographic profiles of export intermediaries in the United States, none had rigorously examined the determinants of their performance (see Table 4.1).

The second finding that struck me was the tremendous number of entries and exits in this volatile industry. Every year, numerous new intermediary firms were founded, while a large number went inactive or out of business. Although most practitioners I interviewed had a "theory in use" about what determined export intermediary performance, they usually could not articulate such a view clearly. If they did, they always added the caveat that it was based only on their personal experience. Therefore, in order to answer an unexplored but important question and fill a gap in the literature, I decided to focus on the export intermediary performance issue.

PHASE I: SIX CASE STUDIES

Because the topic of intermediary performance had not been previously explored, qualitative case studies were deemed to be an ideal launching pad to initiate this research. However, given the pitfalls of qualitative studies, namely, small sample size, nonrandom selection of the cases, and, hence, lack of generalizability, I also wanted to employ quantitative methods to provide a more definitive answer to the research question. As a result, I adopted a two-phase hybrid methodology, which maximized the benefits from the strengths of these two methods while minimizing the exposure to their limitations.

A Comparative Case Study Design

I followed the clinical field research methodology to undertake the six case studies (Eisenhardt, 1989b; Glaser and Strauss, 1967; Miles and Huberman, 1984; Strauss, 1987; Yin, 1989). The purpose of this phase was to build cases and examine the integrated model of export intermediary performance in a qualitative way. The clinical field research methodology required a purposive rather than a random sampling design. I considered several factors in selecting the cases. First, the firms selected for comparative case studies included examples of both successful and unsuccessful ones. The list of potential candidates was compiled through conversations with trade officials and practitioners. An attempt was made to obtain consent from the most successful firms nominated by a large number of interviewees. If the most desired firms declined to participate, I went down the list to recruit other successful firms. As expected, it was easier to recruit successful firms to participate than to recruit unsuccessful ones.

Second, I limited the sample to intermediaries which primarily dealt with relatively simple (low-tech), commodity-type exports, such as apparel, foodstuffs, and pulp/paper, in order to minimize what Eisenhardt (1989b) called "extraneous variation" that might be derived from differences between the distribution of simple products and that of complex ones. The distribution of technology-intensive, complex (high-tech) products requires a great deal of transaction-specific investment, thus calling for more channel integration (Williamson, 1975, 1985). According to previous studies using U.S. samples, manufacturers of relatively complex products are more likely to use integrated channels to exercise greater control over distribution, thus leaving little room for intermediaries (Anderson and Coughlan, 1987; Anderson and Schmittlein, 1984; Majumdar and Ramaswamy, 1995; Rangan, et al., 1993). Similar results held when British (Nicholas, 1982, 1983), Canadian (Klein, et al., 1990), and Spanish (Campa and Guillen, 1995) samples were used. Even in Japan, where the tradition of using trading companies for exports has deep roots, manufacturers of complex products such as electronics and automobiles, due to the extensive sales force training and postsale service requirements of their products, were among the first ones to break away from trading companies and establish integrated channels (Yoshihara, 1982). As a result, I selected intermediaries dealing with less complex products as a way to broadly control for industry and product variations.

Third, I chose a group of firms focusing on the same set of markets. Five firms in the sample were located in the Seattle area, which during the time of study was ranked as the country's number one city for international trade by *Fortune* magazine (1992). Moreover, the location dictates that most exporters in the area focused on the booming Asian markets (Washington State, 1994). In addition, I added another firm located in Hawaii, which also has significant trade relationships with Asian markets (Hook and Czinkota, 1988; *Market Facts Hawaii*, 1995).

Finally, I ensured that the sampled firms were consistent with the operational definition of export intermediaries specified in Chapter 2. Specifically, they must (a) be located in the United States; (b) be independent; and (c) engage in export sales.

In summary, both successful and unsuccessful firms were included in the sample for comparative case studies. Although it was a convenience sample, I did attempt to broadly control for product industry, location, and markets in the case selection process.

Data Collection and Analyses

Given the drawbacks of using a single informant (Huber and Power, 1985; Schwenk, 1985), I sought to interview multiple informants of the same firm to ensure internal consistency of the data. Since the six firms in the sample were all relatively small, two informants, who were owners, principals, or managers, per firm were deemed adequate. All together, twelve individuals from six firms agreed to participate. Some of them were interviewed multiple times.

Incorporating the information obtained from the interviews during the problem definition stage, I prepared a survey instrument for case studies. The format of the case study interview was semi-structured, in that all questions on the survey were covered, while I left room to raise other issues. I mostly queried the participants on the underlying reasons for their performance to ensure that important explanatory variables were included, thus seeking to achieve "the intimate connection with empirical reality" (Eisenhardt, 1989b: 532). Examples of these questions included (a) how many years they had been in the export business; (b) how they would rate their own negotiation skills; and (c) whether they took title to the goods. In terms of performance, a number of measures were sought, including both "objective" (e.g., sales, margin) and "subjective" (e.g., self-rated performance) measures. Each interview typically lasted between sixty and 120 minutes, and two interviewers were present. All impressions, comments, and notes were discussed and documented soon after the interviews, as "the observations from multiple investigators enhance confidence in the findings" (Eisenhardt, 1989b: 538). In addition, company documents, sales material, follow-up interviews, and phone calls were also used to obtain more data and clarify some issues.

Following recent clinical field research practices (Briggs, 1986; Peng, 1997b; Rangan, et al., 1993; Yan and Gray, 1994), I used an iterative approach to constantly compare, contrast, and clarify discrepant observations. Such an approach is especially useful for an exploratory inquiry like this one (Eisenhardt, 1989b; Glaser and Strauss, 1967; Strauss, 1987; Van de Ven, 1992). Although materials in Chapters 5, 6, and 7 were presented in an almost linear fashion, progressing from model building to case studies and then to a mail survey, the real process was more "messy" (Parkhe, 1993). Model building and case studies were actually intertwined, which was expected for an exploratory inquiry such as this one in search of a grounded model. According to Glaser and Strauss (1967), a grounded theory or model emerges from (a) the observation of relevant empirical data; and/or (b) the combination of empirical data and concepts developed from a review of the literature. In this inquiry, model building and case studies were undertaken almost concurrently.

I started with a resource-based model, based on a review of the recent strategic management literature on firm performance. The initial list of resources and capabilities, however, proved to be no more than a laundry list of all sorts of explanatory variables with a potential to affect export intermediary performance. It was not clear how and why some of these would create value while others would not. Attempts to organize these resources and capabilities in any theoretically meaningful fashion met with little success. Then interview data suggested the usefulness of viewing export intermediaries as transaction-cost-minimizing devices for manufacturers. This view eventually led to an extension which regarded intermediaries as agents and manufacturers as principals according to agency theory. Once I was equipped with such an analytical lens, it became easy to organize the contribution of different resources and capabilities according to their abilities to minimize export-related transaction costs and agency costs. As a result, an emergent model of export intermediaries, which I later called "the integrated model" in this book, gradually took shape.

While the case studies generally supported the validity of the emergent model, field data were also useful in generating insights that refuted some of my original thinking. For example, initially I was led to believe that firms holding an export trading company certificate issued by the Department of Commerce, as envisioned by the ETC Act of 1982, would have better performance. This view was found to be erroneous (and, according to a case study participant, "laughable"—much to my embarrassment!). Most practitioners in the industry largely ignored this issue. As a result, the eventual integrated model made no reference to the provisions of the ETC Act.

In summary, the analytical approach undertaken was largely consistent with the grounded theory approach, which advocates that the collection and analysis of data be carried out simultaneously in search of a grounded theory or model. The end result was not only a theoretically sound and empirically grounded model, but also a number of ways to measure certain constructs which were building blocks of the model.

PHASE II: A MAIL SURVEY

Compared with the more flexible approach used during the first phase, the second phase was more orthodox, involving several incremental steps, such as model specification, construction and administration of the survey, data reliability tests, and hypothesis tests.

Model Specification

The basic multiple regression model took the following form:

$$\text{Performance}_{(93, 94)} = \beta_0 + \\ \beta_1 \text{ Export knowledge } + \\ \beta_2 \text{ Negotiation ability } + \\ \beta_3 \text{ Ability to take title to goods } + \\ \beta_4 \text{ Specialization in commodity products } + \\ \beta_5 \text{ Firm size } + \\ \beta_6 \text{ Firm age } + \\ e \qquad \text{(equation A1)}$$

A principal feature of this model was that the dependent variable (Performance $_{[93, 94]}$) represented measures averaged over two years in order to increase the reliability of this important construct. A one-year snapshot of performance might not be an accurate reflection of overall firm performance, given the inherent fluctuations of the global marketplace. Therefore, by averaging performance over time, I was in effect smoothing out temporal fluctuations (e.g., Hill, Hitt and Hoskisson, 1992; Mosakowski, 1991). A two-year average was used because I wanted a consistent number of years per firm, and I expected that two years were sufficiently long to achieve the benefits of averaging. Moreover, at the time of the survey (1995), respondents were believed to have better recall of organizational performance and firm capabilities for the two most recent years (1993–94). The draw-back of such an approach was that I had to accept a smaller sample size: The sample was reduced from 195 firms which responded to 166 firms whose performance data were complete for the two most recent years. I also attempted to obtain averaged performance over the three most recent years (1992–94). While the results were largely similar, the sample size was further reduced to 129 firms, due to missing performance data at some firms (Peng, 1996).

The specifications of the model and data were based on the following assumptions (Neter, et al., 1989):

1. The relationships among the variables were linear and additive. This ruled out curvilinear, multiplicative, and interactive relations. The current literature, as well as the six case studies, did not give any a priori reason to suspect that the relationships were nonlinear. The assumption of noninteraction was one of convenience.

2. The structural equation residual (e) was independent of the variables. I suspected that no systematic intervening variables existed. Other than those specified in the model, the current literature and the case studies did not provide any significant reason to believe that there are others.

Construction and Administration of the Survey: The Total Design Method

Organizational surveys often have fairly low response rates. Among various surveys, those requesting financial information can easily trigger nonresponse (Tomaskovic-Devey, et al., 1994). There-fore, this survey focusing on the performance of privately held firms created a major challenge to obtaining the desired response rate. In order to improve the survey response rate, I followed the total design method (Dillman, 1978) in designing, organizing, and administering the survey. The questions were designed to be (a) easy to under-stand, (b) concise (only four pages), and (c) neutrally worded.

The development of the survey questionnaire took several steps. After I incorporated information gathered from the case studies, a draft questionnaire was designed and critiqued by several academic experts. Then I revisited the ten case study participants in Seattle and asked for their reaction. The instrument was separately admini-stered to these participants to check interrater reliability (r) in each of these five firms—defined as the weighted average of the corre-lations of response for each item. I found that the interrater r calcu-lated for the correlations was better than 0.90, thus suggesting no significant difference among individual respondents at each firm (Nunally, 1978). These results, in addition to the knowledge that the sampled firms in the mail survey were usually small and that the respondents tended to be knowledgeable about their firms, led me to believe that multiple respondents from one firm were not necessary; one respondent per firm was deemed adequate. In other words, pre-test results, the small size of the sampled firms, and the level of respondents I sought gave me confidence in the accuracy of the information provided by a single informant per firm.

To improve the response rate and encourage more accurate responses, several steps were taken following Dillman (1978). First, anonymity of the participating firms was guaranteed, and respondents were not asked to reveal their identity in returned surveys. Second, a summary of the findings was promised to be sent to participating firms.[1] In order to track respondent firms, questionnaires were mailed with postage-paid postcards which the respondents could send back separately, identify themselves, and request a copy of the findings. Third, postage-paid envelopes were enclosed for the convenience of the respondents. Finally, two rounds of mailings were used. Dillman (1978) reported consistently high response rates from the use of this mailing method.

In addition, careful consideration was given with sensitivity to respondents' possible reactions. Specifically, I offered the option of a telephone interview, which was indicated on the postcard should the respondents be too busy to sit down and fill out the questionnaire. Providing such a choice increased survey response not only because it created a more flexible opportunity to respond, but also because, by giving respondents a choice that was not a flat refusal, researchers could increase their involvement in the interaction and made it more awkward to refuse (Tomaskovic-Devey, et al., 1994: 454). In the end, three respondents chose to be interviewed on the phone and filled out the survey questionnaire this way. In addition, a choice of refusal to participate was given to the respondents on the postcard, with one line of blank space asking for a brief reason. Among nonrespondents, these reasons included "too busy," "no interest," and "ready to retire."

Out of a total of 1,046 surveys sent out in two rounds of mailing, 131 were returned because of incorrect addresses or expired mail-forwarding orders. Therefore, the effective sample was reduced to 915. Among these, 195 surveys were returned, thus yielding a response rate of 21.31 percent (195/915). As shown in Table A.1, this response rate compared very favorably with those obtained by other studies, except the U.S. Department of Commerce (1990) survey. As an official survey, the Department of Commerce survey yielded a response rate of close to 50 percent. But this survey, together with other known studies, did not ask for sensitive financial data from their respondents. In the current survey, the careful consideration of

Table A.1
Response Rates of Survey Studies
of U.S. Export Intermediaries since the 1970s

Studies	Total Sampled	Total Responded	Response Rates
Hay Associates (1977)	287	85	29.6%
Brasch (1978)	1,000	198	19.8%
Coopers and Lybrand (1984)	1,178	209	17.7%
Bello and Williamson (1985a, 1985b)	1,100	258	23.5%
Howard and Maskulka (1988)	453	115	25.4%
U.S. Department of Commerce (1990)	513	254	49.5%
Batra (1991)	1,130	175	15.5%
This Study	915	195	21.31%

response sensitivity and close adherence to the total design method resulted in a similar response rate despite my interest in obtaining performance data.

Data Reliability

Whether the results of the survey could be generalized at the national level depended on whether responses came from firms across the country. If substantial regional response bias was found, then this survey, at best, could only be regarded as a regional one.

Targeting a nationwide sample, surveys were sent to a random sample of 1,046 export intermediary firms in forty-nine states and the District of Columbia (DC) listed in the "Trading Companies" section of the 1994 edition of *The Export Yellow Pages* published by the U.S. Department of Commerce (Table A.2). The selection process did not generate any firm located in Delaware, a small state on the East Coast. Inaccurate addresses of the only two firms sampled in Vermont eliminated an additional state from the sample and resulted in an effective sample of firms in forty-eight states and DC. The 195 responses came from firms in thirty-eight states and DC. None of the sampled firms in the remaining ten states returned the survey. Out of a total of 915, there were only twenty-two firms sampled in these ten "missing" states (Alaska, Mississippi, Montana, Nebraska, Nevada, North Dakota, South Dakota, Tennessee, West Virginia, and Wyoming) and two in Vermont, and none of these states appeared to

Table A.2
Firms Sampled and Firms Responding

State	Original Sample	Effective Sample	Response	Response %
Alabama	6	6	2	33.33%
Alaska	1	1	0	0.00%
Arizona	9	9	1	11.11%
Arkansas	4	4	1	25.00%
California	169	140	29	20.71%
Colorado	7	6	3	50.00%
Connecticut	27	21	9	42.86%
District of Columbia	17	14	3	21.43%
Florida	116	93	22	23.66%
Georgia	21	21	3	14.29%
Hawaii	13	12	2	16.67%
Idaho	1	1	1	100.00%
Illinois	41	34	12	35.29%
Indiana	8	8	1	12.50%
Iowa	8	6	3	50.00%
Kansas	13	9	1	11.11%
Kentucky	3	3	1	33.33%
Louisiana	5	5	1	20.00%
Maine	5	5	1	20.00%
Maryland	33	32	4	12.50%
Massachusetts	39	34	5	14.71%
Michigan	25	22	3	13.64%
Minnesota	9	8	3	37.50%
Mississippi	3	3	0	0.00%
Missouri	18	16	2	12.50%
Montana	1	1	0	0.00%
Nebraska	1	1	0	0.00%
Nevada	3	1	0	0.00%
New Hampshire	6	5	1	20.00%
New Jersey	48	45	8	17.78%
New Mexico	6	6	1	16.67%
New York	100	94	14	14.89%
North Carolina	16	14	2	14.29%
North Dakota	2	2	0	0.00%
Ohio	33	29	6	20.69%
Oklahoma	6	5	2	40.00%
Oregon	9	8	3	37.50%
Pennsylvania	23	21	6	28.57%

Table A.2
Firms Sampled and Firms Responding (Continued)

State	Original Sample	Effective Sample	Response	Response %
Rhode Island	5	4	2	50.00%
South Carolina	6	2	1	16.67%
South Dakota	2	2	0	0.00%
Tennessee	9	9	0	0.00%
Texas	70	59	10	16.95%
Utah	9	9	1	11.11%
Vermont	2	0	0	N/A
Virginia	35	31	11	35.48%
Washington	40	38	13	34.21%
West Virginia	1	1	0	0.00%
Wisconsin	11	10	1	10.00%
Wyoming	1	1	0	0.00%
Total	1,046	915	195	21.31%

be a "major league" player in exporting. As a result, their omission was judged to be insignificant to the results of the survey, and information provided by the respondents was used for the analyses.

While response rates varied from state to state (Table A.2), a clear pattern emerged when the responses were organized according to the ten different regions as defined by the Small Business Administration (SBA) (Table A.3). With the exception of firms in Region X which includes Washington state, home of the survey sponsor, the University of Washington, responses from all the other nine regions ranged between 15.83 and 26.09 percent, none of which was significantly different from the sample response mean at 21.31 percent. Therefore, it was safe to observe that the response rates did not substantially differ from region to region when Region X was excluded.

Then how strong was the "home state" effect which might have resulted in disproportionately more responses from Washington-based firms? As shown in Table A.3, the response rate from Region X (Alaska, Idaho, Oregon, and Washington), at 35.42 percent, indeed was the highest among all the regions surveyed. However, after examining the list of the states which had the top ten highest response rates in Table A.4, one would find that the response rate for Washington-based firms, at 34.21 percent, was barely at the tenth. One explanation was that if a few firms that were sampled in a small

Table A.3
Response Rates by SBA Geographic Regions

Regions*		Effective Sample	Total Response	Response Rate
I.	6 States (CT, ME, MA, NH, VT, RI)	69	18	26.09%
II.	2 States (NJ, NY)	139	22	15.83%
III.	5 States (DE,** MD, PA, VA, WV) and DC	99	24	24.24%
IV.	8 States (AL, FL, GA, KY, MS, NC, SC, TN)	155	31	20.00%
V.	6 States (IL, IN, MI, MN, OH, WI)	111	26	23.42%
VI.	5 States (AR, LA, NM, OK, TX)	79	15	18.99%
VII.	4 States (IA, KS, MO, NE)	32	6	18.75%
VIII.	6 States (CO, MT, ND, SD, UT, WY)	21	4	19.05%
IX.	4 States (AZ, CA, HI, NV)	162	32	19.75%
X.	4 States (AK, ID, OR, WA)	48	17	35.42%
	Total	915	195	21.31%

* The ten-region division was specified by the Small Business Administration. An underlined state indicates that no response was received from firms located there. None of these eleven "missing" states appears to be a significant exporter.
** The random selection process did not generate any firm located in Delaware.

Table A.4
Top Ten Response Rates by State

Rank	State	Response Rate	Number of Responses
1.	Idaho	100.00%	1
2.	Colorado	50.00%	3
	Rhode Island	50.00%	2
4.	Connecticut	42.86%	9
5.	Oklahoma	40.00%	2
6.	Minnesota	37.50%	3
	Oregon	37.50%	3
8.	Virginia	35.48%	11
9.	Illinois	35.29%	12
10.	Washington	34.21%	13
	Total	21.31%	195

state all returned the survey, then the response rate for that state could be inflated. This might explain a few of the top ten cases, such as Idaho (where the only firm sampled answered the survey and, therefore, yielded a 100 percent response rate), Colorado, and Rhode Island. However, this could not explain the high response rates from firms in Connecticut, Virginia, and Illinois, at 42.86, 35.48, and 35.29 percent, respectively. Compared with 13 responses from Washington, these high response rates were also based on a substantial number of returned surveys (9 for Connecticut, 11 for Virginia, and 12 for Illinois).

In addition, the locational effect of the survey sponsor could be further discounted because seven of the top ten highest response states were located in regions where the University of Washington could not claim to have strong visibility and influence, such as Connecticut, Rhode Island, and Oklahoma. Therefore, I could rule out the explanation that some of the high response rates were caused by only one or two firms sampled in a small state that answered the survey. Thus, I concluded that response rates did not systematically differ from one state to another and that Washington-based firms did not have a higher propensity to return the survey. In short, there was little regional bias in survey responses.

Testing nonresponse bias in this study, however, was difficult, because there exist no publicly available comprehensive databases, such as COMPUSTAT, for U.S. export intermediaries. Therefore, checking the characteristics of the respondent firms against those published in databases (e.g., Hill, et al., 1992; Phan and Hill, 1995) was not feasible. To solve this problem, the chronological order according to which responses were received was recorded. All of the 195 returned surveys were divided into four equal subgroups—the first subgroup contained the first batch of responses received; the second subgroup contained the second batch; and so on. Then, following Bello and Lohtia (1995) and Dutta, et al. (1995), Chi-square (χ^2) tests were used to determine the significance of the differences along each of the five key demographic dimensions of the first and last batches: (a) firm age; (b) number of people at the firm; (c) total export sales; (d) type of clients; and (e) average export sales margin. The assumption was that the first batch of respondents could be proxies for "typical" respondents and that late respondents (the last batch) were similar to nonrespondents. As shown in Table A.5, results of these tests indicated that there were no significant differences between these two batches. The p-value for all the five tests was greater than 0.15, well above the 0.05 standard by which most results would be regarded as significant (Neter, et al., 1989; Nunally, 1978).

Table A.5

Chi-Square (χ^2) Two Sample Tests between the First Batch (50) and Last Batch (50) of Respondents: Proxy Tests for Nonresponse Bias

Variables	χ^2	Significance	Degree of Freedom
Firm age*	2.823	0.2825	3
Number of people at the firm**	1.629	0.7433	4
Total export sales***	0.047	0.9370	4
Type of client firms****	2.826	0.2431	3
Average sales margin*****	3.732	0.1857	5

* Firm age was classified into 4 categories: 0–5 years, 6–10 years, 11–20 years, and 21 and over.

** Number of people at the firm was classified into 5 categories: 1–4, 5–9, 10–24, 25–49, and 50 and over.

*** Total export sales was classified into 5 categories: under $500,000, $500,000–$1 million, $1 million–$4.99 million, $5 million–$9.99 million, and over $10 million.

**** Type of client firms was classified into 4 categories: Uninterested in exporting, occasional exporters, established exporters, and globalized firms.

***** Average export sales margin was classified into 6 categories: Under 1%, 1–10%, 11–25%, 26–50%, 51–100%, and over 100%.

This method for assessing nonresponse bias in the data was an indirect test. Although the method is not the most perfect way of examining nonresponse bias, it has been widely accepted in the survey methodology literature (Armstrong and Overton, 1977; Churchill, 1979; Kerlinger, 1986; Tomaskovic-Devey, et al., 1994). Therefore, it was inferred from the results of these tests that nonresponse bias was not significant. Moreover, the similarity between the demographic characteristics of the firms in this survey and those reported in earlier studies (see Table 4.1) further reinforced the belief that nonresponse bias was not a substantial problem that might cause concern for further analysis in this study.

In summary, the integrity and reliability of the data obtained from the nationwide mail survey were assessed. Examinations of regional response bias suggested that the data could be considered as representative of the national population of U.S. export intermediaries since no significant regional response bias was detected. Similarly, nonresponse bias was inferred to be minimal.

Hypothesis Tests

Frequently in regression analysis, the data set contains some outlier cases that will heavily influence the overall model. Therefore, examining the outlier cases is important. For the 166 firms which were founded in or before 1993 and whose performance data were complete, an outlier analysis using Cook's distance measure D was first performed. It was found that Cook's Ds were all less than one, thus posing little undue impact on the overall results (Neter, et al., 1989).

In order to carry out hypothesis tests, it was necessary to transform the raw data reported by respondents into a smaller set of key factors and also to validate the measures used in the survey. This technique is called factor analysis (Kim and Mueller, 1978). Although an attempt was made to use measures that were validated by previous studies, some were either unavailable or were limited in their applicability to this study. Therefore, several new measures specific to this study had to be developed. The multi-item questions in the survey were designed to elicit specific response patterns. In the coded data, a single underlying dimension (e.g., ability to reduce search costs) might be reflected in several items (e.g., experience in exporting, experience in overseas environment, and foreign language proficiency). There were too many items to analyze with the number of observations available and many of these items were highly correlated, particularly where a number of questions reflected the same underlying dimension of behavior. Consequently, factor analysis was attempted to explain the variance in the set of coded items as a function of a much smaller set of underlying variables (factors). In other words, a large number of coded items were essentially replaced by a smaller number of estimated variables (factors), each of which was closely related to a set of the original items.

In addition to data reduction, factor analysis also has the benefits of examining the plausibility of the constructs developed (Kim and Mueller, 1978). If a given factorial hypothesis is supported, one would have greater confidence in the appropriateness of the factor analytic model for the data collected from the survey. In that sense, factor analysis can provide self-validating information (Tan and Litschert, 1994).

Summarized in Tables A.6 and A.7, all the multi-item scales used in the study showed reasonable internal consistency, as evidenced by the *alpha* scores of 0.89, 0.72, 0.88, and 0.77, which were all above the minimum benchmark of 0.70 specified by Churchill (1979) and Nunally (1978). In order to further assess the construct validity of the four independent variables, the items across the scales were sub-

Table A.6
Multi-Item Measures Used in Factor Analyses
and Regression Runs

Independent Variables	Measures

Hypothesis 1: Knowledge of foreign markets and export processes

	1	2	3	4	5
a. Respondent's export experience [Year]	0	1–5	6–10	11–20	> 20
b. Top 3 managers' average export experience [Year]	0	1–5	6–10	11–20	> 20
c. Percentage of foreign-born personnel [%]	0	1–25	26–50	51–75	75–100
d. Top 3 managers' foreign travel frequency [Frequency]	None in past 2 yrs.	Once every 1–2 yrs.	Once every 6 mo.	Once every 3 mo.	Once every mo.
e. % of multilingual personnel at your firm [%]	0	1–25	26–50	51–75	75–100
f. The firm's overseas connections [Relative to your top 3 competitors]	Very little	2	3	4	Very extensive
g. The firm's experience in product industry [Relative to your top 3 competitors]	Very little	2	3	4	Very extensive
h. Top 3 managers' exp. in product industry [Relative to your top 3 competitors]	Very little	2	3	4	Very extensive

Hypothesis 2: Negotiation ability

	1	2	3	4	5
a. Top 3 managers' negotiation skills [Relative to your top 3 competitors]	Very little	2	3	4	Very extensive
b. Top 3 managers' negotiation frequency [Relative to your top 3 competitors]	Very little	2	3	4	Very extensive

Table A.6
Multi-Item Measures Used in Factor Analyses
and Regression Runs (Continued)

Independent Variables					Measures

Hypothesis 3: Ability to take title

a. Your firm's willingness to take title to goods *[Relative to your top 3 competitors]*	1 *Very* *little*	2	3	4	5 *Very* *extensive*
b. Your firm's ability to take title to goods *[Relative to your top 3 competitors]*	1 *Very* *little*	2	3	4	5 *Very* *extensive*

Hypothesis 4: Product specialization*

(a) The amount of training manufacturers provide to your sales force	1 *Very* *little*	2	3	4	5 *Very* *extensive*
(b) The amount of training your sales force provides to foreign customers	1 *Very* *little*	2	3	4	5 *Very* *extensive*
(c) The amount of postsale services that your typical products require	1 *Very* *little*	2	3	4	5 *Very* *extensive*

* Reverse coded.

jected to factor analysis. Results of the oblimin rotated factor analysis are provided in Table A.7. Cumulatively, the prespecified four-factor solution accounted for 58.83 percent of the variance and represented all the derived factors with eigen values greater than one. The pattern of observed loadings indicated that the scales represented independent measures of the underlying construct, thus further supporting unidimensionality and discriminant validity of the scales. Summary statistics can be seen in Table A.8.

Due to the lack of support for a composite measure of export intermediary performance from the literature and from the case studies, no attempt was made to create a composite measure of firm performance. The practical difficulty was the inability to assign weights to different measures, such as per capita export sales and ex-

Table A.7
Rotated Factor Matrix for Multi-Item Independent Variables

	Factor 1	Factor 2	Factor 3	Factor 4
For Hypothesis 1: Export knowledge				
a. Respondent's export experience	**0.77***	0.32	0.06	0.10
b. Top 3 managers' average export experience	**0.73**	0.35	0.01	-0.07
c. % of foreign-born personnel	**0.61**	0.17	0.18	0.02
d. Top 3 managers' foreign travel frequency	**0.67**	0.21	0.23	0.05
e. % of multilingual personnel	**0.84**	0.42	0.08	0.12
f. The firm's overseas connections	**0.59**	0.34	-0.07	0.08
g. The firm's experience in product industry	**0.72**	-0.04	0.04	0.02
h. Top 3 managers' exp. in product industry	**0.91**	0.07	0.03	-0.29
For Hypothesis 2: Negotiation ability				
a. Negotiation skills	0.27	**0.87**	0.21	0.01
b. Frequency of negotiations	0.04	**0.62**	0.02	0.13
For Hypothesis 3: Ability to take title				
a. Willingness to take title to goods	0.02	0.04	**0.91**	0.03
b. Ability to take title to goods	0.11	0.07	**0.87**	0.05
For Hypothesis 4: Product specialization				
a. Training provided by manufacturers	0.01	0.09	-0.11	**0.81**
b. Training provided to foreign customers	0.15	0.23	0.20	**0.78**
c. Amount of post-sale services	0.17	0.01	0.04	**0.67**
Alpha	0.89	0.72	0.88	0.77
Eigen value	4.23	1.32	4.22	3.91
% of variance explained	24.91	9.35	15.66	8.91
Cumulative % of variance	24.91	34.26	49.92	58.83

* **Boldface** indicates items that load on factors.

port sales margins, if an overall composite measure had to be created. As a result, similar to the approach used by Mosakowski (1991), three performance measures were used as different dependent variables in regression runs, resulting in a triangulation of the findings (see Tables 7.13–7.16).

More detailed discussions of the research process can be found in a number of papers written for academic audiences (Peng, 1996, 1997c; Peng, et al., 1997). In deriving the conclusions, I have not only

Table A.8
Summary Statistics and Correlations (N=166)

Variables				Mean	Standard Deviation			
1.	Export knowledge			3.28	0.95			
2.	Negotiation ability			3.13	0.74			
3.	Taking title			3.11	0.80			
4.	Specialization			0.50	0.48			
5.	Firm size			0.30	1.00			
6.	Firm age			9.43	5.62			
7.	Net sales margin			0.14	0.16			
8.	Per capita sales			0.31	0.25			
9.	Self-reported performance			3.53	1.09			

Variables	1	2	3	4	5	6	7	8	9
1.									
2.	.31*								
3.	.13	.23							
4.	.24	-.06	.09						
5.	.11	.10	.10	.05					
6.	.29*	.18	.21	.06	.32**				
7.	.31*	.25*	.20	.19	.07	.21			
8.	.32**	.12	.34**	.20	.18	.15	.26*		
9.	.51***	.54***	.46***	.22	.20	.26*	.16	.21	

* $p < 0.05$
** $p < 0.01$
*** $p < 0.001$

been governed by the findings from a particular method or a specific test, but also by the overall learning from the entire research process involving a hybrid methodology with both qualitative and quantitative methods. The conclusions, therefore, are supported by the findings in a holistic way.

NOTE

1. A six-page summary report, entitled "U.S. Export Intermediary Firms: The State-of-the-Art, 1995," was sent back to all 195 respondents after the preliminary analysis was completed in early 1996. The report was

well received and was featured in the editorial of the May 1996 issue of *The Exporter Magazine* (Stroh, 1996).

Caves, Richard E. (1995). *Multinational enterprise and economic analysis*, 2nd ed. New York and Cambridge: Cambridge University Press.

Cavusgil, S. Tamer (1984a). Differences among exporting firms based on their degree of internationalization. *Journal of Business Research*, 12: 195–208.

Cavusgil, S. Tamer (1984b). Organizational characteristics associated with export activity. *Journal of Management Studies*, 21: 3–22.

Cavusgil, S. Tamer, and V. H. Kirpalani (1993). Introducing products into export markets: Success factors. *Journal of Business Research*, 27: 1–15.

Cavusgil, S. Tamer, and Shaoming Zou (1994). Marketing strategy-performance relationship: An investigation of the empirical link in export market ventures. *Journal of Marketing*, 58 (1): 1–21.

Chandler, Alfred D. (1990). *Scale and scope: The dynamics of industrial capitalism*. Cambridge, MA: Harvard University Press.

Chen, Ming-Jer, and Donald C. Hambrick (1995). Speed, stealth, and selective attack: How small firms differ from large firms in competitive behavior. *Academy of Management Journal*, 38: 453–482.

Chi, Tailan (1994). Trading in strategic resources: Necessary conditions, transaction cost problems, and choice of exchange structure. *Strategic Management Journal*, 15: 271–290.

Chiles, Todd H., and John F. McMackin (1996). Integrating variable risk preferences, trust, and transaction cost economics. *Academy of Management Review*, 21 (1): 73–99.

Cho, Dong-Sung (1984). The anatomy of the Korean general trading company. *Journal of Business Research*, 12: 241–255.

Cho, Dong-Sung (1987). *The general trading company: Concept and strategy*. Lexington, MA: Lexington Books.

Christensen, Sandra (1989). The Export Trading Company Act of 1982: An effectiveness study. Ph.D. diss., University of Washington.

Churchill, Gilbert A. (1979). A paradigm for developing better measures of marketing constructs. *Journal of Marketing Research*, 16: 64–73.

Coase, Ronald H. (1937). The nature of the firm. *Economica*, 4: 386–405.

Cohen, Stephen D., Joel R. Paul and Robert A. Blecker (1996). *Fundamentals of U.S. foreign trade policy: Economics, politics, laws, and issues*. Boulder, CO: Westview.

Collis, David J. (1994). How valuable are organizational capabilities? *Strategic Management Journal*, 15 (winter special issue): 143–152.

Conner, Kathleen R. (1991). A historical comparison of resource based theory and five schools of thought within industrial organization economics: Do we have a new theory of the firm? *Journal of Management*, 17: 121–154.

Conner, Kathleen R., and C. K. Prahalad (1996). A resource-based theory of the firm: Knowledge versus opportunism. *Organization Science*, 7: 477–501.

Contractor, Farok J., and Peter Lorange (eds.) (1988). *Cooperative strategies in international business*. Lexington, MA: Lexington Books.

Cook, Karen S., Richard M. Emerson, Mary R. Gillmore, and Toshio Yamagishi (1983). The distribution of power in exchange networks. *American Journal of Sociology*, 89: 275–305.

Cook, T. D., and D. T. Campbell (1979). *Quasi-experimentation*. Boston: Houghton Mifflin.

Cooper, Arnold C., and William C. Dunkelberg (1987). Entrepreneurial research: Old questions, new answers and methodological issues. *American Journal of Small Business*, 11 (3): 11–23.

Cooper, R., and E. Kleinschmidt (1985). The impact of export strategy on export sales performance. *Journal of International Business Studies*, 16 (1): 37–55.

Coopers and Lybrand (1984). *Export management companies: A new look at a changing industry*. Washington, DC: Coopers and Lybrand.

Cosimano, Thomas F. (1996). Intermediation. *Economica*, 63: 131–143.

Coughlan, Anne T. (1985). Competition and cooperation in marketing channel choice: Theory and application. *Marketing Science*, 4 (2), 110–129.

Czinkota, Michael R. (1984). The business response to the Export Trading Company Act of 1982. *Columbia Journal of World Business*, 19 (3): 105–111.

Czinkota, Michael R., Ilkka A. Ronkainen and Michael H. Moffett (1996). *International business*, 4th ed. Ft. Worth, TX: Dryden.

Daft, Richard L., and Arie Y. Lewin (1990). Can organization studies begin to break out of the normal science straightjacket? *Organization Science*, 1 (1): 1–9.

Daniels, John D., and Lee H. Radebaugh (1998). *International business*, 8th ed. Reading, MA: Addison-Wesley.

da Rocha, Angela, Carl H. Christensen and Carlos E. da Cunha (1990). Aggressive and passive exporters: A study in the Brazilian furniture industry. *International Marketing Review*, 7 (5): 6–15.

D'Aveni, Richard A. (1994). *Hypercompetition*. New York: Free Press.

D'Aveni, Richard A., and Anne Y. Ilinitch (1992). Complex patterns of vertical integration in the forest products industry: Systematic and bankruptcy risks. *Academy of Management Journal*, 35: 596–625.

D'Aveni, Richard A., and David J. Ravenscraft (1994). Economies of integration versus bureaucracy costs: Does vertical integration improve performance? *Academy of Management Journal*, 37: 1167–1206.

Davies, K. (1957). *The Royal African Company*. London: Longman.

Day, G. S., and R. Wensley (1988). Assessing advantage: A framework for diagnosing competitive superiority. *Journal of Marketing*, 52 (2): 1–20.

Delacroix, Jacques (1984). Export strategies for small American firms. *California Management Review*, 26 (3): 138–153.

Denis, Jean-Emile (1990). A research agenda on the internationalization process for smaller Ontario firms: Comment. *Research in Global Strategic Management*, 1: 99–111.

Denis, Jean-Emile, and D. Depelteau (1985). Market knowledge, diversification and export expansion. *Journal of International Business Studies*, 16 (3): 77–90.

Denis, Jean-Emile, and H. Mallette-Lafreniere (1987). Trading companies and freight forwarders as export intermediaries. In P. Rosson and S.

Reid, eds., *Export entry and expansion: Concepts and practices*, 269–281. New York: Praeger.

DeNoble, Alex F., and Michael A. Belch (1986). Bank involvement with export trading companies. *American Journal of Small Business*, 10 (1): 19–28.

Dess, Gregory, and Robert Robinson (1984). Measuring organizational performance in the absence of objective measures. *Strategic Management Journal*, 5: 265–273.

Destler, T. M. (1986). *American trade politics: System under stress*. New York: The 20th Century Fund.

Dichtl, Erwin, Hans-Geoorg Koeglmayr and Stefan Mueller (1990). International orientation as a precondition for export success. *Journal of International Business Studies*, 21 (1): 23–40.

Dierickx, Ingemar, and Karl Cool (1989). Asset stock accumulation and sustainability of competitive advantage. *Management Science*, 35: 1504–1511.

Dillman, D. A. (1978). *Mail and telephone surveys: The total design method*. New York: Wiley.

Directory of leading U.S. export management companies (1987). Westport, CT: Bergano.

Donaldson, Lex (1985). *In defense of organization theory*. Cambridge and New York: Cambridge University Press.

Donaldson, Lex (1990). The ethereal hand: Organizational economics and management theory. *Academy of Management Review*, 15: 369–381.

Douglas, Susan, and Samuel Craig (1995). *Global marketing strategy*. New York: McGraw-Hill.

Drazin, Robert, and Andrew H. Van de Ven (1985). Alternative forms of fit in contingency theory. *Administrative Science Quarterly*, 30: 514–539.

Dunning, John H. (1980). Toward an eclectic theory of international production. *Journal of International Business Studies*, 11: 9–31.

Dunning, John H. (1988). The eclectic paradigm of international production: A restatement and some possible extensions. *Journal of International Business Studies*, 19 (1): 1–31.

Dunning, John H. (1993). *Multinational enterprises and global economy*. Reading, MA: Addison-Wesley.

Dutta, Shantanu, Mark Bergen, Jan B. Heide and George John (1995). Understanding dual distribution: The case of reps and house accounts. *Journal of Law, Economics and Organization*, 11: 189–204.

Dziubla, Robert W. (1982). International trading companies: Building on the Japanese model. *Northwestern Journal of International Law and Business*, 4: 422–496.

Egan, Mary L. (1987). The ETCA of 1982: An analysis of firms' responses in relation to the goals of the Act. Ph.D. diss., George Washington University.

Economist, The (1995). Japan's trading companies: Sprightly dinosaurs? February 11: 55–57.

Eisenhardt, Kathleen M. (1988). Agency and institutional theory explanations: The case of retail sales compensation. *Academy of Management Journal*, 31: 488–511.

Eisenhardt, Kathleen M. (1989a). Agency theory: An assessment and review. *Academy of Management Review*, 14: 57–74.

Eisenhardt, Kathleen M. (1989b). Building theories from case study research. *Academy of Management Review*, 14: 532–550.

Emerson, Richard M. (ed.) (1983). *Contemporary field research*. Prospect Height, IL: Waveland.

Entrepreneur Magazine (1995). *The Entrepreneur guide to starting an import-export business*. New York: Wiley.

Erramilli, M. Krishna (1991). The experience factor in foreign market entry behavior of service firms. *Journal of International Business Studies*, 22: 479–502.

Exporter Magazine, The (1996). Ex-Im report. May: 34–35.

Fairbank, John K., Edwin O. Reischauer and Albert M. Craig (1989). *East Asia: Tradition and transformation*. Boston: Houghton Mifflin.

Fama, Eugene F. (1980). Agency problems and the theory of the firm. *Journal of Political Economy*, 88: 288–298.

Far Eastern Economic Review, The (1994). One province, no system. June 2: 46–48.

Fayerweather, J., and A. Kapoor (1976). *Strategy and negotiation of the international corporation*. Cambridge, MA: Ballinger.

Federal Trade Commission (1967). *Webb-Pomerene associations: A 50-year review*. Washington, DC: FTC.

Feldstein, Martin (1987). Correcting the trade deficit. *Foreign Affairs*, 65: 795–806.

Fortune (1992). The best cities for business. November 2: 40–70.

Fortune (1995). Export: Redefining home turf. September 4: S1 (special advertising section).

Fortune (1996). The *Fortune* global 500 list. August 5: F1–42.

Foss, Nicolai J., Christian Knudsen and Cynthia A. Montgomery (1995). An exploration of common ground. In Cynthia A. Montgomery, ed., *Resource-based and evolutionary theories of the firm: Towards a synthesis*, 1–18. Boston: Kluwer.

Friedman, Milton (1953). *Essay in positive economics*. Chicago: University of Chicago Press.

Galbraith, Craig S., and C. Stiles (1984). Merger strategies as a response to bilateral market power. *Academy of Management Journal*, 27: 511–524.

Galenson, David W. (1986). *Traders, planters, and slaves: Market behavior in early English America*. Cambridge and New York: Cambridge University Press.

Gerbing, David, and James Anderson (1988). An updated paradigm for scale development incorporating unidimensionality and its assessment. *Journal of Marketing Research*, 25: 186–192.

Gerlach, Michael L. (1992). *Alliance capitalism: The social organization of Japanese business*. Berkeley: University of California Press.

Ghoshal, Sumantra, and Peter Moran (1996). Bad for practice: A critique of the transaction cost theory. *Academy of Management Review*, 21: 13–47.

Glasser, B. J., and A. L. Strauss (1967). *The discovery of grounded theory*. Chicago: Aldine.

Godfrey, Paul, and Charles W. L. Hill (1995). The problem of unobservables in strategic management research. *Strategic Management Journal*, 16: 519–533.

Goffman, Erwin (1969). *Strategic interaction*. New York: Ballantine.

Gomez-Mejia, Louis R. (1988). The role of human resources strategy in export performance: A longitudinal study. *Strategic Management Journal*, 9: 493–505.

Gomez-Mejia, Louis R., and David B. Balkin (1992). Determinants of faculty pay: An agency theory perspective. *Academy of Management Journal*, 35: 921–955.

Goodnow, James D., and W. Elizabeth Goodnow (1990). Self-assessment by state export promotion agencies: A status report. *International Marketing Review*, 7 (3): 18–30

Graham, John (1983). Business negotiations in Japan, Brazil and the United States. *Journal of International Business Studies*, 14 (1): 47–61.

Graham, John (1987). A theory of interorganizational negotiations. *Research in Marketing*, 9: 163–183.

Graham, John, Alma Mintu and Raymond Rodgers (1994). Explorations of negotiation behavior in ten foreign cultures using a model developed in the United States. *Management Science*, 40: 72–95.

Granovetter, Mark S. (1985). Economic action and social structure: The problem of embeddedness. *American Journal of Sociology,* 91: 481–510.

Green, Robert T., and Ajay K. Kohli (1991). Export market identification: The role of economic size and socioeconomic development. *Management International Review*, 31 (1): 37–50.

Grimwade, N. (1989). *International trade*. London: Routledge.

Gripsrud, Geir (1990). The determinants of export decisions and attitudes to a distant market: Norwegian fishery exports to Japan. *Journal of International Business Studies*, 21: 469–486.

Grossman, Sanford J., and Oliver D. Hart (1986). The costs and benefits of ownership: A theory of vertical and lateral integration. *Journal of Political Economy*, 94: 691–719.

Gulati, Ranjay (1995). Does familiarity breed trust? The implications of repeated ties for contractual choice in alliances. *Academy of Management Journal*, 38: 85–112.

Haigh, Robert W. (1994). Thinking of exporting? Export management companies could be the answer. *Columbia Journal of World Business*, 29 (4): 66–81.

Hall, Richard (1992). The strategic analysis of intangible resources. *Strategic Management Journal*, 13: 135–144.

Hall, Richard (1993). A framework linking intangible resources and capabilities to sustainable competitive advantage. *Strategic Management Journal*, 14: 607–618.

Hambrick, Donald C. (1994). What if the Academy actually mattered? *Academy of Management Review*, 19: 11–16.

Hannan, Michael, and John Freeman (1989). *Organizational ecology*. Cambridge, MA: Harvard University Press.

Hansen, Gary S., and Birger Wernerfelt (1989). Determinants of firm performance: The relative importance of economic and organizational factors. *Strategic Management Journal*, 10: 399–411.

Harrigan, Kathryn Rudie (1985). *Strategic flexibility*. Lexington, MA: Lexington Books.

Hay Associates (1977). *A study to determine the feasibility of the ETC concept as a viable vehicle for expansion of U.S. products*. Philadelphia: Hay Associates.

Heide, Jan B. (1992). Interorganizational governance in marketing channels. *Journal of Marketing*, 58 (1): 71–85.

Heide, Jan B., and George John (1988). The role of dependence balancing in safeguarding transaction-specific assets in conventional channels. *Journal of Marketing*, 52: 20–35.

Heide, Jan B., and Anne S. Miner (1992). The shadow of the future: Effects of anticipated interaction and frequency on buyer-seller cooperation. *Academy of Management Journal*, 35: 265–291.

Hennart, Jean-Francois (1982). *A theory of the multinational enterprises*. Ann Arbor: University of Michigan Press.

Hennart, Jean-Francois (1989). The transaction cost rationale for countertrade. *Journal of Law, Economics and Organization*, 5: 127–153.

Hennart, Jean-Francois (1993). Explaining the swollen middle: Why most transactions are a mix of "market" and "hierarchy." *Organization Science*, 4: 529–547.

Hennart, Jean-Francois, and Erin Anderson (1993). Countertrade and the minimization of transaction costs: An empirical examination. *Journal of Law, Economics and Organization*, 9: 290–313.

Hesterly, William S., Julia Liebeskind and Todd R. Zenger (1990). Organizational economics: An impending revolution in organization theory. *Academy of Management Review*, 15: 402–420.

Hesterly, William S., and Todd R. Zenger (1993). The myth of a monolithic economics: Fundamental assumptions and the use of economic models in policy and strategy research. *Organization Science*, 4: 496–510.

Hill, Charles W. L. (1990). Cooperation, opportunism, and the invisible hand: Implications for transaction cost theory. *Academy of Management Review*, 15: 500–513.

Hill, Charles W. L. (1997). *International business*, 2nd ed. Chicago: Irwin.

Hill, Charles W. L., Michael A. Hitt and Robert E. Hoskisson (1992). Cooperative versus competitive structures in related and unrelated diversified firms. *Organization Science*, 3: 501–521.

Hill, Charles W. L., Peter Hwang and W. Chan Kim (1990). An eclectic theory of the choice of international entry mode. *Strategic Management Journal*, 11: 117–128.

Hill, Charles W. L., and W. Chan Kim (1988). Searching for a dynamic theory of the multinational enterprise: A transaction cost model. *Strategic Management Journal*, 9 (special issue): 93–104.

Hill, Charles W. L., and Scott A. Snell (1989). Effects of ownership and control on corporate productivity. *Academy of Management Journal*, 32: 25–46.

Hirsch, Paul, R. Friedman and Mitchell Koza (1990). Collaboration or paradigm shift? Caveat emptor and the risk of romance with economic models for strategy and policy research. *Organization Science*, 1: 87–98.

Hofstede, Geert (1980). *Culture's consequences: International differences in work-related values.* Beverly Hills, CA: Sage.

Hofstede, Geert (1994). Management scientists are human. *Management Science*, 40: 4–13.

Holmstrom, Bengt (1989). Agency cost and innovation. *Journal of Economic Behavior and Organization*, 12: 305–327.

Holmstrom, Bengt, and Paul Milgrom (1991). Multitask principal-agent analyses: Incentive contracts, asset ownership, and job design. *Journal of Law, Economics and Organization*, 7 (special issue): 24–53.

Hook, Ralph C., and Michael R. Czinkota (1988). Export activities and prospects of Hawaiian firms. *International Marketing Review*, 5 (3): 51–57.

Hoskisson, Robert E., and Thomas A. Turk (1990). Corporate restructuring: Governance and control limits of the internal capital market. *Academy of Management Review*, 15: 459–477.

Howard, Donald G., and James M. Maskulka (1988). Will American export trading companies replace traditional export management companies? *International Marketing Review*, 5 (3): 41–50

Huber, George P., and D. J. Power (1985). Retrospective reports of strategic-level managers: Guidelines for increasing their accuracy. *Strategic Management Journal*, 6: 171–180.

Huber, George P., and Andrew H. Van de Ven (eds.) (1995). *Longitudinal field research methods.* Thousand Oaks, CA: Sage.

Hunt, S. D., and R. M. Morgan (1995). The competitive advantage theory of competition. *Journal of Marketing*, 59 (2): 1–15.

Hymer, Stephen (1976). *The international operation of national firms: A study of direct foreign investment.* Cambridge, MA: MIT Press.

Ilinitch, Anne Y., and Mike W. Peng (1993). Developing intangible resources: The new battleground for export success. *CINTRAFOR Newsletter*, 8 (1): 4–5. Seattle: University of Washington, Center for International Trade in Forest Resources (CINTRAFOR). [Also reprinted in the *British Columbia Wood Specialist Newsletter*, Vancouver, Canada.]

Ilinitch, Anne Y., and Mike W. Peng (1994). A resource-based model of export performance. Paper presented at the Academy of Management annual meeting, Dallas, August.

Ireland, R. Duane, and Philip M. Van Auken (1987). Entrepreneurship and small business research: An historical typology and directions for future research. *Entrepreneurship Theory and Practice*, 11 (4): 9–20.

Itami, H. (1987). *Mobilizing invisible assets.* Cambridge, MA: Harvard University Press.

Jacobson, Robert (1992). The "Austrian" school of strategy. *Academy of Management Review*, 17: 782–807.

James, Lawrence (1994). *The rise and fall of the British Empire.* London: Abacus.

Jensen, Michael C. (1983). Organization theory and methodology. *Accounting Review*, 50: 319–339.

Jensen, Michael C. (1987). The cash flow theory of takeover: A financial perspective on mergers and acquisitions and the economy. In Lynn Browne and Eric Rosengren, eds., *The merger boom*, 102–143. Boston: Federal Reserve Bank of Boston.

Jensen, Michael C. (1989). Eclipse of the public corporation. *Harvard Business Review*, 67 (5): 61–74.

Jensen, Michael C., and William H. Meckling (1976). Theory of the firm: Managerial behavior, agency costs and ownership structure. *Journal of Financial Economics*, 3: 305–360.

Jensen, Michael C., and Kevin Murphy (1990). Performance pay and top management incentives. *Journal of Political Economy*, 98: 225–264.

Jensen, Michael C., and Robert S. Ruback (1983). The market for corporate control: The scientific evidence. *Journal of Financial Economics*, 11: 5–50.

Jick, Todd D. (1979). Mixing qualitative and quantitative methods: Triangulation in action. *Administrative Science Quarterly*, 24: 602–611.

Johanson, Jan, and Jan-Erik Vahlne (1977). The internationalization process of the firm: A model of knowledge development and increasing foreign market commitments. *Journal of International Business Studies*, 8 (2): 23–32.

John, George, and Barton A. Weitz (1988). Forward integration into distribution: An empirical test of transaction cost analysis. *Journal of Law, Economics and Organization*, 4: 337–355.

Johns, R. A. (1985). *International trade theories and the evolving national economy*. New York: St. Martin's Press.

Johnson, Chalmers (1982). *MITI and the Japanese miracle*. Stanford, CA: Stanford University Press.

Jonnard, Claude M. (1996). *Keys to starting an import-export business*. New York: Barron's.

Joskow, Paul L. (1991). Asset specificity and structure of vertical relationships: Empirical evidence. *Journal of Law, Economics and Organization*, 7 (special issue): 53–83.

Kaikati, Jack G. (1984). The Export Trading Company Act: A viable international marketing tool. *California Management Review*, 27 (1): 59–70.

Kamath, S., P. J. Rosson, D. Ratton and M. Brooks (1987). Research on success in exporting: Past, present and future. In P. J. Rosson and S. D. Reid (eds.), *Managing export entry and expansion: Concepts and practices*, 398–421. New York: Praeger.

Keats, Barbara W., and Jefferey S. Bracker (1988). Toward a theory of small firm performance: A conceptual model. *American Journal of Small Business*, 12 (4): 41–57.

Kerlinger, F. N. (1986). *Foundations of behavioral research*, 3rd ed. New York: Holt, Rinehardt & Winston.

Kim, Jae-On, and Charles Mueller (1978). *Factor analysis*. Beverly Hills, CA: Sage.

Kim, W. Chan (1986). The global diffusion of the general trading company concept. *Sloan Management Review*, 27 (2): 35–43.

Kirzner, I. M. (1973). *Competition and entrepreneurship*. Chicago: University of Chicago Press.

Kirzner, I. M. (1979). *Perception, opportunity, and profit.* Chicago: University of Chicago Press.

Klein, Benjamin, Robert A. Crawford and Armen A. Alchian (1978). Vertical integration: Appropriate rents and the competitive contracting processes. *Journal of Law and Economics,* 21: 297–326.

Klein, Saul, Gary L. Frazier and Victor T. Roth (1990). A transaction cost analysis model of channel integration in international markets. *Journal of Marketing Research,* 27: 196–208.

Klein, Saul, and Victor Roth (1990). Determinants of export channel structure: The effects of experience and psychic distance reconsidered. *International Marketing Review,* 7 (5): 27–38.

Kogut, Bruce (1989). A note on global strategies. *Strategic Management Journal,* 10: 383–389.

Kogut, Bruce (1991). Country capabilities and the permeability of borders. *Strategic Management Journal,* 12 (special issue): 33–47.

Kogut, Bruce, and Udo Zander (1992). Knowledge of the firm, combinative capabilities, and the replication of technology. *Organization Science,* 3: 383–397.

Kojima, Kiyoshi, and Terutomo Ozawa (1984). *Japan's general trading companies: Merchants of economic development.* Paris: Organization for Economic Cooperation and Development (OECD), Development Studies Centre.

Kotabe, Mosaaki (1984). Changing role of the *sogo shosha,* the manufacturing firms, and the MITI in the context of the Japanese "trade or die" mentality. *Columbia Journal of World Business,* 19 (3): 33–42.

Kotabe, Mosaaki, and Michael R. Czinkota (1992). State government promotion of manufacturing exports: A gap analysis. *Journal of International Business Studies,* 24 (4): 637–658.

Kotler, Philip (1983). *Principles of marketing,* 2nd ed. Englewood Cliffs, NJ: Prentice-Hall.

Kreps, D. M. (1991). *Game theory and economic modeling.* Oxford: Clarendon.

Kreps, D. M., P. Milgrom, J. Roberts and R. Wilson (1982). Rational cooperation in the finitely repeated prisoner's dilemma. *Journal of Economic Theory,* 27: 245–252.

Krugman, Paul (1990). *The age of diminished expectations: U.S. economic policy in the 1990s.* Washington, DC: The Washington Post Company.

Kryzanowski, Lawrence, and Nancy D. Ursel (1993). Market reaction to the formation of export trading companies by American banks. *Journal of International Business Studies,* 24: 373–381.

Kuhn, Thomas (1970). *The structure of scientific revolutions,* 2nd ed. Chicago: University of Chicago Press.

Kvint, Vladmir (1994). Don't give up on Russia. *Harvard Business Review,* 72 (2): 62–74.

Lacy, J. V. (1987). The effect of the Export Trading Company Act of 1982 on U.S. export trade. *Stanford Journal of International Law,* 23: 177–202.

Lafontaine, Francine (1993). Contractual arrangements as signaling devices: Evidence from franchising. *Journal of Law, Economics and Organization,* 9: 256–289.

Lardy, Nicholas R. (1992). *Foreign trade and economic reform in China, 1978–1990.* Cambridge and New York: Cambridge University Press.

Lasser, Walfried M., and Jeffrey L. Kerr (1996). Strategy and control in supplier-distributor relationships: An agency perspective. *Strategic Management Journal,* 17: 613–632.

Lax, D. A., and J. K. Sebenius (1986). *The manager as negotiator.* New York: Free Press.

Lee, W.-Y., and J. Brasch (1978). The adoption of export as an innovative strategy. *Journal of International Business Studies,* 9 (1): 85–93.

Lenway, Stephanie A. (1985). *The politics of U.S. international trade.* Boston: Pitman.

Leonard-Barton, Dorothy (1995). A dual methodology for case studies. In George P. Huber and Andrew H. Van de Ven, eds., *Longitudinal field research methods,* 38–64. Thousand Oaks, CA: Sage.

Leonidou, Leonidas C., and Constantine S. Katsikeas (1996). The export development process: An integrative review of empirical models. *Journal of International Business Studies,* 27: 517–551.

Levi, D. (1985). The transaction cost approach to vertical integration: An empirical examination. *Review of Economics and Statistics,* 67: 438–445.

Levinthal, Daniel A. (1988). A survey of agency models of organizations. *Journal of Economic Behavior and Organization,* 9: 153–185.

Levinthal, Daniel A., and Mark Fichman (1988). Dynamics of interorganizational attachments: Auditor-client relationships. *Administrative Science Quarterly,* 33: 345–369.

Levitt, S. (1995). Optimal incentive schemes when only the agents' "best" outcome matters to the principal. *RAND Journal of Economics,* 26: 744–760.

Levitt, Theodore (1983). The globalization of markets. *Harvard Business Review,* 61 (3): 92–102.

Li, Jiatao (1995). Foreign entry and survival: Effects of strategic choices on performance in international markets. *Strategic Management Journal,* 16: 333–351.

Li, Jiatao, and Stephen Guisinger (1992). The globalization of service multinationals in the "Triad" regions: Japan, Western Europe and North America. *Journal of International Business Studies,* 23: 675–696.

Liang, Neng (1995). Soliciting unsolicited export orders: Are recipients chosen at random? *European Journal of Marketing,* 29 (8): 37–59.

Lieberman, Marvin B., and David B. Montgomery (1988). First mover advantages: A survey. *Strategic Management Journal,* 9 (summer special issue): 41–58.

Lilien, Gary L. (1979). Advisor 2: Modeling the marketing mix decision for industrial products. *Management Science,* 25: 191–204.

Lilien, Gary L., Philip Kotler and K. Sridhar Moorthy (1992). *Marketing models.* Englewood Cliffs, NJ: Prentice Hall.

Lippman, S. A., and Richard P. Rumelt (1982). Uncertain imitability: An analysis of interfirm differences in efficiency under competition. *Bell Journal of Economics,* 13: 418–438.

Loge, G. C., and W. C. Crum (1985). U.S. competitiveness: The policy tangle. *Harvard Business Review*, January–February: 34–52.

Luo, Yadong, and Min Chen (1996). Managerial implications of *guanxi*-based business strategies. *Journal of International Management*, 2 (4): 1–23.

Luo, Yadong, and Mike W. Peng (1998). First mover advantages in investing in transitional economies: Two tests from China. *International Executive* (in press).

MacBean, Alsdair (1996). China's foreign trade corporations: Their role in economic reform and export success. In John Child and Yuan Lu, eds., *Management issues in China: International enterprises*, 183–200. London: Routledge.

Macneil, I. (1978). Contracts: Adjustments of long-term economic relations under classical, neoclassical and relational contract law. *Northwestern University Law Review*, 72: 854–906.

Mahoney, Joseph T. (1992). The choice of organizational form: Vertical financial ownership versus other methods of vertical integration. *Strategic Management Journal*, 13: 559–584.

Mahoney, Joseph T., and J. Rajendran Pandian (1992). The resource-based view within the conversation of strategic management. *Strategic Management Journal*, 13: 363–380.

Majumdar, Sumit K., and Venkatram Ramaswamy (1995). Going direct to market: The influence of exchange conditions. *Strategic Management Journal*, 16: 353–372.

Mansfield, Erwin (1988). The speed and cost of industrial innovation in Japan and the United States: External versus internal technology. *Management Science*, 34: 1157–1168.

Market facts Hawaii: All about business in Hawaii (1995). Honolulu: Department of Business, Economic Development and Tourism.

Masten, Scott E. (1984). The organization of production: Evidence from the aerospace industry. *Journal of Law and Economics*, 27: 403–418.

Masten, Scott E. (ed.) (1996). *Case studies in contracting and organization*. New York: Oxford University Press.

Masten, Scott E., James W. Meehan and Edward A. Snyder (1991). The costs of organization. *Journal of Law, Economics and Organization*, 7: 1–26.

Mattson, Jan (1990). Trading companies and small and medium-sized firms: Functional roles in international commercial relations. *European Journal of Marketing*, 24 (3): 42–56.

McFadden, M. (1987). Protectionism can't protect jobs. *Fortune*, May 11: 128.

Melin, Leif (1992). Internationalization as a strategy process. *Strategic Management Journal*, 13 (winter special issue): 99–118.

Miles, M., and M. Huberman (1984). *Qualitative data analysis*. Beverly Hills, CA: Sage.

Miles, Robert (1980). *Macro organizational behavior*. Santa Monica, CA: Good-year.

Mill, James (1958). *The history of British India*. London: James Madden.

Miller, Danny, and Jamie Shamsie (1996). The resource-based view of the firm in two environments. *Academy of Management Journal*, 39: 519–543.

Miller, Larry (1981a). Looking at EMCs? Check internal stability, operations. *American Import and Export Management*, October: 50–84.

Miller, Larry (1981b). Taking the EMC gamble? Figure the financial odds first! *American Import and Export Management*, September: 48–50.

Miller, Larry (1981c). To unlock new export markets, consider the "EMC" key. *American Import and Export Bulletin*, August: 82–105.

Mintzberg, Henry (1979). An emerging strategy of "direct" research. *Administrative Science Quarterly*, 24: 580–589.

Mintzberg, Henry (1989). *Mintzberg on management*. New York: Free Press.

Mitchell, Will, J. Myles Shaver and Bernard Yeung (1994). Foreign entrant survival and foreign market share: Canadian companies' experience in U.S. medical sector markets. *Strategic Management Journal*, 15: 555–567.

Mitsui & Co. (1991a). *Mitsui & Co., Ltd*. Tokyo: Mitsui & Co., Ltd.

Mitsui & Co. (1991b). *Mitsui USA: The Trading Company*. Tokyo: Mitsui & Co., Ltd.

Monteverde, Kirk, and David J. Teece (1982). Supplier switching costs and vertical integration in the automobile industry. *Bell Journal of Economics*, 12: 206–213.

Montgomery, Cynthia A., Birger Wernerfelt, and S. Balakrishnan (1989). Strategy content and the research process: A critique and commentary. *Strategic Management Journal*, 10: 189–197.

Mosakowski, Elaine (1991). Organizational boundaries and economic performance: An empirical study of entrepreneurial computer firms. *Strategic Management Journal*, 12: 115–133.

Moxon, Richard W. (1975). The motivation for investment in offshore plants: The case of the U.S. electronics industry. *Journal of International Business Studies*, 6: 51–66.

Moxon, Richard W. (1995). International business in the Russian Far East. Paper presented at the Academy of International Business annual meeting, Seoul, Korea, November.

Nayyar, Preet R. (1990). Information asymmetries: A source of competitive advantage for diversified service firms. *Strategic Management Journal*, 11: 513–519.

Nelson, Richard (1991). Why do firms differ and how does it matter? *Strategic Management Journal*, 12 (winter special issue): 61–74.

Nelson, Richard R., and Sydney G. Winter (1982). *An evolutionary theory of economic change*. Cambridge, MA: Belknap.

Neter, John, William Wasserman and Michael Kutner (1989). *Applied linear regression models*, 2nd ed. Homewood, IL: Irwin.

Nicholas, Stephen (1982). British multinational investment before 1839. *Journal of European Economic History*, 11: 605–630.

Nicholas, Stephen (1983). Agency contracts, institutional modes, and the transition to foreign direct investment by British manufacturing multinationals before 1939. *Journal of Economic History*, 40: 675–686.

North, Douglas C. (1961). *The economic growth of the United States, 1790–1860.* Englewood Cliffs, NJ: Prentice-Hall.

North, Douglas C. (1985). Transaction costs in history. *Journal of Economic History,* 42: 566–576.

North, Douglas C. (1990). *Institutions, institutional change and economic performance.* Cambridge, MA: Harvard University Press.

Nunally, J. C. (1978). *Psychometric theory.* New York: McGraw Hill.

Ohmae, Kenichi (1985). *Triad power: The coming shape of global competition.* New York: Free Press.

Ohmae, Kenichi (1989). Managing in a borderless world. *Harvard Business Review,* 67 (3): 152–161.

O'Rourke, A. Desmond (1985). Differences in exporting practices, attitudes and problems by size of firm. *American Journal of Small Business,* 9: 25–29.

Oviatt, Benjamin M., and Patricia P. McDougall (1994). Toward a theory of international new ventures. *Journal of International Business Studies,* 25: 45–64.

Oviatt, Benjamin M., and Patricia P. McDougall (1995). Global start-ups: Entrepreneurs on a worldwide stage. *Academy of Management Executive,* 9 (2): 30–44.

Parkhe, Arvind (1993). "Messy" research, methodological predispositions, and theory development in international joint ventures. *Academy of Management Review,* 18: 227–268.

Peng, Mike W., ed. (1992). *Doing business with the Chinese: Readings from Chinese and English sources.* Seattle: University of Washington, Center for International Business Education and Research.

Peng, Mike W. (1994a). Organizational changes in planned economies in transition: An eclectic model. *Advances in International Comparative Management,* 9: 223–251.

Peng, Mike W. (1994b). Organizational form, hypercompetition and competitive advantage: The case of trading companies. Paper presented at the Academy of International Business annual meeting, Boston, November.

Peng, Mike W. (1995a). Foreign direct investment in the innovation-driven stage: Toward a learning options perspective. In Milford B. Green and Rod B. McNaughton, eds., *The location of foreign direct investment,* 29–41. London: Avebury.

Peng, Mike W. (1995b). Tracking the global diffusion and U.S. development of export intermediary organizations: Evolution, rationale, and implications. Paper presented at the Academy of Management annual meeting, Vancouver, Canada, August.

Peng, Mike W. (1996). Behind the success and failure of U.S. export intermediaries. Ph.D. diss., University of Washington (Ann Arbor, MI: UMI Dissertation Services).

Peng, Mike W. (1997a). The China strategy: A tale of two firms. In Charles W. L. Hill, *International business,* 2nd ed., 107–118. Chicago: Irwin.

Peng, Mike W. (1997b). Firm growth in transitional economies: Three longitudinal cases from China, 1989–96. *Organization Studies,* 18 (3): 385–413.

Peng, Mike W. (1997c). Transaction cost economizing and firm performance: A new test. Working paper, University of Hawaii at Manoa, Honolulu.

Peng, Mike W. (1997d). The winning structures. *China Business Review*, 24 (1): 30–33.

Peng, Mike W., and Peggy S. Heath (1993). Strategic advantages of export planning: A contingency framework. Paper presented at the Academy of International Business annual meeting, Maui, Hawaii, October.

Peng, Mike W., and Peggy S. Heath (1996). The growth of the firm in planned economies in transition: Institutions, organizations, and strategic choice. *Academy of Management Review*, 21 (2): 492–528.

Peng, Mike W., Charles W. L. Hill and Anne Y. Ilinitch (1997). The determinants of export intermediary performance: A transaction cost perspective. Paper presented at the Academy of Management annual meeting, Boston, August.

Peng, Mike W., and Anne Y. Ilinitch (1995). Exploring the performance of U.S. export intermediaries: Transaction costs and resource-based perspectives. Paper presented at the Academy of International Business annual meeting, Seoul, Korea, November.

Peng, Mike W., and Anne Y. Ilinitch (1997). Export intermediary firms: A missing link in export development research. Working paper, The Chinese University of Hong Kong.

Peng, Mike W., and Yadong Luo (1997). Managerial networks and firm performance in a transitional economy: A micro-macro link. Working paper, The Chinese University of Hong Kong.

Peng, Mike W., and Richard B. Peterson (1994). Multinational triangulation in management theory building. Paper presented at the Academy of International Business annual meeting, Boston, November.

Peng, Mike W., and Oded Shenkar (1997). The breakdown of trust: A process model of strategic alliance dissolution. Paper presented at the Academy of Management annual meeting, Boston, August.

Penrose, Edith T. (1959). *The theory of the growth of the firm.* New York: Wiley.

Perrow, Charles (1986). *Complex organizations: A critical essay,* 3rd ed. New York: Random House.

Perry, Anne C. (1990). The evolution of the U.S. international trade intermediary in the 1980s: A dynamic model. *Journal of International Business Studies,* 21: 133–154.

Perry, Anne C. (1992). *The evolution of U.S. international trade intermediaries: The changing international environment.* Westport, CT: Quorum.

Peters, Thomas (1987). *Thriving on chaos.* New York: Alfred A. Knopf.

Pettigrew, Andrew M. (1995). Longitudinal field research on change. In George P. Huber and Andrew H. Van de Ven (eds.), *Longitudinal field research methods,* 91–125. Thousand Oaks, CA: Sage.

Pfeffer, Jeffrey (1993). Barriers to the advance of organizational science: Paradigm development as a dependent variable. *Academy of Management Review,* 18: 599–620.

Pfeffer, Jeffrey, and Gerald Salancik (1978). *The external control of organizations.* New York: Harper.

Phan, Phillip, and Charles W. L. Hill (1995). Organizational restructuring and economic performance in leveraged buyouts: An ex post study. *Academy of Management Journal*, 38: 704–739.

Piore, Michael J., and Charles F. Sabel (1984). *The second industrial divide: Possibilities for prosperity*. New York: Basic Books.

Podsakoff, P. M., and D. W. Organ (1986). Self-reports in organizational research: Problems and prospects. *Journal of Management*, 12: 531–544.

Popper, Karl (1972). *Conjectures and refutations: The growth of scientific knowledge*. London: Routledge.

Poppo, Laura, and Todd Zenger (1995). Opportunism, routines, and boundary choices. *Academy of Management Best Paper Proceedings*: 42–46.

Porter, Michael E. (1980). *Competitive strategy*. New York: Free Press.

Porter, Michael E. (1985). *Competitive advantage*. New York: Free Press.

Porter, Michael E. (1990). *The competitive advantage of nations*. New York: Free Press.

Porter, Michael E. (1991). Towards a dynamic theory of strategy. *Strategic Management Journal*, 12 (winter special issue): 95–117.

Powell, Walter W. (1990). Neither market nor hierarchy: Network forms of organization. *Research in Organizational Behavior*, 12: 295—336.

Prahalad, C. K., and Gary Hamel (1990). The core competence of the organization. *Harvard Business Review*, 68 (3): 79–93.

Prahalad, C. K., and Gary Hamel (1994). Strategy as a field of study: Why search for a new paradigm? *Strategic Management Journal*, 15 (summer special issue): 5–16.

Prakash, O. (1985). *The Dutch East India Company and the economy of Bengal, 1630–1720*. Princeton, NJ: Princeton University Press.

President's Commission on Industrial Competitiveness (1985). *Global competition*. Washington, DC: Government Printing Office.

Pusteri, C. Joseph (1988). *A history of American business*, 2nd ed. Arlington Heights, IL: Harlan Davidson.

Pye, Lucian W. (1982). *Chinese commercial negotiation style*. Cambridge, MA: Oelgeschlager Gunn & Hain.

Quinn, James B. (1992). *Intelligent enterprise*. New York: Free Press.

Rangan, V. Kasturi, E. Raymond Corey and Frank Cespedes (1993). Transaction cost theory: Interfaces from clinical field research on downstream vertical integration. *Organization Science*, 4: 454–477.

Rao, C. P., M. Krishna Erramilli and Gopala Ganesh (1990). Impact of domestic recession on export marketing behavior. *International Marketing Review*, 7 (2): 54–66.

Reed, Richard, and Robert J. DeFillippi (1990). Causal ambiguity, barriers to imitation, and sustainable competitive advantage. *Academy of Management Review*, 15: 88–102.

Reich, Robert B. (1991). *The work of nations*. New York: Alfred A. Knopf.

Reid, Stan D. (1981). The decision-maker and export entry and expansion. *Journal of International Business Studies*, 12 (3): 101–111.

Reischauer, Edwin (1974). *Japan: The story of a nation*. New York: Alfred A. Knopf.

Richardson, J. David, and Karin Rindal (1995). *Why exports really matter?* Washington, DC: Institute for International Economics.

Ricks, David A. (1993). *Blunders in international business*. Cambridge, MA: Blackwell.

Ricks, David A., Brian Toyne and Zaida Martinez (1990). Recent developments in international management research. *Journal of Management*, 16: 219–253.

Ring, Peter S., and Andrew H. Van de Ven (1994). Developmental processes of cooperative interorganizational relationships. *Academy of Management Review*, 19: 90–118.

Robins, James A. (1987). Organizational economics: Notes on the use of transaction cost theory on the study of organizations. *Administrative Science Quarterly*, 32: 68–86.

Root, Franklin R. (1994). *Entry strategies for international markets*, 2nd ed. Lexington, MA: Lexington Books.

Rosenberg, Emily S. (1982). *Spreading the American dream: American economic and cultural expansion, 1890–1945*. New York: Hill and Wang.

Rosenbloom, Bert (1987). *Marketing channels*. Chicago: Dryden.

Rosson, Philip J., and I. David Ford (1982). Manufacturer-overseas distributor relations and export performance. *Journal of International Business Studies*, 13 (3): 57–72.

Rubner, Alex (1987). *The export cult: A global display of economic distortions*. Aldershot, UK: Gower.

Rugman, Alan M. (1981). *Inside the multinationals: The economics of internal markets*. London: Croom Helm.

Rumelt, Richard P. (1991). How much does industry matter? *Strategic Management Journal*, 12: 167–186.

Rumelt, Richard P., Dan E. Schendel and David J. Teece, eds. (1994). *Fundamental issues in strategy: A research agenda*. Boston: Harvard Business School Press.

Salacuse, J. W. (1988). Making deals in strange places: A beginner's guide to international business negotiations. *Negotiation Journal*, 4: 5–13.

Sappington, David (1991). Incentives in principal-agent relationships. *Journal of Economic Perspectives*, 5: 45–66.

Sarathy, Ravi (1985). Japanese trading companies: Can they be copied? *Journal of International Business Studies*, 16 (2): 101–119.

Schendel, Dan E., and Charles W. Hofer (1979). *Strategic management: A new view of business policy and planning*. Boston: Little Brown.

Schumpeter, Joseph A. (1942). *Capitalism, socialism and democracy*. New York: Harper.

Schwenk, Charles R. (1985). The use of participant recollection in the modeling of organizational decision process. *Academy of Management Review*, 10: 496–503.

Scott, B. R., and G. C. Lodge, eds. (1985). *U.S. competitiveness in the world economy*. Boston: Harvard Business School Press.

Seabright, Mark A., Daniel A. Levinthal and Mark Fichman (1992). Role of individual attachments in the dissolution of interorganizational relationships. *Academy of Management Journal*, 35: 122–160.

Seringhaus, F. H. Rolf (1986). The impact of government export marketing assistance. *International Marketing Review*, 3 (2): 55–66.

Servan-Schreiber, J. J. (1968). *The American challenge*, translated by R. Steel. New York: Athenum.

Sharma, Anurag (1997). Professional as agent: Knowledge asymmetry in agency exchange. *Academy of Management Review*, 22 (3): 758–798.

Shelanski, Howard A., and Peter G. Klein (1995). Empirical research in transaction cost economics: A review and assessment. *Journal of Law, Economics and Organization*, 11: 335–361.

Simon, Hebert A. (1991). Organizations and markets. *Journal of Economic Perspectives*, 5: 25–44.

Small Business Administration (1989). *The state of small business: A report of the President*. Washington, DC: SBA.

Small Business Administration (1991). *The state of small business: A report of the President*. Washington, DC: SBA.

So, Alvin, and Stephen W. K. Chiu (1995). *East Asia and the world economy*. Thousand Oaks, CA: Sage.

Spender, J.-C., and Robert M. Grant (1996). Knowledge and the firm: Overview. *Strategic Management Journal*, 17 (winter special issue): 5–10.

Staff, Pfeiffer (1994). *Start your own import-export business*. San Francisco: Jossey-Bass.

Stalk, G., P. Evans and L. Shulman (1992). Competing on capabilities: The new rules of corporate strategy. *Harvard Business Review*, 70 (2): 57–69.

Stern, Louis W., and Adel I. El-Ansary (1992). *Marketing channels*, 4th ed. Englewood Cliffs, NJ: Prentice-Hall.

Stern, Louis W., and Torger Reve (1980). Distribution channels as political economies: A framework for comparative analysis. *Journal of Marketing*, 44: 52–64.

Stigler, George J. (1961). The economics of information. *Journal of Political Economy*, 69: 213–225.

Stopford, John M., and Louis T. Wells (1972). *Managing the multinational enterprise*. New York: Basic Books.

Strauss, A. L. (1987). *Qualitative analysis for social scientists*. Cambridge and New York: Cambridge University Press.

Stroh, Leslie (1996). Editorial: Nobody asked me, but. . . . *The Exporter Magazine*, May: 2.

Stross, Robert E. (1990). *Bulls in the china shop and other Sino-American business encounters*. Honolulu: University of Hawaii Press.

Summer, Charles E., et al. (1990). Doctoral education in the field of business policy and strategy. *Journal of Management*, 16: 361–398.

Suzuki, Norihiko (1989). The trading house and the challenge from the Far East. *Advances in International Marketing*, 3: 249–258.

Tan, J. Justin, and Robert J. Litschert (1994). Environment-strategy relationship and its performance implications: An empirical study of the Chinese electronics industry. *Strategic Management Journal*, 15: 1–20.

Teece, David J., ed. (1987). *The competitive challenge: Strategies for industrial innovation and renewal*. Cambridge, MA: Ballinger.

Teece, David J., Gary Pisano and Amy Shuen (1997). Dynamic capabilities and strategic management. *Strategic Management Journal*, 18 (7): 509–533.

Terpstra, Vern, and Ravi Sarathy (1994). *International marketing.* Chicago: Dryden.

Thurow, Lester C. (1993). *Head to head: The coming economic battle among Japan, Europe and America.* New York: Warner.

Tirole, Jean (1986). Hierarchies and bureaucracies: On the role of collusion in organizations. *Journal of Law, Economics and Organization*, 2: 181–214.

Tomaskovic-Devey, Donald, Jeffrey Leiter and Shealy Thompson (1994). Organizational survey nonresponse. *Administrative Science Quarterly*, 39: 439–457.

Tosi, Henry L., and Louis R. Gomez-Mejia (1989). The decoupling of CEO pay and performance: An agency theory perspective. *Administrative Science Quarterly*, 34: 169–189.

Toyne, Brian (1989). International exchange: A foundation for theory building in international business. *Journal of International Business Studies*, 27: 1–17.

Tung, Rosalie (1982). U.S.-China trade negotiations: Practices, procedures, and outcomes. *Journal of International Business Studies*, 13 (2): 25–38.

Tung, Rosalie (1988). Toward a conceptual paradigm of international business negotiations. *Advances in International Comparative Management*, 3: 203–219.

Tyson, Laura D'Andrea, William Dickens, and John Zysman, eds. (1988). *The dynamics of trade and employment.* Cambridge, MA: Ballinger.

U.S. Department of Commerce (1985). *A competitive edge for U.S. exports: The export trade certificate of review program.* Washington, DC: Department of Commerce, International Trade Administration.

U.S. Department of Commerce (1987). *Partners in export trade: The 1987 directory for export trade contacts.* Washington, DC: Department of Commerce, International Trade Administration.

U.S. Department of Commerce (1990). *Report to Congress on export trade intermediaries.* Washington, DC: Department of Commerce, International Trade Administration.

U.S. Department of Commerce (1994). *The export yellow pages.* Washington, DC: Department of Commerce, International Trade Administration.

U.S. Senate (1982). Committee on Banking, Housing and Urban Affairs, Sub-committee on International Finance and Monetary Policy. Hearings on the Export Trade Act of 1982. 97th Congress, 1st Session.

U.S. Senate (1986). Committee on Banking, Housing and Urban Affairs, Sub-committee on International Finance and Monetary Policy. Hearings on the Export Trading Company Amendments Act of 1986. 99th Congress, 2nd Session.

Van de Ven, Andrew H. (1989). Nothing is quite so practical as a good theory. *Academy of Management Review*, 14 (4): 486–489.

Van de Ven, Andrew H. (1992). Suggestions for studying strategy process. *Strategic Management Journal*, 13 (special issue): 169–188.

Vernon, Raymond (1966). International investment and international trade in the product cycle. *Quarterly Journal of Economics*, 80: 190–207.

Vernon, Raymond (1971). *Sovereignty at bay: The multinational spread of U.S. enterprises*. New York: Basic Books.

Vernon, Raymond (1977). *Storm over the multinationals: The real issues*. Cambridge, MA: Harvard University Press.

Waldinger, Roger, Howard Aldrich, and Robin Ward (1990). *Ethnic entrepreneurs: Immigrant businesses in industrial societies*. Beverly Hills, CA: Sage.

Walker, Gordon, and David Weber (1984). A transaction cost approach to make-or-buy decisions. *Administrative Science Quarterly*, 29: 373–391.

Walker, Gordon, and David Weber (1987). Supplier competition, uncertainty, and make-or-buy decisions. *Academy of Management Journal*, 30: 589–596.

Wall Street Journal, The (1994). Small companies look to cultivate foreign business. July 7: B2.

Wall Street Journal, The (1997). U.S. trade gap hit eight-year high in 1996. February 20: A2, A4.

Walters, Peter G. P. (1993). Patterns of formal planning and performance in U.S. exporting firms. *Management International Review*, 33: 43–63.

Walters, Peter G. P., and Saeed Samiee (1990). A model for assessing performance in small U.S. exporting firms. *Entreprenuership Theory and Practice*, 15 (2): 33–50.

Washington State Department of Trade and Economic Development (DTED). 1994. *Washington state international trade directory*. Seattle: DTED.

Weber, Max (1947). *Theory of social and economic organization*, translated by A. R. Henderson and T. Parsons. New York: Macmillan.

Weiss, Stephen E. (1993). Analysis of complex negotiations in international business: The RBC perspective. *Organization Science*, 4: 269–300.

Weiss, Stephen E. (1994). Negotiating with "Romans." *Sloan Management Review*, 35: 51–62.

Wells, L. F., and K. Dulat (1996). *Exporting: From start to finance*. New York: McGraw Hill.

Wernerfelt, Birger (1984). A resource-based view of the firm. *Strategic Management Journal*, 5: 171–180.

Westney, Eleanor (1987). *Immitation and innovation: The transfer of Western organizational patterns to Meiji Japan*. Cambridge, MA: Harvard University Press.

Wilkins, Mira (1970). *The emergence of multinational enterprise: American business abroad from the colonial era to 1914*. Cambridge, MA: Harvard University Press.

Wilkins, Mira (1974). *Maturing of multinational enterprise, 1914–1970*. Cambridge, MA: Harvard University Press.

Williamson, Oliver E. (1975). *Markets and hierarchies*. New York: Free Press.

Williamson, Oliver E. (1985). *The economic institutions of capitalism*. New York: Free Press.

Williamson, Oliver E. (1991a). Comparative economic organization: The analysis of discrete structural alternative. *Administrative Science Quarterly*, 36: 269–296.

Williamson, Oliver E. (1991b). Strategizing, economizing, and economic organization. *Strategic Management Journal*, 12 (winter special issue): 75–94.

Williamson, Oliver E. (1993a). Calculativeness, trust, and economic organization. *Journal of Law and Economics*, 36: 453–486.

Williamson, Oliver E. (1993b). Opportunism and its critics. *Managerial and Decision Economics*, 14: 97–107.

Williamson, Oliver E. (1996). Economic organization: The case for candor. *Academy of Management Review*, 21: 48–57.

Willsher, Richard (1995). *Export finance*. London: Macmillan.

Woodcock, C. Patrick, Paul Beamish and Shige Makino (1994). Ownership-based entry mode strategies and international performance. *Journal of International Business Studies*, 25: 253–274.

Wortzel, Lawrence, and Heidi Vernon-Wortzel (1983). Using general trading companies to market manufactured exports from LDCs and NICs. *Management International Review*, 23 (2): 72–77.

Yan, Aimin, and Barbara Gray (1994). Bargaining power, management control and performance of U.S.-China joint ventures: A comparative case study. *Academy of Management Journal*, 37: 1478–1517.

Yin, Robert K. (1989). *Case study research*. Beverly Hills, CA: Sage.

Yoshihara, K. (1982). *Sogo shosha: The vanguard of the Japanese economy*. Oxford: Oxford University Press.

Young, A. (1978). *The sogo sosha: Japan's multinational marketing companies*. Boulder, CO: Westview.

Young, Stephen, James Hamill, Colin Wheeler and J. Richard Davies (1989). *International market entry and development*. Englewood Cliffs, NJ: Prentice-Hall.

Zaheer, Srilata (1995). Overcoming the liability of foreignness. *Academy of Management Journal*, 38: 341–363.

Zajac, Edward J., and C. P. Olsen (1993). From transaction cost to transactional value analysis: Implications for the study of interorganizational strategies. *Journal of Management Studies*, 30: 131–145.

Zodl, Joseph A. (1995). *Export import: Everything you and your company need to know*. Cincinnati, OH: Betterway Books.

Index